A DIVIDED HEART

JB

For you both
with happy memories

MATHEW THORPE

A DIVIDED HEART

Mathew.

WALKING THE JAKOBSWEG IN AUSTRIA:
THE PILGRIM PATHS TO SANTIAGO
DE COMPOSTELA

First published in the UK in August 2021 by
Journey Books, an imprint of Bradt Guides Ltd
31a High Street, Chesham, Buckinghamshire, HP5 1BW, England
www.bradtguides.com
Text copyright © 2021 Mathew Thorpe
Edited by Robina Pelham Burn
Cover illustration/cover design by James Nunn
Text design by James Nunn
Layout and typesetting by Ian Spick
Production managed by Sue Cooper, Bradt & Jellyfish Print Solutions

ISBN: 9781784779993

British Library Cataloguing in Publication Data
A catalogue record for this book is available from the British Library
Digital conversion by www.dataworks.co.in
Printed in the UK by Jellyfish Print Solutions

To find out more about our Journey Books imprint, visit bradtguides.com/
journeybooks

DEDICATION

TO AUSTRIA.

BELLA GERANT ALLII, TU FELIX AUSTRIA NUBE
NAM QUAM MARS ALIIS, DAT TIBI VENUS.

While other powers sought to expand their lands by conquest,
you, fortunate Austria, achieved your rise by marriage.

This couplet, generally said to extoll the emperor Maximilian
I, expresses and explains my love for Austria. She sits serene,
a sun-lit beauty. She gained her great Empire by luck and
guile: she lost it by misjudgement on the turning of the tide
of humanity. Still she sits serene, without rancour at having
lost in wars so much that she had gained in marriage. Winter
has shrunk her days but still she is dressed in fur-trimmed silk
velvet, adorned by glowing emeralds and surrounded by the
treasures of her glorious past.

CONTENTS

THE SECOND WALK
Graz to Innsbruck: the Southern Tributary.................141

THE THIRD WALK

THE FOURTH WALK

INTRODUCTION

I DISCOVERED THE Jakobsweg quite by chance, as I shall explain in a moment. What, first, is the Jakobsweg?

Improbable legend proclaimed that St James the Greater worked in Galicia before returning to his martyrdom in the Holy Land. After his death his remains were miraculously returned to Galicia for burial. By a further miracle a shepherd in the 9th century was led by a star to his burial place. Spiritual and temporal powers invested in this discovery by building the Cathedral of Compostela over the site. So successful was their investment that by the 12th century only Rome and Jerusalem exceeded the fame of Compostela as pilgrimage shrines. So in the Middle Ages Austria was an artery in the bloodstream that connected all Europe to Santiago de Compostela. Pilgrims from Eastern Europe had to cross Austria, then Switzerland and finally France to reach the Pyrenees. So they entered Austria at the Danube, crossing at modern Bratislava, and left Austria behind at Feldkirch on the Swiss border. The distance between these two points is about 850 kilometres because modern Austria lies east–west across the map of Europe, like a sausage.

The pre-eminence of the pilgrimage, which earned plenary indulgence, waned with the Black Death, followed by the Reformation and its ensuing religious wars, almost to the point of extinction. By 1985 the number registered as reaching journey's end that year stood at 690. In 1987, however, the Council of Europe declared the Way of St James the first European Cultural Route. Then UNESCO named it a World Heritage site. By 2018 the annual number registered at journey's end had risen to 327,378.

In Austria, a Tyrolean, Peter Lindenthal, is credited with promoting the Jakobsweg in the mid 1990s. The Austrian revival has been led by tourism services in each *Land* and by the archbishop or bishop of the nearest diocese. Locally many *Gemeinde* will display maps marking the passage of the Jakobsweg through their administrative area. So the modern Jakobsweg has only a tenuous root in medieval history. What is now offered is the connection of so many local walks to make a continuous path. Wherever possible the chosen path includes any church dedicated to St James, in which a pilgrim stamp will be found by the west door, but it is no longer primarily a Catholic penitential way. I believe the principal contemporary incentives are a search for nature and a rejection of the consequences of industrialisation.

☞

MY CHANCE ENCOUNTER with the Jakobsweg came about as a consequence of my love for Judge Felicitas Paller and my resulting sojourns at her home in Purkersdorf on the very edge of the famous Vienna woods, just beyond the city boundary to the west. *Wanderwege*, or paths for ramblers, are proudly way-marked all over Austria (I say proudly because each commune seems to boast its beauty and charm as it signposts *Sonnenweg, Panoramaweg, Bienenweg,* et cetera). Purkersdorf has a quiverful, as for more than a century it has lured elite city dwellers, and particularly artists and writers, hungering for nature.

When staying with Felicitas I made a survey of the network of the *Wege* and noticed the singular marking, distinct from local markings, of the Jakobsweg with its bright yellow shell on a blue ground – Matisse colours. That led me to the tourist office in the village and the acquisition of a leaflet promoting the section from Purkersdorf all the way to Gottweig at the eastern end of the distant Wachau Valley. I calculated that, at a steady pace, it would be a trip not of hours but of days, with overnight lodgings.

It chanced that Felicitas needed to visit her mother in Stuttgart one weekend, so I decided to use the time to test the water by walking a day out, staying a night and walking back the next day. Little idea had I of where the experiment would lead me.

Never did I imagine that I would be drawn into walking from Purkersdorf to Switzerland with the map of Austria laid flat on the floor and I crawling like an ant across its surface, seeing cities, towns, villages, hamlets, farmhouses, mountains, rivers, lakes, forests, high pastures and arable cultivations – none of which I had seen before and almost none of which I would ever see again. And the ant would crawl an inch or two and then freeze for months before crawling a few more inches. This, as I first followed the path through the Vienna woods, was completely unforeseeable. No less unforeseen was the emergence of this record of my pilgrimage.

☞

WHAT IS THIS record? At its first conception it was intended to be a simple guide for the use of one who reads English but not much German. As one such myself, I had been frustrated by the complexity of the text of the two published guides, both of which, naturally enough, are available only in German. I had reached Linz before I bought the Kompass publication. It was invaluable in suggesting the sensible day stages, the starred sights en route, the hostelries and the cafés. But the text was so dense as to be almost useless. I dare to say that because for a time I prepared translations in advance with the aid of my teacher in England, a native German speaker. Even she struggled with the author's taste for the archaic and the poetic. So, in finding the way, the map rather than the text was my reference when the waymarks were ambiguous or absent.

My intention was to allow my experience to benefit others who were attracted to this great endeavour and similarly handicapped. I fear the concept got lost in the execution, however. Part of the failure, I must own, is the result of my indolence. I did not, as ideally I should have done, write up each day's journey at its conclusion. In mitigation I can plead that I was usually too exhausted to do anything but eat, drink and then sleep. But I have no excuse for failing to write up each three- or four-day stage promptly on my return to England. On occasions I let weeks slide by, until I had difficulty in recapturing one or more of the days at all in my memory. Then I had to resort to the guide to get anything down, and what appeared on the page lacked freshness.

To compensate for these failings I began to embellish the legitimate theme with diversions and digressions into tangentially connected topics that happened to interest or move me. Thus I included impressions and experiences of Stift Kremsmünster, which is not on the walk, a skiing weekend in Pillerseetal, and my brief guide to Vienna and its *Land*.

Even more exorbitant was my introduction of those I loved and lost during the seven years over which I spread the pilgrimage. So there was a drift from guide towards diary. I also lost control of the illustrations. I am a very amateur photographer with a very basic digital camera. Much better architectural photographs, of exteriors and of interiors, are easily available. But I have to express my passionate response to what I see by taking a photograph. Likewise with nature, the photograph captures a moment of rapture or delight that would otherwise be lost. After stringent editing, the plate section includes only a small selection of my photographs.

So that is my explanation and apology for what follows. Nevertheless my original intention survives: to provide a practical guide for those, like me, with little or no German, not for those who are looking for the big walk but for those who would like to try a few days of holiday walking in Austria. For them I would suggest plucking a plum from the duff: for instance, the Wachau from Gottweig Abbey to Melk Abbey. Not only is that a sublime stretch, but it is so accessible from Vienna, a short train ride from the Hauptbahnhof to St Polten and then a local train on to Furth.

Feldkirch Innsbruck Salzburg Linz Vienna

THE FIRST WALK

West from Vienna to Feldkirch: the Main Stream

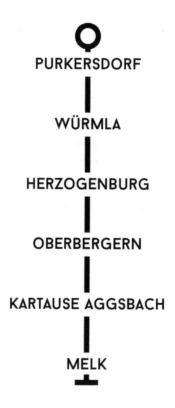

PURKERSDORF

WÜRMLA

HERZOGENBURG

OBERBERGERN

KARTAUSE AGGSBACH

MELK

PURKERSDORF TO MELK

Day 1 – 21 June 2013 – Purkersdorf to Würmla
MY FIRST DAY'S walk took me from Purkersdorf all the way
to Würmla. This is a distance of about 35 kilometres. It divides
into two obvious halves. The first half sees the pilgrim leave
the Purkersdorf parish church to tackle a long walk through
the Vienna woods. It is 12 kilometres from Purkersdorf to
Ried, all through the silent, enveloping woods. The pilgrim
will feel utterly alone. Apart from an occasional bird he will
see no other form of life and the only movement comes from
the trees and running streams. At about the halfway point the
path crosses Troppberg, a high point at nearly 600 metres. Just
off the path to the right stands a viewing tower erected on the
summit. It is only a brief detour and well worth the walk. The
tower is easily climbed and offers spectacular 360-degree views
over forest tops.

At times the way runs along the edge of the woods,
revealing vistas of rich farmlands with crops and livestock, and
approaching the end of the *Wald* the path opens into a clearing
with a spring and the ruins of a minute monastery. Religious
houses, both extant and defunct, are perhaps the dominant

theme of the Jakobsweg. My first photograph was of the nearby sign explaining the significance of the few remaining stones of the monastery.

The second and much longer part of this day's walk is through farmland. Emerging above the village of Ried the traveller surveys a fertile valley through which the Elsbach gently flows. Ried itself is a pretty village and has the useful Gasthof Schmid on the main road. I took a picture of this handsome inn. The trees bordering the road shade a pretty garden, ideal for a midday rest. I also recorded the path that leaves Ried with the Elsbach running quietly only metres to the left of the path.

Once refreshed at the Gasthof Schmid, the walker has an easy 5.5 kilometres beside the brook until reaching Sieghartskirchen. This is the most substantial village encountered on the first day. It boasts two guesthouses and an excellent Café Konditorei, where the cakes and ices rival even the range at Demel in Vienna's Kohlmarkt. A sight of the church confirms the standing of the village.

From there to Siegersdorf is 8 kilometres and the route is more challenging, climbing up into the woods and then sinking down on the approach to Siegersdorf. The larger village of Asperhofen is only skirted on the next phase of 4.5 kilometres to reach the wood at Bildeiche. An equal distance through the wood leads down to Würmla. The prospect with lengthening evening shadows attracted another picture.

If the walker reaches Würmla he will have covered 35 kilometres and will welcome the basic bed and table offered by the *Gasthaus* opposite the church.

All the above is mainly written impersonally. But on that June day when I was the pilgrim it was blisteringly hot as the day wore on and I left the cool of the Wienerwald. The long-distance walker develops techniques to ease or shorten the distance. For instance, on a hairpin section, up or down, it may be possible to cut across from one end of the hairpin to the other. Even on the flat I always favoured the inside of any bend unless only the outside of the bend were in the shade, in which case in any sort of heat I would prefer the shade to saving a few metres. Of course these discoveries lay ahead of me on this trial day but still I found myself looking for shade wherever I could find it as I walked on from Ried.

With hindsight I should have called a halt in Asperhofen but bravado drew me on. I wanted to test what I could cover on a day's march. The result was that I began to struggle as the path climbed into the wood at Bildeiche, and beyond the wood every step was pain. By the time I reached the church at Würmla I was dehydrated and done.

There are two inns beside each other, opposite the handsome church. I booked into the first before I discovered there was no dinner and no staff, and payment was required in advance. But I ate outside at the other, watching some farm workers going home while others were on their way to an evening out. I also watched the growing dusk on the walls and spire of the ochre-washed church. How the church dominates the street! The yellow house opposite is where I found my bed and breakfast; primitive, but excellent value at €25.

Ever optimistic, I assumed I would be right for the return on the next day. It started well enough when the innkeeper's

5

father was friendly in serving a breakfast of bitter coffee and stale bread. And before leaving the village I explored what had once been a manor house in a small park, which had been converted into some sort of community project. It seemed to mourn this transformation. But as soon as I walked away I knew I was in trouble. Like a racehorse that has been jarred up on firm going, I could not find my stride. My legs ached and the ache grew worse with every step. I could save 5 kilometres by taking the highway to Asperhofen and that I did even though the tarmac surface aggravated my pain. I soon recognised that I would never make it back to Purkersdorf and would be pressed even to make it to Reid. That I did, however, by the evening and Anatol, Felicitas' son, kindly collected me from Gasthof Schmid.

An obvious lesson learned was that the pilgrim's feet must be shod with the same care as the racehorse's. Later that summer Felicitas took me to a sports shoe shop in Vienna, Tony's Laufshop, where fitting includes a video of the customer in action and a running escalator on which to perform. That leads to intensive questioning as to the intended use. I emerged with an expensive purchase especially selected for the *Wegwanderung* that proved to be one of the best investments I have ever made. They lasted me until Schärding on the third walk, years on.

Despite the pain I was inspired by the experiment to commit to journey on to Göttweig. It would be achieved in short stages and always by a return to take up the path where I had last left it. All that explains why the second day of my journey came three months after the first.

The resolution to go all the way developed gradually thereafter. It emerged as a challenge, a challenge that could not be fudged and one by which I was determined not to be defeated. As I had discovered, walking in high summer was not ideal. What I was also to discover was that walking in midwinter was impossible. What inspired me at all times and in all conditions was the beauty and variety of the Austrian countryside. Although I have given 5 September as the second day, it was in effect the first day that was purposeful rather than experimental. Between the two dates I had celebrated my seventy-fifth birthday and retirement with a beacon party for the village at home in Seend. (For some jubilee, or perhaps the millennium, we had built a brazier onto a telegraph pole that could be hauled up like a crucifix, after being loaded with kindling and timber offcuts, then to be ignited and to flare as a beacon.) I photographed the setting sun and the beacon primed for lighting when dusk came.

☞

Day 2 – 5 September 2013 – Würmla to Herzogenburg
FROM WÜRMLA IT is only 2.5 kilometres to Diendorf and then 3.5 on to Langmannersdorf. The Austrians are enthusiastic purchasers of garden gnomes and it was on this stretch that I recorded a gnome display that would surely gain a place in the *Guinness Book of Records*. On the next 5 kilometres to Weissenkirchen I passed a stone marking the middle point of the Jakobsweg's distance through the territory of Lower Austria, a point that hardly seemed to merit a significant milestone.

There is then what feels like a long 6 kilometres through woodland and agricultural splendour to reach the village of St Andrä, which boasts a fine church.

On the walk through the woodlands to St Andrä an opportunity presents to make a detour to Heiligenkreuz. This is well worth the additional 3 kilometres since the pilgrim church and adjoining schloss sit in a perfectly preserved feudal village with flower gardens and fruit trees surrounding each dwelling. The chatelaine permits visits to the schloss and its extraordinary staircase and chapel. Her welcome to me, probably the only visitor that day to buy a ticket, was brimming with kindness and ended with an invitation to join her and her workers for their simple lunch laid out in the garden amid the flowers and fruiting plum trees. The invitation seemed the most natural thing in the world and equally natural was my acceptance. The lunch that followed was home-grown and simply cooked, shared by us all easefully. I took so many pictures, expressing my delight at all I saw, that I have had to exercise restraint in restricting the selection to four: of these I have chosen one for the plate section, the grand staircase in the Schloss. There was a programme displayed for concerts in the schloss on summer evenings and I tried to enthuse Felicitas to buy tickets but somehow it never happened. I got no closer than sending a postcard of thanks and then a card the following Christmas.

St Andrä is in the valley of the Traisen, a substantial river, and on leaving the village one must cross it as well as the very main road from St Pölten to Krems. This brings one at once to the historic and magnificent Stift Herzogenburg, which is surrounded by a handsome town. Although only 20 kilometres from Würmla it makes an agreeable short day and allows the traveller to rest the night with the Augustinian canons of the monastery.

At the abbey, I was warmly welcomed by Father Moritz. He spoke perfect English and explained the life of the canons to each of whom is allocated a local parish. Through the day they serve as parish priest, congregating in the evening to rejoin the communal life of the abbey. Guided by Father Moritz I joined the small congregation for vespers in the magnificent abbey church which serves the town as well as the abbey. After vespers came a simple supper to which I was invited by Father Moritz. The next day opened with morning mass in the abbey church followed by breakfast with the canons. There were two other pilgrims, Brazilians, father and son – at least that is how they introduced themselves and I would now find it hard to explain why I found that explanation unconvincing. We shared a dormitory with a capacity of twenty bunk beds and I was grateful that that allowed us to avoid proximity. Although the hospitality is austere it is a privilege to be embraced in the life of the community. On my return to Seend I posted a large box of Darjeeling to Father Moritz.

☞

Day 3 – 6 September 2013 – Herzogenburg to Oberbergern
THE WALK ON day three led me past Stift Göttweig. The way climbs agreeably to Walpersdorf where there is an imposing 16th-century schloss which I noticed only in passing. The path continues across fine country to Eggendorf via Maria Ellend

with its exceptionally pretty little church. At this point the great Benedictine abbey of Göttweig sails into view, and what a view! It merits its place in the plate section.

As I crossed the flat land approaching the hill my mobile rang and I found myself in an acerbic exchange with Carola, then still my wife, on one of the myriad issues raised by separation and divorce. Generally I was fortunate in the rarity of incoming calls. A mobile is of course indispensable in case of accident and perhaps I would have been wiser to have turned it on only in emergency.

The steepness of the hill that must be climbed to reach the abbey is daunting. Nor is there much reward for the effort. The abbey commands a superb site. It was designed by a famous architect, Nikolas von Hildebrandt. I had high expectations but they were all disappointed. I found it altogether over large, lacking in charm and over-commercialised. Perhaps it is happily so, otherwise I would have been tempted to rest a night there after covering only 15 kilometres.

From Göttweig Abbey there is a steep descent through the woods to arrive at Furth. The path then runs through vineyards to Mautern, a large town that takes some negotiation. From Mautern it is an uninteresting road walk to Unterbergern, but from Unter- to Oberbergern the path soars uphill through wild and wooded country. Looking east from a panorama point just off the path, the Danube lies below with Mautern on the south bank and more distant Stein/Krems on the north. Oberbergern is in the midst of the Dunkelsteinwald, some of the most remote and least inhabited country that the Jakobsweg crosses. The reception at Zum Goldenen Hirsch in

Oberbergern, reached in the early evening, was warm; I was fed a hearty supper and slept in a simple room after a walk of 32 kilometres.

☞

Day 4 – 7 September 2013 – Oberbergern to Kartause Aggsbach

BREAKFAST THE NEXT morning was abundant and I set off on what was a three and a half hour stage through the forest to reach Maria Langegg. The beauty of this forest caught my heart with a view of a farm slumbering halfway up a wooded hill.

Maria Langegg is an important pilgrimage church and has an adjoining small museum. I photographed the approach climbing the village street. The church and surrounding forest belonged to the Prince Bishop of Würzburg in the 16th century and he built a substantial dwelling for his land agent. That dwelling now serves as a *Stube* for locals and visitors. It is rare to find a house of this period and of this domestic grandeur in an Austrian village. I took the view of the house coming back from the church. Having rested and drunk two large milky coffees, I set out for the Aggstein ruins.

This stage of the walk was populated by many families who park at Maria Langegg and then walk to the spectacular ruined castle of Aggstein standing high above the Danube. The castle is well managed for tourism and was packed, with many inspecting the view and many more eating hearty meals at long tables set outside in the castle keep. I took a picture of the ruin and another of the Danube flowing far below carrying its traffic. One of the sights of the Danube is its great barges that carry freight, in theory – and perhaps in practice – from Rotterdam to the Black Sea.

From Aggstein Castle comes a long descent followed by a stiff walk uphill from Aggstein village to reach Kartause Aggsbach. The view of the monastery from afar is highly romantic since it has a huge curtain wall behind which rests nothing but a grassy bank. That is how I first saw it as I emerged from the woods, a view I have included in the plate section.

The monastery church is spectacular, however, completely unornamented save for functional necessities (pulpit, altar and lectern), all decorated in sombre black and gold. Nowhere is there any sign of the rich embellishments of the baroque: stucco and painted images on canvas or frescoed on wall or ceiling. I photographed the nave and then the pulpit on its own. I subsequently came to understand that what I saw at the *Kartause* is the traditional Carthusian decorative style with which I was not then familiar.

I was unable to find a room at the traditional Gasthaus zur Kartause opposite the abbey but found satisfactory accommodation in a modern hotel, Gasthaus Haidon, down the high street. The mosquitoes, however, were savage. The next morning my credit card was not acceptable and the proprietor became taxi driver as he charged for a 15 kilometre round trip to the nearest bankomat. This had been a walk of 30 kilometres. I was soon to learn that on the Jakobsweg the tendered credit card was generally refused. A good reservoir of cash is essential to pay for the overnight stays.

☞

Day 5 – 8 September 2013 – Kartause Aggsbach to Melk

I SET OFF early the next morning as soon as the bill was paid. I tried to capture the sights that I would want to remember: the backward glance at the monastery; the window boxes even on the roadside barrier; Highland cattle, incongruous, perhaps, but sporting EU regulation ear tags. I saw them in the wooded terrain that ran past Wolfstein to the riverside town of Schönbühel.

At the edge of the town is an early 19th-century romanticised castle which is still in private ownership. Before I reached it, however, I encountered a most extraordinary site at the Servitenkloster which I had chosen to visit, although it necessitated a detour of about a mile off the pilgrim route. In the field below the monastery I glimpsed a traveller's caravan pulled by a huge bullock. I endeavoured to get close but found the vehicle proceeding at a fast pace and I was unable to catch up until reaching Schönbühel castle. I immediately started taking photographs, which much annoyed the fast-walking woman, the only adult, but accompanied by dogs and young children. Alas, I had accidentally switched the setting from camera to video and the four pictures I took are videos trapped in the memory card.

Having rested in Schönbühel I set out on a steep climb to reach Hub and thence a descent to the Danube riverbank. The remaining walk of some 5 kilometres to gain the centre of Melk was hot, dry and cheerless. In the first place not a single café or shop was open on this Sunday afternoon in any of the suburban approaches. Even in the outskirts of Melk itself there was no respite. By the time I reached the railway station in Melk, itself not easy to find, I could hardly speak, being so dehydrated. I managed to leave my *Wandestaub* in the ticket office but at least found a train with a change at St Pölten which returned me to Vienna Westbahnhof. The airport bus took me to meet Felicitas on her return flight from visiting her mother in Stuttgart.

☞

THIS SECOND STRETCH of the pilgrim way from Göttweig to Melk is undoubtedly the most interesting and the most beautiful that I had encountered, or was yet to encounter before the Alps. This is the famous valley of the Wachau, rich in grapes, apricots and history. The glory of the Wachau lies on the north bank of the Danube where the south-facing flat land and steeply rising terraces are planted with grapevines and apricots. The trees are harvested in June and the vines in September. The main road runs through this Eden, connecting villages, hamlets and towns made prosperous by trade and tourism. The south bank of the Danube is north-facing and has not the softness and ease of the lands across the waters. But in its different way it is no less impressive and better matches the spirit of the Jakobsweg. The main crossings of the Danube are of course the bridges but there are also occasional ferries big enough to transport one or two cars from one bank to the other. It is such a bespoke service that it had for me a powerful charm when driving about with Felicitas in the apricot season.

These ferries only cross the river and make only a tiny increase to the abundant traffic flowing with or against the mighty river, which consists mainly of huge barges for goods, passenger cruise ships (for which Melk and Dürnstein are prime calls), and day trips from Vienna. Another unexpected delight that the Danube offers is its beaches. Occasionally they appear, a sandy strip at the water's edge thronged with children bathing and parents keeping watch.

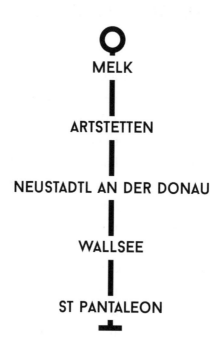

MELK

ARTSTETTEN

NEUSTADTL AN DER DONAU

WALLSEE

ST PANTALEON

MELK TO ST PANTALEON

Day 6 – 3 October 2013 – Melk to Artstetten

IT WAS AT the end of September that I returned to tackle the third section of the Jakobsweg. (The Austrian National Tourist Office has divided the whole into a series of sections for each of which there is a separate guide brochure.) Having taken a train to Melk I called at the very helpful tourist information office, where I was supplied with the map for the next section and indeed a map for the section beyond. Unfortunately, I mislaid that map for the fourth section – or perhaps I left it behind in the tourist office – a mistake that did not become evident until I had reached Persenbeug. Initially I took a route from Melk through water meadows to cross the Danube in search of an easy walk to Emmersdorf and Leiben. I photographed the view of the abbey from the north bank and also the ruin that rises dramatically above the river embankment at Weitenegg. Unfortunately this shortcut, commended by the tourist office, lacked any waymarks and it was with considerable anxiety and hesitation that I eventually succeeded in reaching Leiben. It had been a stiff walk and it was by now mid-afternoon. Leiben boasts a castle but I felt no enthusiasm for the short detour and viewed only its roofs from afar. After finding the only café in the sleepy village I set out to reach a further point, namely the considerable town of Artstetten.

Artstetten is famous for its castle, which was constructed by Archduke Franz Ferdinand in the second half of the 19th century. Here he and his morganatic wife are buried, since she was not eligible for inclusion in the Imperial Vault in Vienna. The town attracts many tourists and the village inn was accommodating a huge party of Germans from Saxony. I was billeted in a relief house but got a good dinner and a good breakfast the next morning. I was sufficiently impressed to change for dinner and wear for the first time the strawberry-red alpaca cardigan. I took a photograph of the castle on the following morning. It is open to the public but the gift shop put me off paying to go further. The royal tombs are accessible in an undercroft without a ticket.

☞

Day 7 – 4 October 2013 – Artstetten to Neustadtl an der Donau

THE NEXT MORNING I set out on a pleasant walk across fields to reach Maria Taferl. This is a pilgrim church of great importance and around it has grown a township devoted to providing services for pilgrims. I took a picture only of the approach to the church, noting the well-mown golf course. Here I received the stamp on my Kompass guide and excellent coffee and cake in a smart café adjoining the pilgrim church, which occupies a magnificent site with huge views over the

Danube valley. The church itself is richly ornamented inside and out in traditional Austrian baroque style. From the church is a sharp and charming descent through deciduous woodland to reach the port town of Marbach on the Danube. I tried to capture the appeal of what I am sure is a very ancient path. At Marbach the waymarking faltered and the outcome was a long trek alongside the river before cutting across a wide bend to arrive at Gottsdorf. The relatively short walk to Persenbeug leads through an industrial wasteland and suburbia before arriving at a delightful town square in the middle of which is a mighty lime tree of extreme antiquity. I photographed the three labels nailed to the tree. One declared its status as a Naturdenkmal tree. One claimed that it was planted in 1300, which seemed to me improbable. The third recorded that Saller, the tree surgeon, had tended it.

My need in Persenbeug, apart from coffee, was to find a map for the next section of the route. This third section had turned out to be surprisingly short and I had achieved in two days what I had expected to take four. Accordingly, I took the decision to combine in one walk the third and fourth sections.

My problem was that I had lost the map. I asked the café for help but they offered none. I went to the bank but they only directed me to a guesthouse. In the guesthouse I met a mine of misinformation, not least that I would receive everything that I required if only I called at the tourist office outside Ybbs on the far bank of the river. Thus encouraged I set out and ultimately reached the tourist office, only to see in the window the helpful sign: "Closed: opening next May". What to do? There was really no choice but to risk it. I was able to pick up the general direction from a road map and thankfully the waymarking thereafter was of a good standard.

The first section to reach Hengstberg was tough. The *Berg* comes in at 571 metres. It is a very rural area with big farms working to high standards. I chose for a photograph a prime example of a local farm, painted in the traditional yellow and white. This tradition dates back to the empire, when official buildings from Bohemia to the Balkans were painted in the same shade of yellow, *Schönbrunner Gelb*.

Thereafter I think I must somewhere have missed a turn and so ended up doing a long stretch on minor roads. My destination was Neustadtl an der Donau. At five o'clock I was dismayed to see that I still had 11 kilometres to travel. I thought that if Neustadtl was on the Danube it would be all downhill. Alas, Neustadtl is far inland and the road was all ascents, with long steep climbs and only occasional descents. I did not reach the village until dusk and on the way my rucksack must have come open and shed my brand new cardigan. The disaster would have been compounded had I not found at least a village pub where in very basic surroundings I managed to negotiate sausages for supper and a bed to sleep.

☞

Day 8 – 5 October 2013 – Neustadtl an der Donau to Wallsee

IN THE MORNING I retraced my steps in the hope of finding my cardigan. But perhaps I had left it at Artstetten? So I soon abandoned the search. Having invested in the vain hope that I had left it in Artstetten, I returned to the way ahead and after this needless loss I developed a way of fastening the rucksack zips to eliminate spontaneous opening from the pressure of the crammed contents. I set out in better heart and much enjoyed the cross-country walk to arrive at the charming village of Kollmitzberg. The church is particularly fine and included a stamp for my pilgrim card. It was harvest festival weekend, not just for this parish but for the region. The wonderful decoration before the altar expresses the piety and tradition of the Austrian farming community, qualities that the Anglican parishes of England have let slip during my lifetime.

The walk on to Ardagger Stift was pleasing and the *Stift* itself exceptional. In the church the scene was enlivened by an amateur choir singing their hearts out to an audience of family and friends. I photographed the choir and later a glance back at the *Stift* as I walked on.

Opposite the abbey is an excellent hotel, the first sign of luxury I had so far encountered anywhere on the pilgrim way. The manager was extremely helpful and ultimately provided me with a map of the Moststrasse (a trail for seekers of the traditional local pear cider), which, as well as all other relevant routes, included, in purple, the Jakobsweg. (Lower Austria is divided into four quarters. The south-east quarter is the Mostviertel, hence within it the Moststrasse. These divisions seem to be less administrative and more for the promotion of tourism, regional identity and tradition.) Thereafter I was not relying only on waymarks. Now at least I knew where I needed to go. The hotel is Landhaus Stift Ardagger and the telephone number is +43 (0)7479 65650.

From Ardagger it was another slog to reach Wallsee. Wallsee is distinguished by its schloss, built or renovated by minor royalty in the late 19th century. Seemingly they had a high sense of community, for the main street of the town is distinguished by imperial-style development of great charm. The only hotel open was again an excellent establishment, albeit less luxurious than at Ardagger. The proprietress and her family provided me with a very warm welcome, an excellent supper and a very comfortable bed. The hotel is the Wallseerhof on Alte Schulstrasse, telephone number +43 (0)7433 2223.

☞

Day 9 – 6 October 2013 – Wallsee to St Pantaleon

I HAD AGREED with Felicitas that I would return that Sunday night rather than, as first planned, at some time on Monday. Accordingly, I had to get to the end of the stage at St Pantaleon and find transport back to Vienna. In the hotel in Wallsee there was not much encouragement. There were no bus services on a Sunday, particularly that Sunday, which was a harvest festival all over the region. I decided that I would forsake the Jakobsweg through the countryside and instead take the river route until it joined the Jakobsweg at Mitterau.

I set off in an autumn fog and was lucky in finding my way from the middle of Wallsee onto this river route, much used by cyclists to get from Passau to Vienna. As I walked through the mist I had the good fortune to encounter a local who had excellent English, having worked for many years on merchant shipping oil tankers. We walked together and chatted until he had walked as far as he had planned. He was almost the only human I encountered before arriving at Mitterau. As I walked on to Erla I passed through a farmyard adorned by a gigantic pear tree. The fallen fruit, lying thick on the ground, would have supplied an industrial output of Williams Birne Snapps.

The Jakobsweg thereafter was erratically signed and I am not sure that I hit it off as I struggled through copse and field to reach Erla, almost at journey's end. The monastic church in Erla is particularly distinguished and to my eye far outshines its rival at St Pantaleon, although St Pantaleon alone retains a feature of their shared 12th century origin in its famous crypt beneath the west apse. They are certainly joined historically and there is an excellent guide covering both.

Opposite the church in St Pantaleon was another excellent hotel, Gasthof Winklehner (telephone +43 (0)7435 7584). The restaurant was full to the brim with local people eating their Sunday lunch, proof that I had achieved this final leg in very good time, perhaps by taking the river route. Extraordinarily I encountered for the first time fellow pilgrims in the hotel. Two girls, one of whom was feeling ill, had just enjoyed their annual two-day walk on the Weg. The one who was feeling poorly had decided to abandon the walk and I was able to share her taxi into the big local town of St Valentin. St Valentin boasts a train station and it was a short wait for the express that stopped on its way from Munich to Vienna. Surprisingly, the express stopped again at Hütteldorf. Seizing the opportunity I jumped off and took the local service to Untertullnerbach. Walking thence through the *Wald* I found an amazing green lizard with violent yellow splashes on its back. I gathered it into my cap as a return present but when offering it to Felicitas with considerable pride I discovered that somewhere in the course of the ten-minute walk it had made good its escape.

THE ROUTE AROUND LINZ

Day 10 – 7 January 2014 – St Pantaleon to Luftenberg

DESPITE THE OBVIOUS disadvantages I was determined to tackle the fifth section in January. The days were short and the weather uncertain. The landscape would be in naked frost. However, I had prepared for the experiment by obtaining what seemed to be extremely full and helpful brochures from the Mostviertel tourist service. The *circumambulations* of Linz offered a north and a south route. The south route appeared to be the more attractive and I accordingly decided on the north route in January with a view to testing the south route on some later occasion in the summer.

Having taken the train to St Valentin and then a taxi to St Pantaleon I was relying upon the excellent hotel manager to help me decide where to spend the first night. Alas, Monday and Tuesday were the hotel's rest days. Nor was there a human being in sight anywhere in the deserted streets. With considerable misgiving I set out, finding at least a fingerpost for the Jakobsweg going who knows where: the excellent system of marking the next staging post and the distance and time required to reach it seems not to exist beyond the Vienna

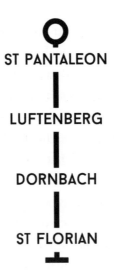

ST PANTALEON

LUFTENBERG

DORNBACH

ST FLORIAN

region. The day was cold and damp with a low mist blotting out the further bank of the Danube. I trudged along country roads and occasional footpaths until reaching an enigmatic sign that showed Jakobsweg to the left and Jakobsweg straight ahead. I concluded that this was the point of division between the northern and southern routes and opted to continue straight ahead.

The assumption was correct and I soon reached a wooden bridge dividing Lower and Upper Austria. Beyond the wooden bridge came a major trunk road that led me across the Danube to the outskirts of Mauthausen. Felicitas had told me that this was the site of a notorious death camp during the Nazi era and I had no inclination to investigate the township, turning sharp left along the bank of the river immediately after the crossing. This at least attracted one sign for the Jakobsweg, the last I saw, pointing to the footpath bordering the Danube. This was hardly idyllic since I was only yards from the huge lorries thundering along the parallel road.

When the footpath died I could not regain the highway but only a tunnel beneath it, which led me all uncertain to a village that turned out to be Langenstein. Here I was fortunate to find a kind man preparing his woodstack and he, understanding my objective, advised that I had best regain the proper path by walking on the road to St Georgen an der Gusen.

This was sound advice, although the highway was unappealing. At least it provided a roadside café and, it being three o'clock, I was in bad need of a drink. A warm welcome, good coffee, rich cake and the lifting of the fog gave me new heart. The late sun shining from a cloudless sky illuminated a heavily developed countryside. This was hardly surprising given the proximity of Linz and the inevitability of a suburban zone.

St Georgen proved more attractive at its heart where the Gusen divides the village and shares that function with the railway track. As I passed traditional *Gasthäuser* to left and right of the road I flirted with the idea of an overnight stop but it was only four o'clock and I had only covered some 15 kilometres. So onward again on a road walk with Luftenberg as the next village ahead. Again it proved to be one with much commuter traffic in both directions. I knew from my guide that Luftenberg offered three addresses for an overnight stay: two B&Bs and one *Gasthaus*. I marched through the village seeing no one and no sign of any commerce. Nor could I find the street that I needed. A return to the guidebook inspired the conclusion that I was in Luftenberg, whereas the hotel was in Luftenberg an der Donau. So, weary and anxious, I pressed on down a steep hill towards the river. At its bottom I faced a long stretch with no sign of any other Luftenberg. I saw a bus stop. I examined the timetable and saw that a bus was due at any minute. When it arrived the helpful driver explained that Luftenberg an der Donau was none other than the Luftenberg at the top of the hill. Being too tired to face the backward climb I crossed the road and waited for the eastbound bus. On entering I explained my goal to the driver, who then revealed that the guesthouse was nowhere near Luftenberg but in the village of Abwinden, close to Statzing, a village I had passed between St Georgen and Luftenberg. Thoroughly confused, I gladly rode with him to Statzing and followed his direction to Abwinden through the gathering dusk.

Entering an Austrian village in early evening is like entering a churchyard. The houses stand in rows like graves but, like graves, they are all shut. The village sprawled ahead, offering neither light nor clue. Only the return of a car to one of the darkened dwellings enabled me to get directions to Gasthaus Radlwirt (+43 (0)7237 27554), which modestly cloaks its whereabouts from the traveller.

It proved well worth the search, bright and crowded. I was shown a room and then became enveloped in the company in the bar, all of them chatting, drinking, smoking and playing an endless card game. After a huge helping of venison and red cabbage with two *Viertel* of wine I was on my way to bed when accosted by a most eccentric figure who, with his straggling beard, approximated a Chinese ancient. Even more surprising was his revelation that he was both a cousin of the landlord and a Yorkshireman, a claim proved by his accent. How he came to be a pensioner on the landlord's charity I never fully understood, but he claimed to be the gardener and plied me with a schnapps made from walnuts from the tree in the garden. Another feature of this curious inn was that the breakfast was entirely self-service. No staff member was anywhere in sight. I put together a substantial meal and even carried off two hard-boiled eggs in my rucksack.

☞

Day 11 – 8 January 2014 – Luftenberg to Dornbach
HAVING REGAINED STATZING I had no heart to repeat my walk through Luftenberg. I knew that the bus would take me

to the next dot on the map, Steyregg. Steyregg is not small and boasts an historic centre. However, when the tourist department at the town hall claimed they had never heard of the Jakobsweg (despite the fact that it runs through the town), I gave up. The way ahead to Linz was entirely either suburban or urban and the suggestion that I should walk the intervening 10 kilometres to the tourist office in the main square seemed ludicrous: so back to the bus stop and a wait for the next bus. Once on board and soon in Linz, the helpful driver put me down as close as he could to the Hauptplatz. The splendour of the column to the Trinity in the square is not matched by anything else in Linz. The incredibly helpful young man behind the counter in the tourist office confirmed that the Jakobsweg brochure was simply misleading. Neither the northern nor the southern route that it proposed offered the walker any attraction. He advised me to delete the Linz section and to resume the Weg at Pausing in the spring. He then provided me with all that I needed for Linz and booked me into the Wilhering Gasthof.

Hugely encouraged, I spent the day seeing the sights of Linz, not in themselves worth a visit but well worth inspection if one is already there. The old cathedral is a handsome baroque church which should never have been abandoned for the construction of the modern neo-gothic pile. The funicular to the pilgrim church on the heights above the city was most enjoyable and enabled me to pass an agreeable hour. I found in the city a bookshop selling a comprehensive Kompass guide in German to the Jakobsweg and with that I set out in the late afternoon by bus for Wilhering. Absurdly I had walked these past ten days guided only by the brochures available in tourist information offices, each covering a section of the Jakobsweg in a sequence of stages.

Having arrived in Wilhering village and having investigated the monastery exterior and located its wonderful church, I bumped into an elderly monk who hobbled out on crutches and invited me to the 6.30 mass the following morning. That settled, I headed for bed and dinner. The experience of the previous night was repeated: the Gasthof Fischer booked by the tourist office was nowhere near Wilhering but in another village, Dornbach, some 5 kilometres distant. I felt compelled to shift to the inn opposite the monastery. My request for bed and board was met with surly refusal from the only Austrian who has ever shown me hostility and rudeness. Eventually I had no alternative but to walk or bus to Dornbach, the neighbouring village. Fortunately I found a bus and was well looked after by the driver. Arriving in the village, however, I found no clue as to where the guesthouse might be and it was only through good fortune that two joggers appeared and put me on to the farm that also serves as guesthouse. Again the door was shuttered and barred, and only by much banging and the barking of a dog did I find a reception. Happily, it proved to be a warm one and the lady of the house showed me to an excellent room. She was not offering anything more, though, and only out of kindness did she provide me with a bowl of soup and a bottle of wine. Off early the next morning for her holiday, she was officially closed and had only taken me in at the request of the tourist office. In season, Gasthof Fischer would be an inviting stop, so I add the telephone number: +43 (0)7221 88094.

☞

Day 12 – 9 January 2014 – Dornbach to St Florian

SO IT WAS that on the next morning there was no breakfast and I made do with the remains of the wine and my hard-boiled eggs from Abwinden. Again it was the bus that carried me back to Wilhering, where I spent a morning digesting the tranquillity of the monastery and the wonders of the monastery church. It is quite simply the best that I have seen in Austria, and that results from the import of decorators not from Italy but from Munich. The resulting rococo grace is on a par with the wonderful churches of Bavaria and its beauty cannot be exaggerated. I took a mass of pictures but again slipped from camera to video. So I have only the fountain in the cloister, the west end and the pulpit. But the latter two record the opulence and delicacy of the work. The monastery has stamped its character on the entire community and there are many handsome buildings and an absence of recent development for which we must be grateful. However it is a misfortune that what has become a busy modern road brushes the length of one facade and divides the abbey from its satellite buildings.

I returned to Linz Hauptplatz by post bus and, having walked across the city to the bus station, found the service to St Florian. St Florian lies about 10 kilometres from the city and the bus set me down in the attractive town square, overlooked by the mighty abbey. Having investigated the various hotels that the town offers, I found myself attracted to Zur Kanne (telephone +43 (0)7224 4288), but decided to defer a decision until all options had been identified. Nowhere could I find 1

Stiftstrasse until came the realisation that it was within the monastery itself and it was a *Keller* with guest rooms (telephone +43 (0)7224 5069). My clear choice then was the monastery accommodation and that gave me the entry to a plea that I might be allowed to see the interior of the monastery, despite the fact that it was not normally available in the winter months. The lady in charge of the gift shop was my salvation and she persuaded one of the fathers of the community to provide me with a guided tour. I was unfortunate indeed in my guide, a monk with virtually no English despite his frequent visits to the cathedral towns of the north of England. Nevertheless we managed, and he showed me all the fine rooms and the treasures of the monastery. The only thing that remained was the monastery church, which I reserved for the following day. Encouraged by the gift shop lady I walked to Zur Kanne for a magnificent dinner of lamb cooked in different ways. The breakfast the following morning was provided in the monastery *Keller* and I was not alone at the table. I made a good breakfast and spent the whole day exploring every corner of the town and the monastery, including the church. The church is justly famous for its size and grandeur but it is the product of Italian painters and decorators, particularly Carlone and Altomonte, neither of whom could be ranked in the first class. However, I must record my admiration for a garden house by Carlone which now stands isolated some 400 metres from the main gates of the abbey. I photographed the facade and the loggia behind. Again my incompetence turned most of my views of the abbey and the town into videos. I have only one view of the west end and one of the pulpit caught by a ray of bright sunlight.

In every Counter-Reformation church in Austria the pulpit was the subject of extravagant expense. Magnificent are the results and they must have inspired the preachers to heights of dramatic oratory. But, as far as I have been able to observe, they are no longer used for their purpose. That may be a necessary reflection of the evolved relationship between priests and laity but for me it tinges their exuberance with sadness.

The village surrounding the abbey has much attraction, reflecting the talent of the many artists and craftsmen employed to glorify the abbey. There is the pretty church and the adjoining well dedicated to St John the Baptist. Close by is the house, built and first occupied by the architect, Prandtauer. Then there is an entrancing walk, at first by road, high above and circling the facade of the abbey church. It soon becomes a footpath and above stands a slumbering old house of almost other-worldly spirit. I never felt so attracted to a home anywhere else on the Weg. It stands in surroundings utterly pastoral and yet within half a mile of one of the most sophisticated imperial creations (I say imperial because the palatial style and scale of the abbey reflected its need to accommodate the Kaiser and other rulers, temporal and spiritual, as they travelled). From this path beyond the bewitching house are the only views of the exterior of the church on its north side and the exterior of the library as it breaks out from the east facade of the abbey. The library is one of the glories of St Florian, both externally and internally; the other is the *Marmorsaal*. The double stairway to the imperial apartments within the great gate is only slightly less glorious. The greatest moveable treasure of the abbey is the series of fourteen paintings by Altdorfer, savage and superb.

St Florian seems to enjoy a surprising local popularity. Legend has it that as a Roman soldier he was condemned for insubordination in adhering to Christianity contrary to orders. He was thrown into the River Enns with a millstone roped to his legs. From this watery grave he became the patron saint of firemen. Since every community has its *Feuerwache* I suppose his popularity is assured. The many statues that venerate him show him emptying a bucket of water over a burning building.

To the north of the abbey church lies an extensive cemetery. My eye was caught by the memorial to:

FRANZ GRAF ZU ELTZ
FRANZISKA GRAFIN CLAM MARTINIC
Geb. 30. vii. 17
Geft. 30. x. 83

The family of Clam Martinic is very familiar to me from the Lawrence portrait of a forebear, Selina Meade, who married Count Clam Martinic in the early 19th century.

I also noticed a memorial to:

GRAF O'HEGARTY

It seemed to me then an invitation to fantasy and the opening line of a novel. But I have since learned of the tradition of British mercenaries enlisting in the imperial armies. Irish families attracted to imperial service included the Butlers, Fitzgeralds, O'Neills, Maguires, O'Byrnes, O'Briens and O'Reillys. Even more noteworthy were the Taaffes and the O'Donnells. Viscount Taaffe, born in Sligo in 1639, served in the imperial army and was ennobled and decorated with the Golden Fleece for his part in the defeat of the Ottoman army at Vienna in 1683. Over the following three centuries many of his direct descendants rose to high office in Vienna and Budapest, counts of the Habsburg empire as well as viscounts in the British peerage. Their seat in the Habsburg lands was Ellischau Castle in Bohemia. This duality ended dramatically when the twelfth viscount served in the Austrian army in the Great War. At its end he was deprived of his Irish viscountcy for what was regarded as disloyalty and his Habsburg title went the way of all Habsburg titles, abolished by the Republic.

Equal distinction was achieved by Count Maximilian O'Donnell, who saved the life of Emperor Franz Joseph in 1853 from an assassin's attack. In imperial gratitude the Emperor permitted him to impale the imperial arms of Austria with his own. (A more manifest expression of gratitude was the building and consecration of the Votivkirche nearby.) I wonder if Joseph Roth had Count O'Donnell in mind as the inspiration for the opening of the Radetsky March: the Emperor's life saved at Solferino by Lieutenant Trotta?

Uplifted by these great monastic houses I returned to Linz by bus and caught the express for Vienna which stopped conveniently at Hütteldorf. I photographed the sleeping youth in the opposite corner, wondering how he would manage the great stretch of life before him. At Hütteldorf I was met by Felicitas and so ended this unusual stage, more sightseeing than walking.

TRAUN TO GAMPERN

Day 13 – 24 March 2014 – Traun to Wels

I ARRIVED AT Linz station in need of advice as to how best to reach the city's edge. I walked to the Hauptplatz and talked again to the helpful young man in the tourist office. On reflection he advised not Pausing but Traun. So I returned to the station and took a local train to Traun. This well-named village is on the outskirts of the city and takes its name from the great river whose course I then followed all day until arriving at the city of Wels. But I only found the river and the way thanks to the kindness of the only human being in the vicinity of the railway station. I was not hopeful when I approached him since he was clearly an immigrant from South East Asia. However, once he had understood my need, he took great trouble to set me on the right road to the river and the Weg.

The Jakobsweg shares its course with the bicycle track from Linz to Traunsee. The river embankment is high and for the first half of the walk I followed the asphalt path in its shadow. The day was fine, if cold, and a wonderful sense of spring came from the scent of the balsam poplars which seemed to spring wild throughout the woodland walk. I eventually discovered

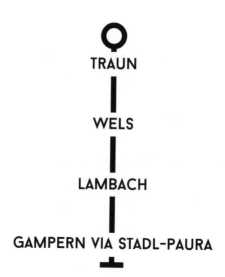

TRAUN

WELS

LAMBACH

GAMPERN VIA STADL-PAURA

that it was possible to walk on top of the embankment to enjoy wide views of the river, albeit in the constant roar of the traffic of the Autobahn on the other side. On balance I preferred the view and the noise to the cloistered silence of the wood. The distance I had undertaken was 20 kilometres, and since I did not leave Traun until 12.15 it was not until 6.30 in the evening that I arrived in the main square of Wels. This is an extremely handsome square since it is entirely composed of baroque facades, many of them undoubtedly without much restoration. I took a poor picture, it being difficult to catch the panorama. There is also in Wels a once-royal residence. I took the view of the gatehouse and, beyond it, the parish church as I stood with my back to the residence on the following morning.

On reaching the market square I examined in my usual fashion the exterior of all the hotels, thinking that I would choose the most desirable. Unexpected was the response to my offer of custom at the eleven hotels within the city centre. Not one had a spare bed. Only recourse to the tourist bureau's guide revealed a seminary situated some 7 kilometres out of the town at Schloss Puchberg. I was eating in a *Gasthof* in the main square and appealed to the manageress who in the kindest way telephoned Puchberg to book a room and sent me off in a taxi at the end of my meal. Schloss Puchberg is an ugly building that seems to serve as a diocesan resource for gatherings of devotees. The atmosphere was austere, and after a rigorous night I shared a frugal breakfast with a group of devout Catholic worthies. This accommodation proved to be surprisingly expensive: austerity usually comes cheap. Although it must be a last resort I add the telephone number:

+43 (0)7242 47537. What a contrast to the generosity and splendour of nights in the *Stifte*! The next morning I took the post bus back to Wels, grudgingly guided by the charmless receptionist at the schloss.

The walk from Traun to Wels is a lovely one and, seen in early spring, it bursts with promise. Two things stand out in my memory. The first is its surprising dedication to the scout movement with frequent way signs telling the life and achievements of Baden-Powell and his widow, Olave. The other was the wonderful scent of the balsam poplars wafting on the spring breeze.

Although Wels is a sizeable town the walker is spared the monotony of a mile of suburbia in and out. The path along the Traun is a delight and precludes much view of industry and the suburbs. From the market square to the Traun path is only a distance of some 100 metres.

☞

Day 14 – 25 March 2014 – Wels to Lambach

THE WALK FROM Wels to Lambach was about 23 kilometres, some 3 kilometres more than the previous day's walk. It was even more delightful, following closely the course of the Traun through wooded paths that were sprinkled with aconites, white and blue windflowers and wild violets. Wild garlic also grows thickly on the woodland floor. The woodland bordering the Traun is almost unbroken, with a mixture of ancient trees and modern planting. The trees run right down to the river and the path is set some 10 to 20 metres from the water's edge.

I was fortunate in walking this path in early spring. While there was the sense of spring bursting with early leaf, forsythia growing wild, and abundant *Cornus mas*, these early shoots did not hamper the constant sight of running water, fast over stones and weirs. Only a month later the river would have been hidden by the canopy of full spring growth.

The Traun leads the pilgrim to the centre of Lambach, indeed to the very gate of Lambach Abbey. I photographed the approach and the view from the abbey gate across the roofs of the town to the distant mountainous snow fields. Although the abbey is huge I had expected some sort of reception, having reserved a room from Puchberg. After a considerable wait I encountered, by chance, one of the Benedictine monks, Brother Albert, who took charge. He gave me a key to the pilgrim dormitory, which looked as if it had been set up in 1945, on the return of the community, and not touched since. He also invited me to the 5.30 vespers and wrote for me a timetable for mass and breakfast on the following morning.

The services tell you much about a community. I counted ten in the stalls at vespers. The music was led and directed by a young monk and the service was performed gracefully. After the service I walked the town, which seems to have had its zenith not in the baroque but in the glorious decade before the First World War. I had an excellent dinner in the abbey cellar, where the menu was all fish and the accompanying white wine excellent. The operator of the franchise was extremely competent and the place was full of local people, some eating, some drinking.

☞

Day 15 – 26 March 2014 – Lambach to Gampern via Stadl-Paurau

THE NEXT MORNING I turned out for the mass, which was held not in the depressing abbey church but in the much more florid sacrament chapel. My contact of the previous evening, Brother Albert, slipped me a note asking me to wait behind at the end of mass. There were ten communicants from the town. My wait ended with the arrival of the young monk who had led the music at vespers. He spoke reasonable English and was my companion at breakfast. He was not optimistic for the future of the abbey or the community within it. His pessimism, where optimism was crucially needed, contributed to my overall impression of the abbey as one to which I would not choose to return. After breakfast he generously showed me the main delights of the monastery, the summer refectory, the library and the early frescos. Alas, he did not show me the theatre. It is the only known instance of a theatre in an abbey, and the first performance in it was graced by Marie Antoinette on her fateful journey to her wedding.

It was nine o'clock before I resumed the path. Almost at once there was the diversion to the church of the Holy Trinity at Stadl-Paura. It stands majestically about 50 metres above the river and its exterior is stunning. The church was locked with a notice that it would open only on Sunday. I could not leave, and was rewarded when a young girl arrived, having business within, and I could hear the organist practising. When she gained admission I slipped in with her and was allowed five minutes to comprehend the extraordinary effect of three entrances, three altars and three organs, all identical and confronting each other. The same pleasing proportions grace the exterior. The ground plan is of course a triangle. Each of the three resulting facades is identical save that the dedication above one door is to God the Father, the next to God the Son, and the third to God the Holy Ghost. The church is to my eye the most beautiful north of the Alps. I have had to make a selection from my enthusiastic pictures. First the church and its adjoining presbytery, then an altar, an organ and the detail of a seat at the base of a column, then one of the three dedications, and finally the backward view from Stadl-Paura of the abbey above the Traun, which shows how close together they stand. Only the last is in the plate section.

Stadl-Paura was built in 1725 as a pilgrim church. The architect was Johann Michael Prunner and it is his supreme achievement. It is the apotheosis of Counter-Reformation triumphalism and that for me is a significant part of its appeal. There is a very clear statement of this message on the altar of God the Father, where Faith is depicted vanquishing a priest holding a bust of Luther.

So in high spirits I set off to cover the 20 kilometres to Vöcklabruck. At the church of the Holy Trinity the Traun bears left and the river at this confluence flowing to the right is the Ager. So this day's walk followed the Ager as the previous day's had followed the Traun. I took a picture of a typical stretch of the Ager. The walk was, if anything, more beautiful, through leafless woods at the point of spring burst, scattered always with the bright flowers of spring and the vivid new-sprung wild garlic. At the halfway point I skirted Schwanenstadt, following the curve of the river to Au. Here the Jakobsweg led away from the river and a kind householder gave me a seat on her terrace and two glasses of water. These I was to need as the route descended from the sublime to the grim. First there was a series of hardworking gravel pits, with clanking machines and gantries moving the shingle into mountains. They gave way to a long walk into increasingly suburban territory around the railway town of Attnang Puchheim. The only delight was on the approach, the sight of the church of St Martin built on an elevation, so standing proud above the sprawl surrounding the railway junction. It became for me a talisman on every train journey west from Vienna.

The route then reached its nadir, following the A1 from Linz to Vöcklabruck with heavy goods transport thundering by. Thank heaven I soon found a bus stop with a timetable showing that soon would come a cross-city line that would take me the 4 kilometres to Vöcklabruck and the 4 kilometres beyond without a change. Thus I found salvation, emerging at Timelkam with the greatest sense of relief. As the bus wound its way through Vöcklabruck I was able to identify the baroque church of St Giles and the city gate built by Maximilian I.

With hindsight I now believe I made my own misfortune. I believe I missed a point at which I should have crossed the railway in Attnang Puchheim to walk through fields to the outskirts of Vöcklabruck. But even that would not have saved me from miles of streets thereafter, since the western outskirts of Vöcklabruck and the eastern outskirts of Timelkan march together.

The sound of Austrian place names impresses me. I dislike Attnang Puchheim and obstinately refuse to master the sound or to commit it to memory. By contrast I delight in the sound of Dunkelsteinwald in the Wachau.

Partly by luck and partly by judgement I found my way from Timelkam to Gampern. My direction was confirmed by a friendly farmer and for 4 kilometres I walked the road through fertile, well-farmed land. However, I was using the country road via Unter- and Obergallaberg, then Weiterschwang, when I should have been finding and following the small river, the Dürre Ager, in the valley.

Gampern is visible from afar thanks to the very un-Austrian late 16th-century spire of its impressive village church. I photographed the church at dusk. As impressive as the exterior is the magnificent flying altar within, which was donated by the prelate responsible for the building of the church. It is extraordinary that so small a farming village should have such a treasure and equally astounding that it has survived unharmed for now five hundred years. I arrived just before the church was locked at six in the evening and was able to return again at eight the next morning. I photographed the altar in the morning light. The fame and importance of the Gampern altar is apparent from the monograph with text in German, English and French which I bought in the church.

In between I found a reasonable bed and dinner at Gasthaus Hugg (telephone +43 (0)7682 8016).

☞

ON THE NEXT morning I spurned the available bus to the main station in Vöcklabruck and attempted to return to Timelkam by the official Jakobsweg. As so often, the waymarking was almost non-existent and I became hopelessly lost. I was forced to use the A1 for nearly a kilometre in order to get back to Timelkam. From there I found a bus to Vöcklabruck and then a slow train to Linz, followed by the express to Vienna. I succeeded in boarding a train run by the private company Westbahn rather than the ÖBB. The guard spurned my ÖBB ticket and I steadfastly refused to pay the single fare that he demanded. In the end he gave up, only insisting that I move to second class. This I did willingly since I had unwittingly chosen first class, there being little to distinguish first from second. The secrets of another country are only slowly learned.

☞

THIS MARCH WALK had taken me from Linz all the way to the beginning of the Salzkammergut. The snow-clad mountains rose in the distance; the rivers were left behind. Ahead, three days' walking would take me to Salzburg itself. Of these March days I will remember the beauty of the river path and the bordering woodland. I will remember Lambach, albeit the least of the monasteries at which I have stayed. I will regret having resisted the temptation to visit Kremsmünster. I will remember the South East Asian man who helped me, isolated outside Traun station, to find my way to the river. I will remember the kind lady in Au. I will remember the young monk at Lambach who viewed the future of the religious life with pessimism. I will remember the beauty of Stadl-Paura. I will remember the horror of Vöcklabruck. I will be grateful for the wonderful walking weather, frost at night and hot sun during the day. I will be grateful for the fact that I can walk 30 kilometres with a heavy rucksack and still feel strong at the end of the day.

GAMPERN

SCHWAIGERN

SEEKIRCHEN

GAMPERN TO SEEKIRCHEN

Day 16 – 5 May 2014 – Gampern to Schwaigern

I SET OUT for Gampern, where my last stage had ended. The journey by train was easy enough: Vienna to Vöcklabruck. But how to Gampern? Outside the station there was no sign of a taxi and the bus shelter was crowded with schoolchildren. Having struggled with an obscure timetable I reached the conclusion that there would be a bus to Gampern in about half an hour. Triumph! The bus duly arrived on schedule and a very friendly driver, exchanging his bad English with my bad German, soon established my provenance and the purpose of my journey to Gampern. He pressed upon me a map of the Salzkammergut, which proved useful, and, once in Gampern, showed me the *Gemeinde*. As with many bus journeys we had wandered from the main road to serve nearby settlements and on this journey diverted to the railway station at Redl-Zipf. This tiny and obscure dot on the atlas is the site of the Zipfer brewery. It illustrates the haphazard distribution of industrial production throughout Austria. Farms and factories often seem to intermingle. There seem to be no industrial heartlands as elsewhere in Europe.

The staff in the *Gemeinde* spoke no English and had very little idea of their distinction as a parish crossed by the Jakobsweg. True, it was marked on the parish map that they gave me, but an inaccurate map is worse than no map at all. I was quickly lost. The village that I had targeted turned out to be not Unteralberting, as I had hoped, but Hörading. I walked on vacuously until confronted by a factory, a busy main road and a tiny *Stube*. Despite the brightness of the day the interior was Stygian and contained only the owner, a man eating a late lunch and what appeared to be a man drinking himself to death. Only when he spoke did I realise that he was a she. My general plea for rescue was met with indifference and bad advice. The heavy drinker urged me to take the main road if I wanted Vöcklamarkt. Emerging like a mole into bright sunlight I knew that whatever I did I would not follow her advice. So I retraced my steps back through Hörading until I reached a sturdy woman in her mid-fifties laboriously picking stones off the ploughed ground and filling the bucket on the fore loader of an old tractor. To her I voiced my despair, which moved her not only to divert the conversation to English but also to offer me her own much-used Jakobsweg guide. Such developments restore faith in the Almighty. We set out for the farmhouse, where we were joined by her daughter and her two grandchildren. Her daughter personified Austrian beauty and chatted confidently both in English and French. I am glad I have a portrait of them, which I have included in the plate section. Armed with her mother's guidebook, and with clear instructions for the immediate path, I set out knowing that I would succeed and that nothing now would prevent me reaching Salzburg. I took this view about a mile on from our parting. On my return to England I was able to return by post to Frau Hollerweg her book, and for some years we exchanged occasional cards. She herself had walked the Jakobsweg westward at least to the Austrian border, if not beyond.

By now it was already past three and I made the best speed I could, bypassing both Vöcklamarkt and Frankenmarkt. Each of these towns is dominated by a magnificent baroque parish church so recognisable as the express trains rush by westwards on the mainline from Vienna. The map suggested that the only hope of a bed would be in Schwaigern, after which the route hardly touched human settlements. Entering Schwaigern, a fair-sized village, I saw no one but a man hurrying back indoors having taken a delivery of firewood. I photographed the load beside his house before calling him. He came. His round ruddy head proclaimed the nature that lay within. No, there was nowhere to stay at Swaigern but he would take me to the inn in Frankenmarkt: Gasthof Kogler (+43 (0)7684 6258). At once he was explaining the plan to his wife and getting the car from the garage. On arrival, my estimation of his character was confirmed by his refusal to take even petrol money. Rather, he led the way inside, explained my needs and introduced me to the landlady. It is sad that I will never again see this good man. Shortly after his departure I was unpacking in a simple room, then eating a dinner of garlic soup and fried fish, accompanied by a good flask of Grüner Veltliner. On that I slept magnificently and was down for breakfast at six o'clock.

☞

Day 17 – 6 May 2014 – Schwaigern to Seekirchen

HAVING LEFT THE inn at quarter past six, I was extraordinarily lucky to jump on a bus that took me back to the outskirts of Schwaigern, so that by half past six I was on my way from where I had stopped the night before. The night had been cold and the frost lay white on the grass where the sun had yet to reach it: heavy enough to show in my picture. I carried on at a good pace over magnificent open land, well illustrated by two photos and, unlike yesterday, where all the farms had been frantic in silage making, here on the second day it was all future promise. The grass crops were heavy but mowing had not begun.

My first setback came in Hochfeld. The hamlet is well named since it commands a view on all sides. I entered and left by the same road. It seemed the obvious thing to do. Absent a sign, there was nothing to suggest the choice of a minor turn to the right in the heart of the village. Three kilometres downhill at a fast pace led me into a hamlet, Reitzing. My map at once showed how great was my mistake: three kilometres in completely the wrong direction. Could I regain the rightful way without returning to Hochfeld, I asked. But there was no denying the farmer's wife who insisted that I must retrace my steps. Facing that relentless hill, desperation drove me to wave down the first approaching car, which proved to be a school minibus. After much hesitation they invited me on board and minutes later set me down at the school gates in Hochfeld.

Given a fresh start, I was soon on a long descent into the edge of Oberhofen where, with luck and local guidance, I found my way through the settlement without further error and there followed a wild walk through farm and forest land to reach, at last, Pfongau. My heart sang at the village sign. In the guide this was only the end of the day stage from Gampern and I was badly behind schedule. Pressing on ahead lay a good walk to reach the edge of Wallersee. As I approached the lake the path ahead seemed unnecessarily sinuous given the sight of the lake only two or three fields away. I therefore plunged off to the left through hay fields and a caravan park to reach the lakeside. The price of any shortcut is uncertainty and, although I knew the Weg followed the shore, the symbol of the shell was nowhere amongst the offered waymarks. I chanced upon a lady of affluence, leaving her convertible and entering a lakeside villa. She was ready and willing to join the hunt for the Weg but bereft of knowledge or ideas. So she took me into her home and gave me a wide choice of drinks. After a good half-litre of water I resolved to ignore the waymark for Seekirchen and simply follow my instinct. I was soon rewarded by the blue and yellow mark of the Jakobsweg. Well on down the lake I met perhaps for only the second time another pilgrim.

My fellow traveller was supremely unsuited to the demands of the pilgrim path. It would not be an exaggeration to say that she was as wide as she was high and determined to ignore the waymark sternly pointing up the hill. She wanted me to give her some encouragement to believe that there was an alternative route along the lake shore. I offered her none. Still less help did she get from two passing men, locals. Seeing no escape from the hill she then suggested that we walk together to Seekirchen. To accept her invitation would have been to jeopardise my objective. Unchristian, but I had to make my best pace and soon left her behind.

The route next reached the lakeside at Frenning and here again I met great good fortune. Outside an upmarket restaurant sat the proprietor. I diffidently asked for water and coffee, a request I expected him to refuse. Instead he produced it with alacrity. Next he asked if he could help. I explained my need to reach Seekirchen station and asked if I might expect to find a local bus as I reached the outskirts of the town. This prompted such a kind response. He installed me in his red Mercedes convertible and we sped off at alarming speed to reach the outskirts of Seekirchen. I was truly lucky, given that the station was hard to find and far from the town centre. Once I had waved him farewell I calculated from the station timetable that it would be quicker to go on to Salzburg and pick up the Vienna Express. That I did. Even without any waiting time the journey from Seekirchen started at two-thirty and did not have me back to Purkersdorf and Felicitas until shortly after seven that evening.

I intended to return at the end of May to walk on from Salzburg, and had allowed a week in the hope of reaching Innsbruck. Felicitas and I agreed to spend two nights in Werfen before I set out on foot and she returned by car to Vienna. But the plan unravelled when she, playing with stilts in Werfen castle yard, fell, broke her ankle and was rushed to hospital. If you are to break a bone there is no better place to do it than in a mountain resort. But however well the emergency has been treated, thereafter patience is at a premium and my walking week became a nursing week. It was not until September that I returned and by then Felicitas, the inspiration for my pilgrimage, had left me and all my efforts to persuade her back had been in vain.

Austria abounds in castles surmounting rocky crags, always of ancient origin, but often like Werfen, heavily restored in the 19th century when social and economic factors combined to make restoration affordable. My photograph of Werfen makes the point but would do so more forcefully had I taken it from the valley floor. Still I have included it in the plate section.

SALZBURG

UNKEN

ST ULRICH

ST JOHANN IN TIROL

GOING AM WILDEN KAISER

SÖLL

BREITENBACH

STRASS IM ZILLERTAL

VIENNA

SALZBURG TO VIENNA

Day 18 – 10 September 2014 – Salzburg to Unken

IN THE MIDDLE Ages the city was safe for the pilgrim and the greatest dangers lay without. In the 21st century the countryside is safe but industrial trade and the suburbs provide a challenge that did not face the pilgrim of ancient times. The solution to the problem is public transport. Accordingly, I would suggest to anyone on the Jakobsweg that a city such as Salzburg would best be navigated by taking the train perhaps from Hallwang into the main station and then a train out to Bad Reichenhall. An exploration of the great wonders that the city offers is better divorced from the Jakobsweg journey.

The frontier between Austria and Germany snakes about Salzburg so that just when you think you are deeper into one country you find you are in the other. Bad Reichenhall lies in Germany and is well worth an extended visit, being a prosperous Bavarian brewery town with a miraculous salt works created by successive Wittelsbach rulers of the Bavarian kingdom. The town is built over the richest natural source of brine in the Alps and the town owes its prosperity to this natural resource. The old salt works can be visited and are a miracle of human ingenuity and engineering skill. I stayed in the Brauereigasthof in the main square (telephone +49 (0)8651 6089). The old town was largely rebuilt after a disastrous fire in the 1830s. As the weather threatened I prudently bought a pair of jeans in a modern clothes supermarket for €6.99. These proved a wonderful investment.

On the next morning I set off, having toured the royal salt works and bought a jar of salt mixed with local herbs for Felicitas. The town bridge crosses the Saalach and immediately to the left a footpath is easily seen. This follows the river until it broadens into a lake. I photographed my first sight of the open water and it gains a place in the plate section. Here the path follows the lakeside through woods of beech, oak and pine. At Fronau the river is crossed and the path, having climbed circuitously through meadows to Unterjettenberg, rejoins the river on its spectacular course. The waters run jade grey and green and as opaque as the precious stone. On the far bank runs a major road but the sound of the traffic is lost in the roar of the river. Sometimes the river is close, sometimes the path prefers a more direct line.

The river is crossed a second time and the approach to Unken is by an old town walk. The Josefsallee from the riverbank to the centre of the town is a gentle climb of only 200 metres. The centre is dominated by the parish church, which is a fine example of baroque, having been built in 1747. I had a comfortable lodging in the adjoining restaurant and pension but sadly left behind my Swatch with a luminous dial, my night watch of many years.

The scenery on this first day was extremely beautiful, with views of towering cliffs and torrents of water. As the day warmed I walked in my shirt. Of the way there is little to record except the tranquillity of this river valley, the senses overwhelmed by the sight and sound of the wonderful Saalach.

☞

Day 19 – 11 September 2014 – Unken to St Ulrich

THE WALK TO Unken was only the second half of the stage from Gois on Salzburg's edge but the stage on from Unken to St Ulrich is a full day of 27 kilometres.

The path from Unken follows the left bank of the Saalach through scenery much as the day before. The day started grey but turned to torrential rain when I was too far on to return. I sheltered in a rock cleft beside the path until its roof dripped as vigorously as the rain outside. The rain eased but not before I was soaked. Soon after, the path leaves the river by the dramatic Innersbachklamm. It is not clear why anyone should wish to construct a walkway through the narrow cleft and above the raging torrent. However, it is certainly a work of strength and ingenuity. The path leads on to Reit, where at the Gasthaus Drei Bruder I found a warm welcome and good coffee. Reit is a beautiful hamlet, traditional down to the little church, and with wonderful views of the encircling mountains.

From Reit there is a pleasant and easy walk following, but distant from, the river to reach Au, with a gem-like baroque church dedicated to St Anthony. From here to Lofer we seemed to part from the Saalach until crossing the river on the outskirts of the town. As a parting tribute to the Saalach I took a picture of an ancient bridge and another of the valley path.

Lofer even has an entry in the *Blue Guide to Austria* for its picturesque town centre and surrounding mountain scenery. A famous pilgrim church nearby is not mentioned in the *Kompass Jakobsweg Guide*. I ate my sandwich on the terrace of a strange hotel, as empty of staff as the *Flying Dutchman* and hardly animated by groups of tourists driven to cards and word puzzles by the dank weather.

The path on from Lofer follows the brook, climbing steadily to Pass Strub. This mountain pass was the scene of a battle in the Napoleonic wars and is well above the village of Strub. Here again I stopped for coffee at a large *Gasthaus* laid out for tourists. The proprietor, Herr Huber, gave me good advice on the road ahead which enabled me to bypass Waidring, taking the alternative route for Schaffenkapelle shortly after the Kneippanlage. As I turned off I met a kind lady who offered me a handful of the *Preiselbeeren* that she was gathering.

The path climbs uphill, then up and down as it circles the Mühlberg, and then fast downhill to reach St Adolari. By now it was half past five and the Gasthaus St Adolari was the obvious option. It was right on the main road, however, and I avoided it, losing the chance to see the medieval church. Instead I resolved to make it to St Ulrich. This meant walking fast on an easy path beside the Pillersee to reach the village at half past six. It had been a long, hard day and I booked in at one of two huge tourist hotels on a half-board contract. I was given a surprisingly attractive double room with a balcony overlooking the mountains.

☞

Day 20 – 12 September 2014 – St Ulrich to St Johann in Tirol

THE NEXT MORNING the clouds were down and I delayed departure by visiting the parish church and admiring the neighbouring presbytery. As is apparent from a photograph of the damp scene, the presbytery abuts the east end of the church and looks as if it could serve as a seminary. The other half of the church carries the tower. The church felt particularly loved and cherished.

I set off as the rain was easing. Half an hour passed as I searched for the tourist office, only to find it closed for two weeks, and then for the Jakobsweg, which, inexplicably, was not way-marked at the crucial point of departure from the village. I found it only thanks to the Kompass guide. The path was initially suburban but then rose through woods to make a good walk of about an hour to St Jakob in Haus.

The whole character of the country changes after St Ulrich. There is ribbon development all the way along the main road running through the valley. Only well off the valley floor does the life and the world of the farmer dominate. These are big prosperous farms and very well managed.

The Church of St Jakob is medieval and, perhaps for lack of funds, the baroque decoration is largely confined to frescos on the medieval walls and ceiling. The Post Hotel facing the church provided generous jugs of coffee and warm milk. Soon after, I stopped for sandwiches, then headed on steadily and without pause through Filzen, Wall and Reitham. These are all small hamlets dominated by their farmhouses. From Reitham there is a long walk into St Johann in Tirol. This is well contrived since the path runs along the riverbank with open fields on the other side of the path right into the heart of the city. Thus the pilgrim is again spared a long entry through outskirts and suburbs.

The local chemist recommended the Hotel Fischer, which proved to be professional if without any frills. It is in Kaiserstrasse and the telephone number is +43 (0)5352 62332.

This was only a four-hour day, partly because of the weather and partly because I needed to go easy on my left leg. This stage should have continued on to Going am Wilden Kaiser, 27.5 kilometres in total. St Johann in Tirol is probably about 15 kilometres from St Ulrich. The Hotel Fischer did not offer dinner and I was directed to the local brewery, Huber Bräu, which has a wonderfully warm eating and drinking floor at the top of the brewery tower.

☞

Pillerseetal – March 2017 – A Digression and an Afterthought

IN PURSUIT OF the pilgrim path from the easternmost point to the westernmost point it is easy to lose sight of passages that stand out as individually independent and complete. So as I moved on from Unken on 11 September 2014 I had nothing in mind save to reach my next stop in St Ulrich and, on the twelfth, little but the need to make it to St Johann by nightfall. My more or less contemporary account does not record that in these two days I had walked the length of the Pillersee valley, famous for its spectacular mountains and its villages that in season transform into ski resorts. Of course in mid-September they were just farming villages with cattle grazing and pastures harvesting for hay and silage. But how did I fail to notice and record the grandeur and majesty of the mountains rising on either side from the valley floor?

At New Year 2017 I resumed my search for the Mecca that lay in my memories of childhood: a mountain village blanketed in and muffled by snow but with the bright lights of shops and cafés along its huddled street – Wengen as it was in 1950. Ramsau had been my choice in 2016, but the hotel had been a factory and the downhill skiing not good enough for Geanina-Maria, with whom I was escaping my sorrow at the great loss of Felicitas and the lesser loss of Renata. So the other recommendation in the brochure was St Jakob in Haus. It sounded quiet and unspoilt, the other side of the mountain from fashionable Kitzbühel and in the hidden valley of the Pillersee. The recommended hotel was fully booked, as was the only other four-star hotel. But there was room at the Schloss Hotel in Fieberbrunn, only 3 kilometres distant. I booked.

Geanina-Maria picked me up at Schechwat from the first flight on Wednesday 8 March, two hours late but no surprise to one who knows her well, and we drove the motorway to Salzburg. Thereafter the route eluded me as we slid in and out of Germany and confidence in the satnav evaporated. I saw signs to Unken and Lofer and realised that I had walked through this terrain. Indeed, at one point I remembered the Saalach valley, with the way through the woods on the left bank and the mingled roar of the traffic on the right bank and the river between. Perhaps we went wrong but eventually I noticed a lake and then we drove through a village marked St Ulrich to reach St Jakob in Haus. Straight through the village we went to reach the Schloss Hotel on the edge of Fieberbrunn. There we received an excellent room (number 330) but a poor dinner.

Thursday was a day of persistent rain in the village but for all who were skiing in the mountains it fell as snow. I scarcely got my bearings as I plodded through slushy snow and torrents on the slopes and puddles like lakes on the flat following the village Rundweg. We had a good dinner at the Alte Post, served by hopeless Dutch girls on what they described as internships.

On Friday it was still raining on the hotel and the mountains were invisible in the mist. But there was a sense that the deluge was easing and I tried the Winterwanderweg to St Jakob. On the path the snow lay dented by many steps. I thought of King Wencelas but there was no miracle in the steps I trod, only slush and slither. Approaching the descent to St Jakob there was a choice between the short course through Mühlau or the longer, round course. Although there were breaks in the clouds, and even glimmers of weak sunlight, I chose the short course and had reached the village of Mühlau when Geanina-Maria rang for me: she had done for the day. I told her where I was and asked her to collect me from the church in St Jakob. I hurried on in expectation, soon disappointed. Here was the church and no sign of the black Audi. I looked at the church. I visited the graveyard adjoining. I penetrated the information office in the *Gemeinde* only to be chased out by the cleaner as of course it was closed. I picked up the village map and identified the two hotels that I had been unable to book. I inspected the adjoining Hotel zur Post and was about to go in for coffee when I realised I had no money. The while I made frequent calls: "Where are you?" "Where am I meant to be?" "St Jakob, I told you." "Where's the church?" and so on. In the end it was an hour from her first call to her arrival.

Back at the hotel I had the text of this Jakobsweg guide and with hours between Kaffee und Kuchen at the great discovery (Hotel Grosslehen, +43 (0)5354 56455) and dinner at the pretentious Meridian I idly thought to look up the Jakobsweg route I caught from Salzburg to Innsbruck. Only as I read did realisation come. The lake along which I had raced, having rejected the Gasthof at St Adolari, was none other than Pillarsee. The huge and gloomy tourist hotel at which I had then stayed was beside the fine church and *Pfarrhof* of St Ulrich. The difficult and delayed start the following morning had taken me up into the forest above the valley floor whence I had dropped down to see the church of St Jakob and to find cans of coffee and hot milk at the Post Hotel.

Until I read those words I had no recollection of what I had seen as we drove in from Vienna and not the slightest sense that I had been to St Jakob in Haus before. Worse still, even the afternoon's visit to the church and the frustrated plan to have coffee at the Post Hotel stirred not the faintest recollection.

Saturday's dawn brought the promised fine weather. The azure orb of the heavens broke on the mountain tops sparkling white in the morning sun. There was but one mountain Winterwanderweg and I had to take it. From the ski lifts it ran along the flat to Lauchsee. Only there did it turn up towards its goal, the Mittelstation Streuböden. The first third of the climb was gentle and along a tarmacked lane from which the snow had melted. That ease foreshadowed pain to come. The waymarker pointed up a track covered in deep snow through the centre of which a narrow path had been trodden. I guess the ascent to the hut was about 600 metres over the course of 6 kilometres from the village. Perhaps the climb up the track from the lane was 500 metres. There the gradient varied from steep to very steep. I hauled myself up from one red marker in the snow to the next. At each marker I had to rest to regain my breath. Had it not been for the challenge I would have given up. The last 50 metres were on the piste with the joyful skiers swooping down. The hut stood on a knoll and commanded a spectacular view of the whole 360-degree, mountain-top panorama. My purse just covered a mineral water, a schnapps and a double espresso. I could hardly have managed without. On the south side of the hut were ranged lines of deck chairs on which many athletes lounged. This was for me a novel sight. That evening we were all ready for a big dinner at the Hotel Grosslehen.

Sunday broke as fine as Saturday and we were up early knowing we must be off by three o'clock. I had my opportunity to make my amends to St Jakob. I walked there by the longer path, dropping down out of the forest to reach the Main Street just east of the church. By the Post Hotel I saw again the familiar blue and yellow waymarker. I was on the Jakobsweg again. I had never before walked the same stretch twice. I did not remember any detail as I climbed out of the village onto the forest path running westwards towards St Johann in Tirol. I did not recognise the spot where I had apparently stopped to eat my piece on that September day. I think I remembered a point at which the forest path turned in towards the mountain in order to cross a stream running down a steep gully. At the stream's side the path rose steeply to gain a bridge over the stream and a wide forest road onwards. It seemed familiar but the feature may be replicated elsewhere on the way through the Tyrol. Because this side of the valley is south-facing the snow had mainly melted and only sporadically was it still lying. Suddenly I came on a warm sunny bank lit by hundreds of daisy-like flowers, deep bright yellow with deeper but dull yellow centres. I picked one for Geanina-Maria. The *Gemeinde* have thoroughly marked the local Wanderweg but the Jakobsweg marking in the Tyrol is poor. At Wall I dropped down into Fieberbrunn near the Hotel Obermair in Rosenegg, not far from the Schloss Hotel. We met at two-thirty but in Geanina-Maria style it was twenty to four before we left, so we had to break all limits to pass the Prandtauer Gate at Kremsmünster five minutes before vespers at six.

I need to reflect on how my passage through such wonderful scenery left so little impression that I forgot not only the names but also the places themselves on return after only some two and a half years. Obviously the seasons count. Particularly in this region of continental climate the contrast between late summer and late winter is extreme. The mountains when snow-covered take on an awesome majesty, the sight of which drives even the ungodly to thoughts of God, especially when lit by the pink lights of the setting sun. Snow changes more than the appearance of the land. The frozen lake, water turned to ice, then snow-covered, no longer reveals its watery substance but appears as a huge and impossibly flat meadow. In the snow-blanketed slopes and forests there is a profound and rare silence that in other seasons is invaded by myriad sounds created by nature and man at work or on the move. Thus in their summer dress the high mountains do not so much impress.

But more profound is the effect of the scale of the Weg. To think of its totality from Bratislava to Feldkirch is not only to reckon 850 kilometres but the fact that it joins the Slavs of the east to the prudent Swiss in the west, encompassing between them the remnants of one of the greatest empires and cultures of human history. That grand scale diminishes any day journey. But there is also the effect of the challenge of the scale: can I do it, will I fail? (Whether ignominious or glorious, failure is not easily accepted.) And that challenge is repeated daily as each day's journey is contemplated and then planned. Can I make the given day's end? Will I find a bed there?

This stress has a profound effect. Sometimes I am going too fast to notice: for example, the dash along Pillersee. Sometimes I am too tired to notice: for example, the struggle to reach Würmla. Sometimes the path is too demanding: for example, the climb from St Anton to St Christoph. And to those instances add the sense that I must travel 1,600 miles – more than 2,500 kilometres – to obtain three or four days' walking on the Jakobsweg. That sense creates a state of mind: not a moment must be wasted and another 100 kilometres becomes the only target. There is no time for deviation, no time to investigate flora and fauna, certainly no time to simply stop and contemplate the scenery. How different might the experience have been were I a Wiener? I would have the language, even the dialects. I would know the life of the woods and the fields. I could take my time and not march to the Jakobsweg's clock.

I wonder too how different the experience would have been in the improbable event that I had absented myself from my life for five weeks of a more genuine pilgrimage?

☞

Return to the Jakobsweg diary and September 2014

Day 21 – 13 September 2014 – St Johann to Going am Wilden Kaiser

THIS WAS NOT a good day. The cloud was down on the mountain and the light drizzle fell all morning until near midday. I whiled away the morning visiting the tourist information, the church and the museum.

About noon I set off, expecting that, as in previous days, the afternoon and evening would hold the best of the weather. Soon out of the town I passed what is the largest farm I saw in Austria. It moves away from the traditional model, which houses humans and cattle under one long roof.

Soon I made a short detour to see the church at Weitau, which was said to hold the oldest surviving gothic window in the Tyrol. The church is small and is now engulfed in modern residential and commercial development. The exterior is plain but within is a characteristic Austrian baroque scene for worship: no sign of an old window anywhere. As I was about to leave there emerged from the sacristy a lady to whom I explained the reason for my visit. She at once lifted a curtain and invited me to walk through the screen to the space behind the high altar. There to my amazement I saw a tall east window entirely filled with 15th-century stained glass. Incredibly, the baroque decorators must consciously have rendered it invisible to all except those who knew how to find it. I photographed the altar and then the window concealed behind, the latter is in the plate section.

The Weg soon climbed away from the river and the highway to return to farmland and woods. Here my expectations were disappointed by the return of the drizzle. It drove me to stop at the cheerful Romerhof, a beautifully maintained stopping point, or even a goal for a planned excursion. The approach and surrounds were made lovely by agapanthus in pots, which, later than with us, were in their prime. Feeling the weight of tradition I ordered a warm *Apfelstrudel* to join an excellent caffè latte.

The respite was temporary as the rain only intensified into a downpour. Gloom was magnified by pangs of protest from my weak leg. However, I had no alternative but to press on through the sodden landscape to reach Going am Wilden Kaiser. In the Kompass guide this is the end of Stage 23. Half past four did not seem a moment too early to call a halt. I booked into the Gasthaus Dorfwirt and was given a poor little room that sufficed. Not only was my rucksack soaked but a good deal of the contents, too. I had the use of the drying room in the basement and my belongings did not need a long stay there. That Saturday evening the dining room was full and cheerful, reflecting the high standard of cooking and service.

☞

Day 22 – 14 September 2014 – Rest Day

SADLY THE WEATHER remained foul, with low cloud and persistent drizzle. It was pointless to continue so I took a rest day in Going. Apart from the need to dry out, I reckoned, rightly as it transpired, that putting my leg up for thirty-six hours would forestall a breakdown. The inn was an added attraction: good cooking and a kindly proprietress. I took a photo not of the Dorfwirt but of a café at the head of the village street. I have never seen the Austrian passion and skill for window-box gardening carried to greater height. Somehow I missed the church in Going, which is praised by the Kompass guide.

My extended stay at Dorfwirt cost €132.20 – excellent value. The telephone number is worth noting: + 43 (0)5358 2411.

☞

Day 23 – 15 September 2014 – Going to Söll

MONDAY BROUGHT THE promised change of weather. Soon after Going the pilgrim reaches the pretty town of Ellmau. Here I stopped for a look at the church, a coffee, the despatch of my postcards and a fruitful visit to the tourist office, which provided the brochure on the Jakobsweg in the Tyrol. The path out of Ellmau climbs into the essential Austrian pastureland. It was at this point that the clouds lifted and the Wilder Kaiser mountains appeared. Their beauty was enhanced by the farmland that filled my foreground view. My photo caught the moment of melting cloud. It is in the plate section.

It is a long walk from Ellmau to Söll and there are no distractions, just a steady march through farmland and forest before one reaches the outskirts of Söll and crosses a major road, the E641, to arrive at the centre.

Söll is rightly described in the Michelin Green Guide as an exceptionally pretty village. The parish church has a handsome and unusual baroque interior where the architect achieved a circular dome above the aisle, which sits on an octagonal base. The richness of this church is extraordinary and I wondered how it came about and how it was financed. The church is dedicated to St Peter and St Paul, celebrated in the high altar painting of 1770 by C.A. Mayr. There are many guesthouses and I was lucky in my choice of Hotel Eggerwirt. It is in the hands of a patroness who showed me exceptional kindness. The talented young chef referred to her as the boss and I came to do the same. During dinner she asked if I had stayed the previous night at Gasthaus Dorfwirt and, when I confirmed, she explained that I had taken a lady's jeans from the drying room. That I understood at once since I had been puzzled at the extent to which they had shrunk in the drying room. The boss from Dorfwirt proposed to drive over to make the exchange when she had closed the kitchens. I waited up and at about half past nine she arrived. Amid much good humour the two bosses and I made the exchange. The service, cooking and comfort at the Eggerwirt are first class. There were a lot of English staying in the hotel and I deduced that the tour company Inghams uses it as a base for its Tyrol tour. I took some views from the village street to illustrate the evening cloud rising off the mountains like smoke.

The boss is Claudia Weiss and the Eggerwirt number is + 43 (0)5333 5236.

☞

Day 24 – 16 September 2014 – Söll to Breitenbach

THE NEXT MORNING I had intended to leave early but found the village shrouded in thick autumn mist. My first goal was the Hohe Salve, two stars in the Green Guide. But what point in ascending in a fog? Fortunately the boss brought up the reality on her computer screen, which revealed the peak well clear of the fog.

The €16 return fare on the cable car is good value for money. The ascent and descent are spectacular and the summit commands spectacular views of mountain ranges through the full 360 degrees. The little chapel on the very summit stands as a testament to the faith and devotion of the clergy and people in long-gone days. My photo of the chapel also shows how popular a place this is. I took the view full circle but I chose only one aspect for the hang-glider soaring high against the cloud.

Not to be missed on the walk to the cable-car station is the *Wallfahrtskapelle* (pilgrim chapel) Stampfanger. Built on top of an erupted rock in the middle of a gorge, it is minute and only reached by a covered bridge from the side of the gorge. The bridge also serves as the nave, with seating for a tiny congregation. Such economy and ingenuity of design only increase the sense of wonder. If I had not photographed it (see the plate section), I would think I had seen it only in a dream.

While on the mountain I felt an urge to linger and spend time with the boss. At the hotel I could not find her and I was beginning to write her a note when she returned. She refused my invitation with grace and kindness. So I journeyed on, setting off at about 12.30 with the intention of reaching Breitenbach am Inn.

It is a long walk to Itter. Initially pleasant, and only briefly uncongenial alongside the 178, it goes through farmland to reach the little village. There I stopped for coffee and unconvincing advice from the proprietor as to the onward route of the Jakobsweg. Here, unusually, the excellent waymarking seemed to die out and I decided to follow a local mark for Wörgl and Kirchbichl. Initially the route was delightful, through forest and farm, until it arrived at a junction with the 178. Having crossed the highway the pilgrim faces a long march through all sorts of development to reach Wörgl. The consolation is that the path runs all the way along the Brixentaler Ache, which seems to flow into the greater River Inn at Wörgl.

This is a recurrent feature of the Jakobsweg. The historic towns are built on a river. The river runs through the heart of the city. There is a footpath along the bank. The banks are invariably lined with trees and bushes. Thus whatever suburban development, commerce and industry outlie the city, the walker passes through with the company and the charm of the river rushing by.

The route through Wörgl is poorly signposted and I took a number of chances, all successfully, to reach a footbridge over the Inn on the far side of the substantial town.

Once leaving the river en route for Breitenbach am Inn the pilgrim is faced with a long upward climb on small roads through small villages to reach the junction with what appears to be a substantial highway at Glatzham. Here I could see from the guide that the route follows the main road for about a kilometre before heading north through farmland to Egg and Berg, then reaching Breitenbach at the point where the main road enters the town.

As I reached Glatzham it was already 6.15p.m. and I could not contemplate this circuitous Jakobsweg route. Indeed I had not time for the direct route along the highway since the 5 kilometres would take me at least an hour even were I fresh. As it was I was hot and tired. So I attempted what I had never done before: hitchhiking. Cars swept by indifferently. Then at last a small car drew up ahead and reversed towards me. The driver was a mother with a boy of about eight by her side. With smiles and kindness she at once offered to be my saviour and within a few minutes we were descending into Breitenbach. She told me that there were five guesthouses and that Gasthof Rappold (telephone + 43 (0)5338 8132) was the best. She dropped me there and went on her way. Only after I had been refused a bed did I realise that I had left my coat in her car. Disaster, but I knew that she would find it and bring it to Rappold. Meanwhile I was given the name of Schwaiger, where I was assured I would find a bed. I was in the midst of explaining that my saviour would surely come in with my coat when the door opened and in she came. She had left her son and insisted that I get back in the car for delivery to Schwaiger. Since it was only a three-minute walk this was indeed proof of her great kindness. She only left me when she was sure that I had a bed for the night.

Schwaiger did not much appeal and, having left my rucksack, I returned to Rappold where indeed the cooking was as good as she had described it.

☞

Day 25 – 17 September 2014 – Breitenbach to Strass im Zillertal

THE BREAKFAST AT Schwaiger proved to be surprisingly good and the €46 for bed and breakfast then seemed reasonable. I was on my way to the church when my saviour chanced to pass. She drew up to make sure that all had been good and to wish me the best for the day ahead before we parted with much goodwill. Such experiences restore faith in human kindness. We will never meet again and I will always be in her debt.

The church in Breitenbach is yet another example of the Austrian baroque, the church far too big for the community. I climbed to a substantial organ and choir loft. The music for a Bach prelude was open on the organ desk. Music and seating at the front of the loft showed the presence of a substantial choir. Where in England would anything comparable ever be found? I took a view of the church in the early morning light.

The walk from Breitenbach is exhilarating, especially on a sunny morning through rich fields and forest before the descent into Voldöpp. From Voldöpp, Rattenberg is the destination, and the designers of the Jakobsweg have chosen a simple footpath through the suburbs which crosses first the tributary and then the Inn itself to deliver the walker into the midst of Rattenberg.

Between Breitenbach and Voldöpp lies the interesting museum Tiroler Bauernhof at Kramsach (telephone +43 (0)5337 62636). This is not on the designated route but on the makeshift one developed to avoid a landslide that had blocked the official Weg. I gained from the accident not only the museum but also a walk through farm and forest as opposed to a long walk along the left bank of the Inn. The museum is extremely authentic and full of virtue but all the structures are so uniformly crude and dark that there is not much to choose between the farmhouse, the smithy, the bathhouse and the granary. To modern eyes they seem scarcely fit for human habitation and use.

Also on this stretch I came upon a wayside shrine which I photographed. The Catholic piety of the Austrian country people accounts for the enormous number of shrines marking not the pilgrim path but Catholic fundamentals: Crucifixions, Calvaries, Holy Marys, and local saints such as St Florian and St John of Nepomuk. They range in size from small chapels to a single figure. Equally varied is their state of preservation. But even those in sore need of restoration will have a plant, a bunch of flowers or a candle at their foot.

What delighted me in the shrine I have illustrated in the plate section is the accompanying hymn to nature and the creation of beauty with the aid of living things. The arch and the seat within are an open invitation to all passersby to enter in and rest a while on a summer's day. In winter and in storm it would offer refuge and shelter from the sudden blast. Every expression was so individual, so personal, that I was sure that it was not the community speaking but a person or even a family inspired by love and perhaps grief.

Rattenberg is quite unlike any other Austrian town I have seen. In the 15th and 16th centuries it rose to riches on the silver trade, which then died as the mines were exhausted. Nothing much seems to have changed in the interim as far as the street scene is concerned. My photograph poorly illustrates the point, but I chose it because it catches the Augustiner Stift tower that commands the four points of the compass.

A north European Renaissance creation, Rattenberg is largely untouched by the Austrian passion for the baroque. The exception to this generalisation is the Augustiner Stift, a medieval monastery modernised in the baroque period in a way that leaves the medieval framework there for all to see. After the reforms of Joseph II, the monastery fell but was later taken over by the Servite Order. They held on until 2000, which then allowed the extremely skilful conversion of the main body of the monastery into a museum of ecclesiastical art and craftwork. There are many interesting things in the museum that were new to me. First, a book of prints, one for each day of the Catholic calendar. Even more remarkable are the large-scale portrait prints that were prepared for the frontispiece of a doctoral thesis. But the real generosity of the museum lies in the access to the upper parts. The first of the upper galleries displaying the picture collection leads to the galleries in the monastic church, from which the abbot and distinguished visitors could attend worship without being seen – very much as though in a box at the theatre. Even more remarkable is the provision of access to the voids between the nave roof and the dome of the church and the ultimate tiled roof above the dome. Although I have visited innumerable monasteries and churches, never before have I had access that reveals the scale and complexity of the frame constructed to hold the nave ceiling and the dome, above which soar the beams and joists that bear the weight of the ultimate tiled roof. With characteristic caution and attention to danger, they have installed in the roof an insulated chamber that would provide ninety minutes of safe shelter should fire break out and prevent descent by ladder. Anyone resorting to this chamber would hope that the fire brigade would be swiftly at the scene. Beyond that there is independent access to the bell tower: in the first chamber, the tower clock; in the second chamber above, the monastery bells; and in the third chamber above that, a viewing platform commanding the four quarters of the compass. All this I had to myself, no one else choosing to climb the ladders.

From Rattenberg there is a walk of some 12 kilometres to Strass im Zillertal. For nine-tenths of the way there is a bicycle path running along the south bank of the Inn. This makes a pleasant walk: level and with a grassy verge and often in the shade of trees to either side. One of my photographs caught the charm of this walk in the afternoon light, and another the might of the River Inn. Another attraction is that there are no choices, no need to look for signs: the way is straight ahead. Only at the end, having reached the Ziller, is there the need to make choices and follow the waymarks. The pilgrim arrives in Strass without the straggle of outskirts before journey's end. By the church I tried a house that declared itself a *Pilgerherberge*. My request for a bed was declined and I was pointed across the road to another house offering rooms. Again I was refused and these refusals were my good fortune as I then walked on to the other end of the village where I encountered the excellent Hotel Post (telephone +43 (0)5244 62119).

☞

Day 26 – 18 September 2014 – Return to Vienna

THE NEXT MORNING, after a good dinner and a good night's sleep, I discovered that the village church is dedicated to St Jakob. The church is of medieval origin but prettily decorated in the baroque period. By chance I found a pilgrim stamp at the back of the church and a book to record a pilgrim visit. After breakfast I boarded the 08.15 Zillertal miniature train, which stopped ten minutes later in Jenbach. My expectation that I would need a local train to connect to the Innsbruck Express was swiftly corrected by the authoritarian ticket officer. He had in just under an hour an express stopping on its way from Bregenz to Vienna. He made me fill in a form, as a result of which he declared that I was eligible for half-price, first-class fare. In second class I would have to pay full fare and by accepting his proposal I would save myself €3. Thence my first experience of first-class rail travel in Austria. It is certainly a lot better than British rail services, with a travelling map, as on a flight, and fulsome information as to speed of travel and expected time of arrival for each station ahead. It is a four-hour journey and the fare of €62 seemed particularly reasonable. I took a photograph of the skyscape as we left the Semmering hills.

☞

Random Thoughts and Generalisations
on this September Walk

WITH HINDSIGHT THE Pension Dorf in Unken was unvarnished but had an excellent kitchen. The two hotels in St Ulrich were industrial, meeting the mass market efficiently but pretentiously and soullessly. The family-run Gasthof Dorfwirt in Going was excellent in all departments. Hotel Eggerwirt in Söll was my favourite, but probably for overall excellence the prize would go to Gasthaus Rappold in Breitenbach. I say probably because I had only dinner there. The Post Hotel in Ziller would not be far below that. I have omitted the Hotel Fischer in St Johann, which was professional but to a fault. It did not attempt charm. The Brauerei in Bad Reichenhall is in a different country and represents a different tradition. It is excellent but that is not to compare like with like.

The walk from Bad Reichenhall up the Saalach is superb until St Ulrich. The route from St Ulrich disappoints all the way to St Johann. It is hard to judge the stretch from St Johann to Going given that I walked in heavy rain. However, the middle section would have been beautiful in fine weather. The glory comes from Going, on past the wonderful Wilder Kaiser peaks. The sense of the sublime really is maintained all the way to Itter until falling into the orbit of the unattractive Wörgl. Beyond Wörgl the walk to Breitenbach is beautiful, as is the walk on to Rattenberg and then the river walk to Strass. All in all this is a supreme section that constantly provokes the judgement that Austria is the most beautiful country in the world.

Weather: cloud, rain and mist ruin the pleasure of walking. If the weather turns foul, rest up rather than lose the experience of walking through sublime country in the sunshine that characterises it. The first day was humid and bright, the middle days were either grey or washed-out and only the final two and a half days were perfect walking weather. The daytime temperature reached 23°C; the night-time temperature never dipped into single figures. When it shone, the sun was strong. Each day banks of glorious cloud, as if created by angels, massed around the ramparts of the surrounding mountains on every side. Those that crossed the ramparts were swiftly dissolved by the heat of the sun and they only achieved their minor victories as the sun sank to lower itself onto, and then beneath, the mountain ramparts.

As soon as the forecast delivered its promise every farmer was out mowing, raking, baling and wrapping. Unlike the English farmer who goes for one main cut, and perhaps a second cut in the autumn, the Austrian farmer cuts as though mowing a lawn. The cut is spread and raked and then baled green. The bales are very dense and hard. They keep their shape. Where the cut is allowed to dry for hay it keeps its natural green to a high degree, without bleaching like an English hayfield.

It is also worth pointing out that on the path from Vienna to Salzburg accommodation and refreshments are generally in short supply. Only in the major cities is there a rich choice of price and quality; between the big cities there is very often little choice or no choice at all. Contrast the country beyond Salzburg which becomes a Mecca for tourism, both in summer and in winter. Here the problem is not to find a bed or a meal but rather to choose the best out of so many on offer.

WINTER INTERLUDE 2014–15

MY EXPERIENCE IN January 2014 drove me to conclude that walking in winter is impossible. The day is too short, the weather too uncertain. It was largely by chance that I developed the solution. For had Wilhering and St Florian not been on the Jakobsweg stretch that I attempted in January, and Linz too, I would not have fallen on selective sightseeing as the ideal January substitute. So in January 2015 I thought, let me return to Melk, which I had resolutely resisted the temptation to visit on line of route. And then I thought, let me visit Kremsmünster. Kremsmünster is only some 8 kilometres from the Jakobsweg as it runs through Lambach, but in walking weather I had resisted the detour.

☞

Melk – January 2015

ON 13 JANUARY I arrived in Vienna in the afternoon, booked into Do & Co and met Renata when she arrived at nine. I photographed the sunset view of the great spire of Stephansdom from Room 313. On the following morning

I was to meet Andrea at ten-thirty in preparation for our meeting at the Justice Ministry at noon. After the meeting, and hospitality from Robert at Café Schulka, I hurried to the West Station and caught the train to Melk. I arrived at dusk and remembered the descent from the station to the main square where I found the Hotel Stadt Melk apparently shut for the winter. I crept in by a side door to find nothing but darkness and silence. In vain I shouted, and as I went to leave the owner returned and greeted me without the barest apology. Yes, his restaurant closed every Wednesday but I could dine at the café opposite the Rathaus. What he did not add was that the café did not cater for anything much beyond a light midday meal. All that was available was a goulash soup and then goulash. There was very little difference between these two courses except that the second had three lumps of beef swimming in the soup.

The hotel redeemed itself with an excellent breakfast, which put me in good spirits for the guided tour of the abbey at eleven. The day was cold and the streets empty. So too was the *Stift*. At the appointed hour came the guide and I thought that we would be but two. However, a young girl hurried up and we were then three. Our guide was a middle-aged lady from the town. She had been educated at the *Gymnasium* and her knowledge was comprehensive and profound. The treasures are laid out in a succession of rooms which formerly served as the imperial guest wing. The display is high class, ultra-modern and thus entirely effective. I cannot say, however, that there was anything on view which amazed or delighted me. What then followed was a parade of the grandest rooms: the marble hall, the terrace leading to the sumptuous library, and the ultimate spiral staircase down to the church. After showing us the church the guide bid us farewell, and the girl and I set out across the huge court towards the entrance gate. Although she had not spoken a previous word she informed me that she was Turkish. She then said that she lived in Istanbul. And when I displayed polite interest she said that her name was Magde and she looked forward to seeing me whenever I might come to Istanbul. She wrote her telephone number down on her ticket with a friendly innocence which touched my heart.

After an excellent lunch in the hotel I was fortified for the train journey from Melk to Amstetten, then a train to Linz, and a third to Kremsmünster. I caught the view of Stift Melk in early light and the street leading out of the Hauptplatz.

☞

Kremsmünster – January 2015

THE ARRIVAL ON 15 January was inauspicious. The local train from Linz stopped at innumerable stations, the identity of which was masked by the dark. With the aid of the guard I eventually established that I must alight at the next stop. I was the only traveller to do so and I had nothing but the sense of a looming mass of masonry elevated above the town. I took the obvious direction until choice began to develop. I asked a man, who interrupted his telephone call to offer voluble instructions that I scarcely caught. Our conversation had been overheard, however, and when I next hesitated an elderly lady emerged and offered herself as a guide. This was timely as I had arranged with Pater Franz that I would attend the six o'clock vespers. My guide revealed that she lived close by the monastery gate and was in any case on her way home. It proved a long climb at her slow pace.

Stift Kremsmünster is huge and even getting from the pedestrian gate to the church proved a puzzle. So half an hour after alighting from the train I deposited my heavy baggage at the rear of the nave and arrived in the Lady Chapel a minute before the Benedictines in their sombre black cowls. Vespers was long and beautifully sung, the verses of psalms and canticles alternating between two tenor soloists and the rest of the congregation. At its close a young monk detached himself and approached. Here was Pater Franz, with whom I had arranged my stay. He showed me to a modest room with shared use of the WC in the passage. He had explained that this was the best that could be done given a prior booking by a group of young people. He then led me to the guest dining room for a very basic supper. I had given him my professional card and he soon returned saying that he had moved my luggage to a better room. He said that he had not appreciated that I would stay three nights and I therefore deserved a better room. I wondered if he had been impressed by my boastful card and had decided in favour of rank over youth. The better room to which he led me after supper was indeed worthy of a visiting prelate. The furniture was all aged, as were the paintings on the wall. There was a particularly handsome marquetry chest of drawers and desk above from the 18th century with its original gilt-brass handles and locks. Pater Franz showed me his recent discovery: that an apparently innocuous side table in fact concealed a backgammon board in its well. In my photograph the gaming table is concealed beneath the decorous lace cloth. The chest of drawers deserves its prominence in the other view of the room.

I then fell into a routine over the following two days: mass at 6.30 a.m., Mittagshore at noon and vespers at 6 p.m. After each service a simple meal was available in the guest dining room. There I encountered not just the young visitors but also the lady who worked in the shop and several Benedictine Sisters who appeared to be loosely attached to or perhaps even stationed within the *Stift*. I spent the mornings working in my room. In the afternoons I ventured out. On the first I had a guided tour of the monastery. Again there were three on the tour: an elderly lady guide, a clever and kind middle-aged Austrian man, and myself. Unfortunately our guide was of an autocratic nature and accelerated to high speed, stopping only at things that interested her and parrying questions on anything else. That is not intended as a criticism. She was elderly and the day was cold.

The abbey's greatest treasure is the Tassilo Chalice. It is so old and venerable that its date and origins remain a mystery. In the treasury room they display only a copy. There are other lovely things, however, particularly a gold chalice of the 14th century.

The abbey has a large collection of pictures, all periods and all schools. We were rushed through at such a pace that I was unable to see anything arresting. From the galleries the guide led us into the Marble Hall, used, I suspect, only in summer as a grand dining room. For like the other great abbeys, Kremsmünster required the facilities to receive the Emperor and a court of 250. Thence we passed into a series of rooms containing a wide variety of exhibits including an armoury. It seems that in the 18th century the abbots were fond of deer stalking. There are also Turkish weapons seized after the defeat at the walls of Vienna.

The library is of massive length but no great height. Typically it contains some very rare manuscripts and books as well as the necessary terrestrial and celestial globes. The entry is through a concealed wide door disguised as book shelves. That completed our tour, our guide showing no intention of taking us to the abbey church. The guidebook that I had bought in the shop described the very fine church as baroque, but I would rather say sumptuous classicism. This is because it was built in the late 17th century before the influence of von Erlach. I grew fond of the Lady Chapel by Carlone where vespers is always sung.

Kremsmünster has two assets, not to be found in any other monastery to the best of my knowledge. The first is the succession of fish ponds which were first four in number and then enlarged to six in the late 16th century. The tanks are square in profile, each dominated by some water-spouting head or statue or godhead, and in each tank still there are fish actively bred for the table, either for internal consumption or for commerce. Then along the walls enclosing the tanks, a long esplanade, are the heads of deer, shot by the abbots largely in the 18th century. Each head is dated and remembered no doubt with pride in the lifetime of the abbot. This area, open to the sky but walled off on all sides, is a private world of fantasy and delight. It demands three photos to convey its unique quality.

The other wonder is the nine-storey observatory built by the monks in 1750. What was its purpose? To enable the monks to come closer to heaven and to observe the gyrations of the heavenly bodies. Later the ground and upper floors were developed as a natural history museum to display minerals and shells and fossils and all the wonders of the natural world. Unfortunately the observatory is not open in the winter months so I could admire it only from afar.

The entrances to the *Stift* and its courts are lavish. The main entrance is a deep gatehouse by Jakob Prandtauer that I illustrated from the second gatehouse, which leads into the principal court where the abbey church, the abbot's quarters and the entry to the grand quarters are to be found. Again I pictured the second gatehouse, from the arch into the third court, which contains the domestic and work places. The simple door seen through this arch led to my rooms as well as to the guest dining room.

Jakob Prandtauer, architect and master builder, was born in 1660 in the Tyrol but he worked extensively in or near the Wachau. While Melk was his masterwork, he also worked on St Andrä an der Traisen and built much in St Pölten, where he lived. Then he built Herzogenburg and the monastery at Dürnstein, as well as being responsible for the great ranges at St Florian after the death of Carlo Carlone. At Kremsmünster he built domestic ranges in addition to the main gatehouse, which is distinguished by its bold depth. So you see that the majority of his commissions, and certainly those for which he will always be celebrated, were monastic. He built on a monumental scale, and to last, but plainly and without the spark of originality or genius. His portrait at Melk fits that estimation. So I think of him as more a builder than an architect.

The town of Kremsmünster is unremarkable but no doubt meets the needs of the inhabitants and the neighbouring countryside. This countryside is undulating and is properly described as alpine foothills.

My second day was not as the first, which had been mist-shrouded until midday and then bright winter sunshine. The second day was clouded and drizzling. Nevertheless, after lunch I set out to explore the satellite, that is a chapel raised on a neighbouring hill and reached through a stairway of Stations of the Cross. I found the beginning of the assent through trial and error and by skipping across an intervening dual carriageway. Each station had its own miniature chapel, and all are in a good state of recent repair. The same is true of the chapel on the hill, although sadly I was unable to gain entry on a bleak winter's afternoon. I could hardly complain that it was securely locked.

On this my second day and third night I was invited by Pater Franz to dine in the refectory. So after vespers he gathered me up and I followed the dark procession as it swept out of the Lady Chapel and ascended a wide and rich staircase in the marble which I know as French Red. This led us into a magnificent refectory, I would guess some 30 metres long and 15 metres wide. Father Franz admitted that its recent conservation had been costly. For the grace all stood in a semi-circle at the end of the room and devoutly intoned a long Latin grace which I could follow on a printed and laminated card that Father Franz handed me. Then we took our places.

The meal was served by one of the two monks who had sung tenor at vespers. His black cowl was fronted by a snow-white apron. As we sat at the inward-facing table he served the soup and in due course cleared the plates. As a guest I was provided with a bottle of beer brewed in some other monastery. Throughout this first course one of the brethren read from the pulpit what I was told was a biography of a Czech priest and philosopher. This reading resumed after the main course, so that conversation was only possible for one of the three courses. The main course consisted of a dish of over-fried eggs, nutty-brown at the edges and completely solid in the yolk, which were accompanied by a dish of chopped spinach so liquid that it could only be ladled onto the plate. This and a basket of dark bread was the evening meal. (When I returned to England a friend, to whom I had described the scene, suggested that it was symbolic since it could be described as eggs Benedict.) The final course consisted of tubs of fruit yoghurt straight from the supermarket shelf. This I declined, as, I noticed, did many of the community. With this abstinence the meal concluded and we grouped again for the second grace. Since it was still only ten to seven, once I had parted from Pater Franz I hastened to the *Stiftschank*. Here I indulged myself with a *Viertel* of Heideboden, an excellent wine from the Burgenland.

Taking Pater Franz's advice, I waited for the 10.15 high mass on Sunday morning. I managed to sit next to Schwester Lydia Suss, who, as before, kindly helped me follow the mass in the prayer book. Clouds of incense thick as a garden bonfire ascended in stately pace to the frescoed ceiling high above. In the organ loft orchestra and choir sanctified the creed, the Gloria, the Agnus Dei and all other choral parts. The service was taken by the abbott, who preached with dramatic conviction. The service lasted an hour and a quarter but was richly appreciated by a large congregation. After the service I waited in the hope of seeing Pater Franz to say farewell but at noon I decided that I must head for the station and the 12.36 fast train to Linz. I left Linz on the Zurich–Budapest express and by 2.30 I was buying flowers at the boutique in the West Station. From there I hastened to the Opernring Hotel and there left my luggage. Fortunately remembering that the Kunsthistorische Museum is shut on Mondays I managed to catch the final two hours of opening which gave me ample time to absorb the extensive exhibition of Velasquez, half of which had been gifts from the Spanish to the Austrian branch of the Habsburg family, the other half having been borrowed from Spain and elsewhere. London richly contributed with the *Rokeby Venus* and the two great paintings from Apsley House: the water seller and the portrait of the virile man in middle age. I whiled away the early evening until meeting Renata at dinner time. I was back in the Opernring Hotel and Room 305, so full of significance for me.

Monday was a day of early breakfast, leisurely shopping and a full visit to the Van Mytens exhibition in the Prince Eugen winter palace. The paintings were indifferent but the setting magnificent. I left the hotel at 3.00 for a 4.30 meeting with Andrea Ciserova at the airport. Then safe back to King's Bench Walk.

☞

Second Stay at Kremsmünster – February 2015

ON SUNDAY 8 February I arrived in Vienna with flowers for a birthday evening with Renata. Snow lay patchily, and more threatened. I woke next morning to a blizzard from the force of which I was sheltered by a long meeting at the Justice Ministry. It struck me as I walked to the Opernring and then on by U-Bahn to Westbahnhof that I had a choice between ÖBB and Westbahn. I chose the latter shrewdly since the fare to Linz was only €18.50. I boarded ten minutes before departure and noticed, first, passengers leaving the train and then no movement at the appointed departure time. There were tannoy announcements in German which I did not understand. At first I worried: should I join the departing, was it a ghost train? Then, as the blizzard surged down the platform, I disconnected. I became calm and indifferent to choice. What would be would be. After perhaps an hour the train began to refill and then departed. The line had been blocked between Westbahnhof and Hütteldorf. We did not arrive at Linz until six o'clock and I reached Kremsmünster just before seven. A long walk through what here was slush brought me to the deserted abbey where I was lucky to find Schwester Lydia walking away from the abbot's door. She found my room and later Pater Franz sought me out in the *Schank*. He took me to meet Frau Stadlhuber, who he had found to give me German lessons. She was employed part-time by the State to teach Turkish immigrants who aspire to acquire a basic level that ignores all the rules of German grammar. That sounded good enough for me but lessons did not long continue as my friendly teacher had not a word of

English. I had not realised that success depended on teacher and pupil having a common tongue.

Following my arrival on the night of 9 February it transpired that the tenth was the day of St Scholastica, the Sister of St Benedict. Accordingly, this was a most significant feast for the nuns. They were given a major part in the morning mass and at breakfast we ate brioche in the shape of doves with two cloves as eyes. These symbolise the legend that St Scholastica ascended to heaven in the form of a dove. The statue of the saint was dramatically decorated with a carpet thrown over the steps, a mighty candle, and flowers at her feet and on the carpet.

I had an exploratory walk past the *Brauhaus* and found the *Gärtnerei*, the Turkish pavilion and the amazing heating plant run entirely on huge quantities of wood chippings. At lunch I met a lady administrator employed to prepare what would be an open competition for the design of a spectacular abbey garden for the summer of 2017. This was being funded by the government of Upper Austria as a tourist investment. The *Schank* is closed on Tuesdays and in the café at the Prandtauer Gate I bumped into Felix who gallantly offered me an insider's tour of the abbey. Before vespers I lit a candle for Joyce, and another for Bill, at the hour of her cremation.

The second day was distinguished by the appearance at mass of a very seductive girl, and by a tour, thanks to Felix and Sister Lydia, of the abbot's apartments. Therein are some extremely rare and valuable chattels. The summer rooms are distinguished by a double cube with paintings framed by the panelling throughout the room. Even more remarkable is the adjoining print room, where the prints are not simply stuck to the wall in English fashion but framed and glazed within the panelling to be flush to the wall. Thus presented, the prints are very well preserved. Schwester Lydia demonstrated that there was a large collection of prints in folders stored either in the four built-in chests or in the spaces under the window steps. After vespers at six o'clock there was an additional compline at eight.

On this February visit the weather was typically Viennese. The blizzard of Monday gave way to unbroken leaden skies that never released the snow that they presaged. Then on my final two days came the blue skies, the chill wind and the bright sunlight.

On Saturday 14 February I had returned to Vienna and in the afternoon I again found shelter in an angle of the imperial palace, where I smoked a leisurely dinner cigar, relishing the returning heat of the February sun. Later we celebrated St Valentine. Very early the following morning I heard a rattle of the door handle and thought that it was Renata returning. That led me to the balcony overlooking the Ring. As I searched the empty street I heard the song of the first dawn chorus of the year, performed by a single blackbird.

☞

Third Visit to Kremsmünster – March 2015

ON 12 MARCH I arrived in Vienna on the early flight to spend the evening with Renata. The next day I muddled the connection at Linz and found myself on the Prague train.

In Austria the platforms have letters as well as numbers. So, for example, there is 4A–F. There may be two trains on platform 4 simultaneously, one on 4A–C and another on 4D–F. I had simply boarded the wrong train on platform 4. As we travelled the perception of error and a growing anxiety developed from the unfamiliar landscape. I found the guard, who confirmed my fear and put me out at the next station. I hoped there might be a bus or taxi to link the lines but the stationmaster was adamant: I must wait for the next train back to Linz. At least at this small deserted station there was an authority: in Austria stations are controlled by the master in smart uniform and peaked scarlet cap.

So the outcome was a return to Linz and a fresh start with the result that I did not reach Kremsmünster until nearly seven o'clock. In the main court I found Schwester Lydia waiting, not by chance, I think. And so my life at the *Stift* resumed. On the following night we went to the school play with Felix in the lead. On Sunday I started to write the major paper commissioned by Slovakia. In the afternoon I walked to Kalvarienberg, to find the chapel open now that winter had passed. It is a fitting addendum to the great abbey. I photographed the rear view to show its relationship to the abbey, at the end of which rises the extraordinary observatory.

The week continued with lessons from Frau Stadlhuber and some exploration of the local *Wanderweg*, which proved to be pretty inadequate.

Thursday was enlivened by Felix's birthday, St Joseph's Day, and another tour of the monastery, this time conducted by the assistant librarian. Have I introduced Felix? He and Leopold Czernin Kinsky were the only boarders among hundreds at the *Gymnasium*. They were boarding because Felix's home was in Innsbruck and Leopold's near the Czech border. But the reputation of the *Gymnasium* is founded on its long history. Wilhering also supports a large *Gymnasium* and the continuing influence and relevance of these two abbeys rests in part on their schools. Leopold was to complete his schooling at Ampleforth and he and his parents were about to visit the school. For some reason they flew to Manchester and then had a horrendous onward journey in a winter blast. Quite unnecessarily I felt some responsibility for such a bad beginning.

During this stay I continued to photograph the abbey. I took the canal between the first and second courts. The crane in the sky marks the building of a major extension to the school. Next comes the imposing west front of the abbey church. Finally I photographed the *Rosenkranz* above the altar in the vespers chapel, which has for me a powerful beauty. I have not included my Kremsmünster photographs in the plate section as any reader can see all on the website.

☞

TO MEET RENATA I returned to Vienna on the 20th only to find that she was ill, so I extended my stay and changed my flight in hope, which was rewarded when she texted me and telephoned as I left the Albertina to say that she was much better. Thus we were together on the twenty-first; she leaving for Brno early the following day to spend time with her brother. We made plans for Krems in April when I would greet the spring and return to the Jakobsweg.

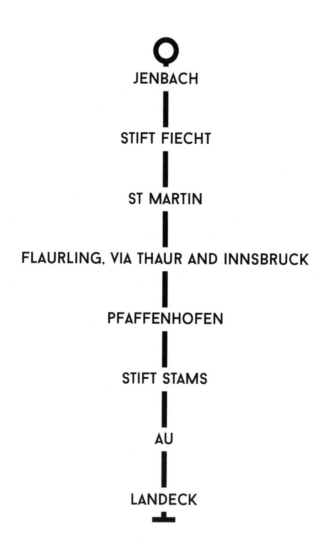

JENBACH

STIFT FIECHT

ST MARTIN

FLAURLING, VIA THAUR AND INNSBRUCK

PFAFFENHOFEN

STIFT STAMS

AU

LANDECK

JENBACH TO LANDECK

Day 27 – 12 April 2015 – Jenbach to Stift Fiecht

I HAD ARRANGED to stay the night at Krems having planned to meet Renata there. Although our plan was frustrated and she had had to return home to Slovakia I had the booking at the Alte Post and, partly out of sentiment and partly in homage to her, on the eve I had taken the train through Tulln to Krems. The Alte Post has the expected picturesque location and a reasonable restaurant but the accommodation above strikes all the wrong notes. The antiquity ensures deficiencies of comfort and convenience. The furnishings and decorations consist of an assembly of old kitsch in varying states of decay. This induced a state of unease and I was glad to walk out into the air and the main street the next morning. Perhaps the atmosphere of the hotel matched my sense of transience at the loss of Renata.

Thus on this first morning of spring walking I took the early train from Krems to St Pölten, where I changed onto the Westbahn express to Salzburg. In Salzburg I transferred to the ÖBB express to Innsbruck, stopping at Jenbach.

The main station in Jenbach lies to the east of the town and I could hardly face an hour of suburban east–west walking. I managed to find a bus leaving in only seven minutes which conveniently conveyed me west of Jenbach to Schloss Tratzberg. There the map showed the possibility of a woodland path and so there proved to be, carrying me pleasantly all the way to the outskirts of Stans. My destination was the Benedictine monastery at Fiecht, which lies some 4 kilometres west of Stans. The day was closing, since I had not reached Jenbach until twenty to three. Accordingly there was little option but to take the highway on to Fiecht from the edge of Vomp. This was a hard and unlovely conclusion to a day of some enterprise.

At Stift Fiecht the lady in charge of the *Pforte*, pleasant but almost slow-witted, had kindly waited for me and I was in good time for the 5.30 vespers. Her directions to the chapel were completely confused, almost incomprehensible, and accordingly I burst into the chapel through the wrong door as the service was about to begin. Nobody paid the least notice. Vespers developed into evening mass, which consumed the hour before the evening meal in the guest dining room.

Two others came in for dinner; a strange couple. He barked in a strong baritone, she vouchsafed sheepish responses. The dinner was surprisingly good, what we used to call *Bouchées à la Reine*. I took the offer of a bottle of German wine for €7. It was described as Spätburgunder Blanc de Noir. It was also said to be *Spätlese*, which accounted for it being between dry and sweet. It tasted of nothing but honey. It well suited my thirst and my need for alcohol.

I slept well in the monastic bed and got up without any clue as to when or where the morning office would be. Since no bell rang at 6 I assumed it must be at 6.30. But when I arrived at 6.25 the office was well underway, indeed half completed. The singing was no better than the night before, although on this occasion led by a monk who accompanied himself on a portable organ that played repetitive long-drawn chords. I was quite relieved when it ended.

Breakfast was as good as dinner and I set to work to plan the day ahead.

☞

Day 28 – 13 April 2015 – Stift Fiecht to St Martin

FIRST I TRIED to interrogate the lady gatekeeper on how and where to proceed, given what seemed to be miles of suburbia in the valley beyond the motorway, which roared incessantly on the eastern boundary of the monastery. But as on the previous evening my effort was in vain.

Then I had a piece of that luck which had so often saved me on my pilgrimage. Into the gate lodge came a quiet man in a pullover. I recognised him from the two offices that I had attended and indeed was not surprised to hear him addressed as Father Johannes. He immediately asked if we could speak English and thereafter became my guide and friend. His first endeavour was to find me a room in a religious house in Innsbruck. The Redemptorists had been recommended to me by Pater Franz. My email bounced back, however, and none of the telephone lines that the brochure offered was live, so we tried the Servites. They were full, as was the Marillac House. Father Johannes suggested another house that was not in my brochure, but like all the others it was fully booked.

We moved, therefore, to the next problem: how to continue the Jakobsweg. Father Johannes took me to the bus stop and we identified a possible bus into Schwaz. I photographed the view of the abbey from the bus stop. Then he had a better idea. A secretary would finish at 12.30 and her road home led past the village of Terfens. But when asked, alas, she declined to give me the proposed lift. She had decided to go shopping on her way home. So I boarded the bus for Schwaz. In Schwaz I had to change to another route in order to reach Terfens. To pass the twenty-minute wait between buses, I had coffee in a sunny shopping centre beside the bus station. When the bus for Terfens arrived, the driver was young and attractive so I was soon explaining my presence on her bus and my need to recover the Jakobsweg in Terfens. Father Johannes had advised that, were I to start in Terfens, after a sharp climb I would reach a plateau which would carry me all the way through almost to Innsbruck.

The driver took a close look at the guidebook and declared that she knew exactly where I should alight. Eventually she put me down at what seemed to me to be an unpromising point, but with great assurance she directed me to a leisure centre and lake that proved to be a twenty-minute walk downhill. When I sought reassurance at her recommended destination a confident man cried, Onward, ever onward, and I complied. The road ran alongside the small lake and I have never seen so many frogs squashed flat on the highway. Suddenly the motorway loomed alongside me and I knew that I must be wrong. The driver had misread the map. Had I looked I would not have made the mistake but I had simply trusted her confidence and local knowledge. The error cost me forty-five minutes and it made the climb from Terfens to the plateau seem particularly arduous. I paid the price for flirtation.

Once the plateau was gained I had three hours of walking in paradise. It was without any doubt the most lovely stretch of the Jakobsweg that I had ever encountered. I photographed this chapel standing right on my path, lovingly preserved in the middle of nowhere. Then I walked through glades of larch and pine, the larch just springing to life. The new shooting grass was an unearthly green. The sky was cerulean blue flecked with occasional cotton-wool clouds. On all sides the mountains rose majestically, most partially snow covered, some completely so. One photograph I selected for the plate section from several, all equally illustrative of the landscape and the day. This clump of larch silhouetted on a high mound showed me for the first time a landscape scene that I imagine would have been familiar to Altdorfer and from which he might have found his inspiration.

It was six o'clock before I returned to the living world in the hamlet of St Michael. The guidebook said that there was a habitation there for the pilgrim but I could see nothing. I hurried on for the half hour that was required to reach St Martin. Here things started to go wrong. The attractive *Stuberl* was enjoying its *Ruhetag*. The swagger hotel catering for the Austrian haute bourgeoisie was fully booked. Neither of the two pilgrim houses in the guide was operating. With the grudging aid of the receptionist in the hotel I was directed to the bus stop where, according to the timetable, I had missed the last bus of the day.

Once again the heavens intervened and suddenly there came the bus some five minutes late. There was no passenger on board, so at some length I explained my predicament to the driver. He was a man of sympathy and sense. He decided that I was better suited to a small local *Gasthaus* than to another posh hotel. So he sped down the road, swooshing round mountain bends to come to a breathless halt at Walderbrücke. The guesthouse there proved as good as his recommendation. I was shown to a simple three-bedded room where I washed and changed. I went down to a supper of smoked tongue and potatoes cooked in wild garlic. I ordered a salad, generous in proportion, instead of the *Kraut*. With this I had half a litre of sparkling water and half a litre of white wine. Thus restored, I slept a sound sleep from nine until six. The breakfast was surprisingly poor after so fine a supper. After breakfast I sought the aid of the owner to identify the bus stop for St Martin. An early inspection had shown that there was no sign for an uphill bus on the far side of the road to match the sign at which I had alighted the evening before. My questions of the owner produced a voluble response in an incomprehensible dialect. I abandoned her, paid my bill and set off. I took a picture of the house that had saved me from disaster.

☞

Day 29 – 14 April 2015 – St Martin to Flaurling, via Thaur and Innsbruck

I SOON FOUND the bus stop, the explanation being that the bus on its uphill journey took a different route which converged with the downhill one about 50 metres short of the point at which I had been set down. The stop was some 20 metres short of that convergence. So, having found the stop, I consulted the timetable attached to the halt sign. It told me that I had missed the first bus of the day and that there was not another for three hours. Since I had missed the first bus by only some two or three minutes I was distraught. My despair drove me to what I hate – thumbing a lift. As I expected, car after car swung by without a glance. Then, again, the heavens came to my aid when the bus swung up to the T-junction. The driver recognised me and stopped. It was my friend from the previous evening, and again he was driving an empty bus. Reunited, we swung round the hairpin bends to St Martin and beyond to St Michael. I knew that in St Michael the Jakobsweg crossed the road and I was therefore bound to find it. There he set me down and we parted with hearty thanks from me and many mutual expressions of goodwill. I resumed the Jakobsweg where I had left it the night before and there followed two hours of magical walking through the woods with all the mountain splendour in those hours between eight and ten. The air was cold, despite the mounting sun. The woods were carpeted with violets and *Anemone blanda*, both white and blue. This paradise ended more or less as I regained Walderbrücke. Thereafter the path dropped through the forest line into the farmland below. Far away I could see my destination of Thaur. Here, where most needed, the Jakobsweg waymarking evaporated. I struck what seemed to me to be the best line. As so often in Austria I was steeplechasing or, more accurately, domed-tower chasing. For every village has its magnificent village church topped with a copper onion dome raised on its tower and declaring itself by its proud height from a great distance. Of the three proud projections it was not difficult to decide which was Thaur and I simply struck a line across the farmland.

Here, to the east of Innsbruck, and I was to see it equally to the west, the predominant crop is vegetable. Flat lands on the valley floor with light friable grey soil were almost all tilled for vegetable crops, many under plastic sheeting for early harvest. I walked across a wide strip of radishes that had been neither harvested nor ploughed in. All these fields have sophisticated irrigation systems. I guess that given its fertility the land would permit several crops a year and would be expensive to buy.

I had been refining my technique for combating city sprawl, urbanisation and industrialisation. It is all perfectly avoidable given the excellence of the public bus services. Thaur is a pretty independent village, quite unaffected by its proximity to Innsbruck. After a ten-minute wait a comfortable bus carried me from its market square to the centre of Innsbruck in less than half an hour and at a cost of €2. The evacuation may have been premature, since some of the uplands between Thaur and Mühlau looked attractive, but I had no regrets.

A kind girl in the central tourist information guided my steps ahead. Yes, the whole day's walk from Innsbruck to Inzing should be written off. It would offer no pleasures. Now, she said, Inzing is a pleasing large village completely separate from and independent of Innsbruck. Take the train there and walk on. Accepting this counsel meant forgoing so much that Innsbruck has to offer as well as historic Hall nearby and the great imperial Schloss Ambras. But I had no hesitation.

Long-distance walking and sightseeing cannot be confused. Innsbruck demanded and merited its own pilgrimage.

So I walked immediately to the station and found a train to Inzing. There I ate a little and drank much in an excellent café in the church square. The tables were outside, the sun shone, the waitress was pretty and friendly: what more could a man want?

When I resumed the Jakobsweg it climbed out of the valley and ran along the edge of the forest above. Water rushed off the mountains in racing streams. Farms of prosperity and content lay immediately below. Distant was the invisible river Inn and, though nearer, the scarcely visible and almost inaudible motorway. The sun was glorious and fairy tale snowy mountains rose majestically towards the heavens. It must have been cold up there. There was no visible sign of melt.

After some research I had chosen to make Flaurling my destination. The approach to Flaurling skirts the edge of the forest with pastures below, and beyond them the main road, the motorway and then the river. Just short of the village I came upon a fenced plot leaning on the forest edge. It measured perhaps 30 metres by 20 and was planted up as some compromise between a garden and an allotment. In its midst was a lady busy watering by hand from a tub constantly filling and then overflowing from a tube laid from some spring in the forest above. This very practical arrangement would obviously much increase the productivity of the plot. As ever I stopped for a chat. My introduction soon developed into an English conversation. The proprietor lived in Innsbruck and she explained that accordingly she was confined to bee husbandry.

Any form of livestock farming would require twice-daily visits. "But how have you managed to acquire and develop the site?" I asked. She told me that it was a very Austrian procedure requiring her to go through various bureaucratic hoops before she had qualified as a "farmer" and thus gained planning consent to enclose and cultivate her farm. However complex the procedure I was surprised that she had no followers. Nowhere had I seen anything comparable and what a deep sense of pleasure must it be to quit the city at will and to play as long as it pleased one in the little kingdom, officially classified as a farm.

She pointed me to the outskirts of the village, where, she said, I could not miss the Goldener Adler. So it proved. The facade, facing the street, was almost too good to be true. The front door was no less than 1.5 metres (5 feet) in width and led into a stone vaulted hall. Off the hall to the left and right were *Stuben*. Thereafter the authenticity evaporated with a modern staircase and a general clutter of 20th-century furnishings. The establishment was run by two women, both considerably overweight. I fancied they must be sisters, although one was fair and the other dark. Both had great prettiness in the face, open countenances and a capacity for heartfelt warmth and kindness. The blonde sister admitted me and made my breakfast the next morning. The dark sister was in charge of dinner. The Goldener Adler is well known and I was surprised that I was the only one to stay overnight and that mine was one of only four meals served. The village is pretty and the church especially so with the door flung wide to a flood of evening sunlight. The proportion of very traditional farm buildings in

108

the village was unusually high and I saw for the first time a technique for stacking the next winter's firewood in galleries attached to the outside of the house. I recorded the discovery in a picture. It was after my village walk that I settled to dinner and, as a producer of organic beef at home, was pleased to see rump steak on the menu. I favoured it over the trout, both local produce, and it came as a good, well-cooked piece of meat. Breakfast the next morning was less sophisticated but I was able to make a piece out of a *Semmel*, cheese and *Speck*. The view of the facade and the close-up of the front door show why the Goldener Adler is so famous and so esteemed.

☞

Day 30 – 15 April 2015 – Flaurling to Pfaffenhofen

THE WAY ON from Flaurling is very similar to the approach. The path climbs steeply out of the village to reach the forest edge and thereafter runs true until the descent into Pfaffenhofen. There I took the local train back to Innsbruck with the intention of buying a ticket only to Salzburg for transfer to the cheaper Westbahn service. However, the girl in the Innsbruck ticket office easily persuaded me that I should buy a senior railcard. The investment of €29 entitles the holder to half-price fares on all subsequent journeys. Why did I not receive this advice from any of the endless ticket offices with which I had previously dealt? The only loser will be Westbahn to whose services I will no longer transfer.

I returned to Vienna with a great sense of achievement. In these three days I had put behind me the great sprawl of

Innsbruck, the last city between me and the Swiss border. I felt as though I were at the furlong marker at the end of a Cup race. The weather had been glorious and on the following day would turn to rain. This sense of joy was matched only by my sorrow at the thought of Vienna without the wonderful Renata, now returned to Slovakia and her home far away on the Hungarian border.

Another sense of joy was in the Austrian spring. My days on the Weg perfectly coincided with its evolution. Cherries and magnolias were fully decked. Only the earliest trees had broken into leaf of the brightest green, so the trees still framed rather than hid the distant views. Most remarkable was the Austrian forsythia. This commonplace, almost indestructible shrub was, I think, developed in about 1820 by the head gardener in Hyde Park, Mr Forsyth. I have no idea of its European distribution but in Austria it is everywhere. The Austrian forsythia blooms with a vigour that I have never seen in England or anywhere else. I photographed a typical example. It is a shocking profusion of brilliant golden yellow that is so intense, so lacking in any variety, as to be almost offensive. I would not want the Austrian forsythia in any garden of mine but it remains to me a wonder. Beside the vulgarity of the forsythia is the delicacy of the woodland flowers: the violets, the anemones. In that seasonal link there is, however, a huge gulf, as the woodland flowers are so slender, so tender.

On my return to Vienna I had two meetings on Thursday, with Dr Fucik and with Andrea Ciserova. The first brought me to Café Sluka, adjoining the Rathaus. The Rathausplatz had been transformed into a Styrian fantasy, with wood shavings to cover the tarmac and straw bales to provide rest for the large gathering of drinkers and revellers, most of them in *Trachten*. The brass band thumped out its traditional singsong and all appeared to accept the roles that they were collectively playing as though in a film set, a filming day on which the director had totally lost control of his cast. There was something very Viennese about this fantasy.

☞

Day 31 – 19 May 2015 – Pfaffenhofen to Stift Stams
ON 18 MAY I had arrived in Vienna for a meeting with Roman and later a meeting with Robert Fucik and Philippe Lortie to explore the possibility of The Hague joining the Austro/Slovak partnership. Time will test the product of those meetings.

On 19 May I took the 08.30 train from Wien Westbahnhof to Pfaffenhofen with a change in Salzburg. In Salzburg I had a fifty-minute wait. I tried to find again the area around the Hotel Markus Sittikus and the river embankment. I failed, largely through lack of time, although I got close to the river and glimpsed again the church on the far bank with the startlingly steep roof.

Out of the station at Pfaffenhofen I took a wrong turn. Soon realising my mistake I returned to the village and discovered the welcome Jakobsweg sign but, with the Swarzer Adler in sight I stopped for coffee before walking in earnest.

Was it here that I met a great eccentric? I think so but I made no note and cannot be sure. I remember so clearly the village street running downhill towards a left-hand bend and the house on the right-hand side of the road. He stood outside the house and as I passed he accosted me. Once he had established my origins he spoke in fluent, educated English. He talked with voluble insistence. His aim was to talk and not to listen. I guessed he was a lonely and isolated man who relished the chance arrival of an amiable listener. He expressed his extreme views on the state of Austria and the world, analysing its evils and its woes and identifying the powers and influences responsible for its decline and decadence. Conspiracies abounded in his lecture. I noticed a growing condemnation of Jews and Jewish influences. But the more eloquent he became the more I became convinced that he was himself Jewish, probably born shortly after the Second World War. Around him were stacked a pile of beams, some blackened and charred by fire. He explained that he reclaimed them from fire or demolition sites to provide fuel for the winter. Despite my limited contribution he clung to my ears so that it became increasingly difficult to walk on without discourtesy. Of course in the end I insisted that I must continue my journey and we parted friends.

My destination that afternoon was Stams, which lies only about 8 kilometres from Pfaffenhofen by the main road but a good 10 kilometres by the Jakobsweg. Once out of the village the path, as usual, follows the edge of the forest above the roar of motorway, rail and river in the bed of the valley. Rietz lies halfway and I paid a brief visit to the parish church with its customary baroque interior. Rain was falling in intermittent showers and I needed a dry place to organise my sparse protection. This precaution gained me little since beyond Rietz the rain came on in earnest. Thunder rolled through the mountains and in its wake came heavy and persistent rain. By the time I reached Stift Stams I was drenched and had no change of clothes. Equally drenched was my rucksack and its contents. I rang Father Daniel Katz on his mobile from the gatehouse and he showed me to a simple room, some distance from the WC and shower serving some thirty cells down a wide passage. Yet it was all extremely welcome.

Vespers was at quarter to six and there I was looked after by a young novice with good English. The service was followed by supper, self-served in the refectory, the guest joining the fathers at their table. After the rigours of the previous twenty-four hours I slept soundly and was only half awake for mass at six-thirty the next morning.

I had always planned a rest day so lost nothing by the weather. Throughout the day the rain was heavy and persistent. It was silent and invisible, so that looking from the window the world outside seemed almost inviting. The first step from the porch revealed the reality and the impossibility of walking. I joined the guided tour after the midday meal, the main meal of the day, which was served by one of the fathers. One tour was offered in French and it attracted a large group on a coach tour. Our guide was a French lady who had married an Austrian and now ran the monastery shop. She enlightened the only two rooms on view, the Hall of the Princes and the magnificent abbey church. Nowhere is there marble or semi-precious stone. All the richness is achieved in wood: in carving, in wrought iron, in gilding and in fresco. The quality of the pews and of the marquetry in the nave and the choir is quite exceptional. Whether the choice of materials was one of financial necessity or of a desire to make use of the riches of the region I did not discover.

I also visited the parish church, which is of an unparalleled scale and quality. I was there in the aftermath of a large village funeral, entering as the last of the congregation trickled out.

I had little choice but to write off my intended march on the following day, the twenty-first. No alleviation in the weather was envisaged. At least I had the opportunity to write a paper on the Commonwealth programme and to despatch postcards to family and friends in all corners of the world.

The interlude also allowed me to examine more closely this beautiful abbey and its community. The glory of the abbey is undoubtedly the magnificent *Stiftskirche*. It consists of a nave without aisles and four transepts, the first two dividing the nave from the choir and the second two dividing the choir from the chancel. The church is remarkable for its length, accentuated by its lack of breadth and height. The internal decoration is almost entirely by fresco and ingeniously carved wood. Everything is in wood. All the false marble is painted wood and not scagliola. Wood for functional use is magnificently carved in the shape of pews and lecterns and the wonderful effect of marquetry is achieved by using different shades and varieties of bur wood. Where the wood is for decoration only it is elaborately painted and gilded. It is said that it took five kilos of gold leaf to renovate the interior. The altarpiece in the form of a tree of devotion to the Virgin Mary is all achieved in lime wood and is a veritable masterpiece. At the west end lies a remarkable, decorated crypt to the Dukes of Tyrol, comprising carved-wood images of the dukes, all surmounted by a towering crucifix group of the highest 17th century quality, facing westwards above the crypt and presenting its bare back to the high altar.

The adjoining Blood Chapel is currently under restoration. When complete it will be heated, allowing it to be used in winter. The church is unheated and the temperature in winter sometimes falls to -4°C. While this seems bizarre, it is necessary for the conservation of the remarkable frescos that decorate the ceiling and hall. These 17th-century works are in their original state, having never been overpainted. Heating would destroy their beauty.

The other pride of the abbey is the Room of the Princes. This formal stateroom is decorated from floor to ceiling, and, in a gilded musician's gallery above, with fresco. I assume that it was the cheapest method of achieving a grand impression. If it achieves that, it achieves no more. The staircase banister ascending to the stateroom is a remarkable achievement of wrought iron, matching the quality of the ironwork in the church and chapel. It seems to have been a local speciality and these works within the monastery are by a master of the craft.

As to the community, it is undoubtedly too small for the vast complex. I counted some ten monks. As a community they seem curiously detached and bound individually to the order of the day, which has no variety or variation. A day of prayer commences at six in the morning and concludes at eight in the evening. Mass at six-thirty is followed by breakfast, the midday service by lunch and vespers by dinner. The food is simple but adequate. Unusually in my experience the visitor eats the same food and at the same table as the monks. I would couple with this sense of detachment my impression that no one there was happy in the monastic life, nor seeking happiness. The abbot is much in evidence. That morning at breakfast he told me that he worked without cease from six in the morning to ten at night, managing the affairs of the monastery and its large adjoining *Gymnasium*. I asked him how many weeks a year he took in respite. Swift was his answer: "I have not left the abbey for a day in these past twelve years." I have seldom met a man who could convey such a sense of profound self-satisfaction and friendly condescension. No doubt these skills he acquired during the years in which he served as headmaster of the *Gymnasium*.

I have never seen anything like the rain at Stams. The clouds hung low and dropped their windless load. It fell silently and invisibly, so that looking out from within the day seemed dry and tolerable, but cross the threshold and you were as though in a shower.

The enforced stay at Stams at least enabled me to understand better the *Stift* and the community. I was able to repeat the *Stift* tour and to wander during the exposition by the lovely French guide since, as she said, there was no point in my hearing her twice. What really distinguishes Stams from other great Austrian monasteries is that the richest of ornamentation is all achieved with paint, carved wood and marquetry. Marble, stucco and stone are there almost none. From the exterior the huge buildings, with the exceptions of the entrance at the front and the two curious towers, appear, particularly from a distance, more like Tyrolean farms and barns. It seems that this was not choice but necessity: quite simply the Cistertians did not have the riches of the Benedictines and the Augustinians.

If anything my unease at the fragility of the community increased. Father Daniel was tortured with uncontrollable hiccups and my French friend told me that he had been in that state for weeks. When I met young Thomas, my guide, by chance in Silz, he was there to see the doctor and to collect prescriptions. His pallor signified his pursuit of information technology studies at the university in Innsbruck and of God at Stams. Had he been chasing the girls he might have been rosy-cheeked. The only sturdy individual seemed to be the abbot and the two Vietnamese priests. Thomas told me that the Cistercian monastery in Vietnam is overwhelmed with numbers and that they export them in pairs to increase their chances of assimilation.

☞

Day 32 – 22 May 2015 – Stift Stams to Au

THIS DAY BOUGHT little improvement in the weather but I had to break out. The path passes through what remains of the famous Stams forest of oaks, which efforts are being made to regenerate. The walk to Silz is level and through farmland. What characterises Austrian pastures, wherever you are, is that it is never grass but a riot of wild flowers. Starlight daisies, ox-eyed daisies, yellow marguerites, scabious of various hues, and fifty other varieties only show how much we have lost by our monoculture of grass, even in permanent pasture.

On from Silz to Haiming is less appealing, generally following the country road. In Haiming I stopped for coffee before crossing the river and following hard by its northern bank to reach and skirt Roppen. Here the way rises steeply to higher ground and a forest walk to reach Karres, where I imagined coffee and a rest only to find that it was no more than a large hamlet. I had high hopes then of Karrösten, but found that it was no better equipped. The path down from Karrösten is lovely but ends in a tangle of intersecting main roads, all competing for the narrow strip of flat land immediately north of the river. Emerging from the tangle of overpasses and underpasses, I was let down by the waymark just when I needed it most. I failed to cross the river to find a westward path along the south bank and instead followed the path on the north bank with the river immediately on my left, and, on my right, only metres away, the eastbound carriageway of the Autobahn. Beyond these two carriageways lay a playground for industrialists and retailers, horrible to behold. I was almost at Imsterau before a sinister underpass and then a roaring bridge brought me to the south bank, with no option but to follow the main road into Au. So I arrived exhausted at six-thirty after a walk of some 28 kilometres. The Alpen Rose disappointed. Both the accommodation and the cooking were very basic but at least they met my needs.

☞

Day 33 – 23 May 2015 – Au to Landeck
I SET OFF with the intention of completing the stage to Strengen. The reality is that all roads west are confined to the

Inn valley. The valley floor is narrow, and competing for the space are the river, the Autobahn, the A roads, the railway, quarries and blasting, and a heavy concentration of industry and transport. Generally the Jakobsweg rises clear of the valley floor and in the forest or at the forest edge the heavy sounds merge into an indistinguishable roar of nature and man in motion. Were it not for man there would only be the roar of the mighty river, strong but not swollen by days of persistent rain.

At first the way from Imsterau follows within metres the path of the railway, then rises into the forest with many ascents and descents as rocky bluffs are circumambulated. I managed well enough as I passed Mils on the northern bank and Saurs on the southern bank but then a failure to mark a crucial right turn forced me to a wasted hour on a circular deviation to bring me back to where I had started and I had to cast wide to strike the true path.

This was little respite since the true path rose steeply, scrambling through pine forest to reach St Vigil. This was a penance to celebrate the fact that the tiny church of St Vigil had in the Middle Ages been rebuilt through the generosity of a passing pilgrim. The little church has a pilgrim stamp and the modern *Pilger* must deviate to respect this history.

At least the way onwards, although hard going, bought me to the extraordinary Kronburg, a hamlet of unequalled beauty, consisting only of a tiny church, a convent and a wonderful Gasthof which seemed to be run by the Sisters of the convent. The Gasthof was exemplary, the cooking and the service being of a high order of excellence. I took a brochure, intending one day to return. Zams (incidentally the birthplace of the architect Prandtauer) is the closest railway station. The telephone number of the guesthouse is +43 (0)5442 63478. I could not resist a quick meal of soup and coffee before moving on to a forest road of great beauty, albeit taxing, with ups that shortened and slowed my pace followed by downs of quickened and lengthened strides. Overall the net effect is not much different to the speed that might have been achieved on a level path. The last descent led into the substantial town of Stanz. I rested here in an excellent Café Konditorei.

The way ahead skirted the town, crossed the river onto the north bank and carried on to skirt Landeck. Landeck is a substantial railhead and a town of holiday hotels. I toyed with striking on, but I had no hope of reaching Strengen, and all the intervening villages were high above the valley on the north bank without access to the main railway line. Fortunately I resisted the temptation to continue and found an expensive and unfriendly hotel, the Nussbaumhof, which had the great advantage of lying only ten minutes from the railhead. At least it offered a higher standard of accommodation, a hot bath and a good dinner.

But eight hours of walking achieved only a net advance of some 18 kilometres for 25 kilometres walked. Even catching the 08.56 would not get me to Vienna until 14.30 and it is to Landeck that I would return when I resumed the walk the next month.

LANDECK TO FELDKIRCH

BETWEEN LEAVING LANDECK in May and returning in June, I took a step much influenced by the Jakobsweg and destined to change my future thoughts and experiences as I walked on. On 20 June 2015 I was confirmed at the Church of the Immaculate Conception in Devizes in the Catholic faith. Most fundamental changes result from a balance of the gains and the losses that will result. My winter visits to Kremsmünster had convinced me that I could no longer remain an outsider, a spectator at the worship upon which the life of the abbey is founded. Thereafter visits to Kremsmünster were greatly enriched by the sense that I was in communion with the place and all who made their lives there. So too did their acceptance of my need for Kremsmünster develop. The most significant signs of that acceptance came swiftly with my stay for the weekend of 3 to 5 December 2016, when I was moved from a room in the guest wing to a hospes room in the *Clausur* and given a place (and a napkin) for meals in the refectory, excepting breakfast. I had always breakfasted with Schwester Lydia, probably torturing her with my awful German, but these breakfasts had become highlights of my days and I was loath to lose them. On the Jakobsweg the sense of

LANDECK

STRENGEN

ST ANTON

KLÖSTERLE

FELDKIRCH

pilgrimage became more real for me. Wherever I found myself in Austria I felt a greater sense of belonging. I was also able to develop a closer friendship with Pater Franz, such a kind and wise priest, who guided me on questions of faith and heard my confession on all my stays.

☞

Day 34 – 23 June 2015 – Landeck to Strengen

ON TUESDAY 23 June I took the express from Vienna to Landeck. I knew the road through the town and was soon on the Jakobsweg with a steep climb through the woods before the path levelled out at 150 metres or so above the town. It took about an hour to reach Stanz, a pretty village specialising in schnapps distilleries; around the town lie orchards to supply the necessary fruit. My train had arrived at two-thirty and, it now being four o'clock, I stopped for coffee in what seemed to be a communal café attached to the *Gemeinde*. It claimed to be the last café before Strengen.

Thus strengthened I set off on a good *Feldweg*, a two-hour walk to Grins. Grins is also a pleasant village without, of course, a café. There is then perhaps a kilometre and a half on tarmac before a long stretch of forest on what is said to be a *Romerweg*. It is quite a slog to reach what is billed as Strengen but what in fact is Unterweg. The village has a church, a chapel and many prosperous houses but no shop or *Gasthaus*. Whether it is Upper Strengen or a separate village is not clear but what is clear is that the only *Gasthaus* lies in Strengen, on the valley floor probably 250 metres below.

The road to the valley is a series of loops, each leading to a hairpin bend. A girl in the upper village had told me that I had to go down. She was going herself, but instead of saying, "Follow me," she gave elaborate directions. As we progressed I found myself following her until, frustrated by the loops, I started taking my own line to the church spire below. From the steep grass slopes I tumbled and often descended on my bottom like a child. My final shortcut proved disastrous when the grassland gave way to a belt of trees and dense undergrowth. I could see that the trees ran down to the river below and I had gone too far to retreat. The drop was almost sheer and I was on my bottom all the way, clinging from sapling to sapling to prevent a free fall. The undergrowth obstructed me and tore my skin. At one point I lost my spectacles. At the end I was barred by one of the high steel fences that guard the highway from falling rock. At last I found a gap between two panels and emerged exhausted and shaken on the road. Although the church had been lost to sight for most of the descent I found by happy chance that it was near and beside it stood the Post Hotel. Here my luck turned. A friendly lady at reception, a twinkling waitress and an owner chef with an incredible waxed moustache all preceded an excellent dinner and a comfortable bed. The room cost €40 and the number for reservations is +43 (0)5447 20150.

☞

Day 35 – 24 June 2015 – Strengen to St Anton
THE NEXT MORNING I could not face the climb out of the valley floor and discovered by enquiring at the hotel that there

was no public transport. But at once the lady in charge of reception on the morning shift led me to her car, drove swiftly up the hill and set me down on the Jakobsweg, two miles by road above. Her sense of hospitality and her kindness I will not forget.

Yesterday's walk had been through glorious mountain terrain with some high cloud and a tearing west wind: all in all, perfect walking weather. The going had been fair and the waymarking the same. But today the going was stiffer, with many steep ascents and the waymarking worse. But the weather and the scenery remained glorious and the wind less intense. I chose a photograph which typified the approach to St Anton. I had only 20 kilometres to reach St Anton and the early omens looked good. The way lay through glorious forest but my first error was not long in coming. With the track twisting sharply uphill, I started a long climb. As I neared the ridge a van came down towards me, driven by a friendly soul who stopped to investigate my purpose. As I explained, he laughed at my folly, explaining that the Jakobsweg lay well below. He seemed dubious when I asked for a lift to the true path but then agreed and so saved me from disaster. When he put me on the right road I saw that there was a crossing, easily missed, and a waymarker, almost invisible.

That disaster averted, I continued through the forest on the path, now marked *Romerweg*, until reaching Flirsch. A handsome church stands up above the river and beside it what seemed to be a fine *Gasthaus*. In reality the waiter was unfriendly and the interior tasteless. As the church clock struck eleven, I set out but nowhere was the encouraging sign of St Jakob and his scallop shell. I did my best with the Kompass map. Somehow I found my way to Schnann and on to Pettneu. Here all went haywire and I bumbled and stumbled until I abandoned the search for the track and took to the highway. This carried me to Vadiesen where I regained the track. I had lost so much time that it was almost two o'clock, and I stopped for my piece. The track on to Gand was straightforward but uneven, with many climbs and fewer descents. From Gand I walked in hot sun, again with many steep climbs, to reach St Jakob am Arlberg. Here I left the track to drop down to the church. Of course, being dedicated to St Jakob, its porch has a pilgrim stamp. The church itself has fine baroque decoration and a striking pulpit showing the destruction of a bad black angel at the hands of two putti who sit engagingly shooting golden forks of lightning at him.

Without much enthusiasm I climbed back to the track but I was rewarded with a perfect woodland walk that led me to the Nassereinstrasse, pedestrianised all the way to the parish church in St Anton. I chose at random a guesthouse opposite the church which proved in all respects kind, generous and thoughtful. It is Haus Fallesin and the telephone number is +43 (0)5446 2517. The room was €37. I ate well at the Restaurant Maximilian three houses further on.

☞

Day 36 – 25 June 2015 – St Anton to Klösterle
NORMALLY THE PARISH church is the centre and focus of every village. The St Anton parish church looks the part. I captured the view from my bedroom window. However, the

whole, inside and out, is deceptively modern and by no means central. In the morning, setting off towards the other end of the village, I discovered that the true heart of the town, and the old St Anton, lies well west of the church. Here jostle the hotels large and small, old and modern, awaiting the winter sports trade. In high summer they appear purposeless. The tourist office, however, is outstanding; here an expert answered my every question with the ease of a Wimbledon qualifier playing a challenger in a county game. Her every instruction was illustrated on the village plan with which I set off on what I knew would be a punishing climb to St Christoph.

At first the way is easy as it follows this mountain stream. But overall it is 600 metres that must be achieved. It is akin to climbing a well-designed staircase that rises almost 2,000 feet into the sky. It took me three and a half hours. It was a struggle, but I never despaired. The way was bright with wonderful flowers of every description and colour. Prolific was what appeared to me to be a wild azalea flowering only in pink. I was keen to record such a handsome plant growing in wild profusion. Almost as plentiful were the orchids. A final view shows the glory of these upland pastures.

The highest points on the Jakobsweg are the Maiensee and the Arlbergpass. In the hollow between the two lies St Christoph am Arlberg. So, first sight of St Christoph is a bird's-eye view which reveals a depressing scramble to develop, with huge cranes towering over nascent hotels.

Arriving in the village I planned to take a long café break at the Hotel Hospiz St Christoph. The hotel is the development of what was a religious house and there is an adjoining chapel that remains consecrated and open to public view. It seems to be the chapel of some religious confraternity and I was not surprised to see my acquaintance, the Abbot of Stams, prominent on the roll of its current officers.

The Kompass guide surprised me by including the *Hospiz* in its hospitality recommendation, for I knew from my son's skiing holidays that it was a top-price establishment. So perhaps I should not have been surprised when I was turned away with the announcement that the café and the restaurant were closed. At one o'clock and in high summer season: was this in reality pilgrim discrimination? I went on the attack and called for the manager. A pert and unfriendly superior informed me that she was prepared to offer me a room for the night but not a glass of water now. I might have a room and breakfast for €39, she said smugly. This was true hypocrisy since all travellers will start in St Anton and none would look for a bed at midday. I was particularly irate since I had understood the first girl to say that the nearest café was 7 kilometres further on, when in fact it was 70 metres further on! That was the Gasthof Valuga, whose owners were kind and hospitable in providing coffee and water. I was in sore need since the path from St Anton to St Christoph is easily the most punishing stretch anywhere on the Jakobsweg.

In June even a day on the flat is dehydrating. But add a steep climb and the consequent need for water to replace what the body wastes in sweat, and the importance of water is paramount and easily underestimated. Certainly two litres will be needed in the course of a long June day. But water weighs heavy and I would not choose to stow more than a half-litre plastic bottle in my rucksack. I favour sparkling water and my ideal is a half litre of Romerquelle Prickelnd from the cold cabinet of any supermarket. Romerquelle is the brand and *prickelnd* tells you that it is sparkling and not still. There is also *mild* which is somewhere between the other two. It can be had for a little over half a euro. But supermarkets are few and far between. So, once emptied, the useful plastic bottle needs frequent refilling. In mountainous terrain there is ample opportunity as you cross the streams tinkling down the hill. Otherwise the graveyard surrounding any village church provides the source, for the plants and flowers with which each family vault are adorned require much water. Prominent in every churchyard is a standpipe and an array of watering cans. The water quickly runs chill when the tap is opened; thirst is soon slaked and the bottle refilled. Without water it is not just the mouth that is parched but the whole head, so that I find my ears pop and I seem to inhale not just through mouth and nostril but through an ear as well. This is worth preventing since the air roars unpleasantly through the ear.

What a contrast there is between an English and an Austrian churchyard! The English churchyard is generally in the Grey's "Elegy" vein; crumbling antiquity enhanced by general neglect. This is a special quality impossible to reproduce and one that fittingly inclines our thoughts to our own mortality. But the Austrian churchyard delights for the loving care, everywhere evident, with which the graves are tended. In fact they are more vaults than graves. Each village family has its family shrine to which members are added as they fall. Generally a cross in wrought iron, often in itself a work of art, dominates the shrine and a marble slab records the names and dates of each who has passed on. Notable is the absence of history. Almost all the shrines post-date the last war. Even more notable is the absence of any neglected or forgotten shrine. All without exception are tended as lovingly as any garden. So the scene is one of bright colour and of light, since most carry one or more candles gravely burning. The emotions roused by the Austrian churchyard are joy and delight at nature, life, beauty and family piety.

The Arlbergpass is the border between the Tyrol and Vorarlberg. This is relevant to the walker since the generally impeccable maintenance and waymarking of the Jakobsweg in the Tyrol collapses in Vorarlberg. The waymarking varies between adequate and abysmal. Furthermore, the maintenance of the Weg has long since been abandoned.

The first mile ran through a broad valley springing with water and spongy bog moss. I quickly became wet and cross. On hands and knees I climbed out of the valley. The climb ended in a near vertical slope, at the top of which ran the main highway between the two provinces. As lorries and camper vans clambered up the slope or rocketed down it I walked the stone wall built to retain any errant vehicle. Just as the wall ran out I reached a wide junction and saw, to the left and below, a broad track running alongside a river. Although undeclared this was in reality the Jakobsweg and it carried me easily to my destination in Klösterle. It was easy, although unmarked, because it was running continuously downhill at a gentle gradient, matching the fall of the adjoining river. At teatime I ate the piece that I had been too exhausted to eat in St Christoph. Then pressing on resolutely I reached Klösterle at about 6.30 p.m. I took a view somewhere on this stretch but it is the sequence in the camera that tells me so rather than any memory.

Although quite a place and the capital city of Klöstertal, it lacked a *Gasthaus* or even a pension. The *Pilgerherberge* recommended in the Kompass guide had closed down. A kind man recommended the Stube Johanniter. There, he said, I could at least eat. But without a bed a meal was of no appeal. This I explained to the *Hausfrau* in the *Stube* who immediately rang round the village, eventually procuring a room. However, when I rang the bell the elderly owner announced that she had changed her mind. She felt sufficiently guilty to offer to ring round for a replacement. After a long wait she said she could find none. Then, perhaps her conscience pricking, she changed her mind again and showed me to a bedroom and a sitting room. I ate well in the *Stube* and slept well in the bed. I find that I am walking for ten hours and then sleeping for ten, the remainder being taken up with breakfast, evening meal, much showering and shaving, and the daily packing and unpacking. I write postcards, I dictate my diary, but I find little time for reading. Currently I have Stefan Zweig neglected in my rucksack.

☞

Some Afterthoughts on the Day's Climb

ALTHOUGH THE ALPINE scenery from St Anton to Klösterle is magnificent, it is threatened by all modern demands; the transport network and the power system greedily consume the narrow valley floor. There is little room here for peace and nature and *Wanderwege*. The beauty of the scenery attracts intense tourism, and the style of choice for those who can afford to build is suburban kitsch. There is no respect for the old or belief in conservation; the preference is to demolish and start again. Then, where the valley widens, industry has staked its claim. There is a resulting deprivation of services. Small shops have disappeared and even Hofer or Spar supermarkets are rarities. Many a large village has no café, let alone restaurant, and even rarer is a *Gasthaus*. The predominant commercial fashion is for holiday apartments. Thus the passing traveller, the overnighter, is hard pressed to find a bed. So what would have been blissful nature before the advent of tourism and general affluence is now dull uniformity and a want of kindness to the man who travels on his own.

As a footnote to today's climb and descent, I record that if the climber has one weak leg, then he must use the good leg to raise the weight to the tread above, and not follow through with the weak leg but always conquer the next riser with the good leg. By contrast, when descending it is better always to lead with the weak leg, allowing the strong leg to take the stress of the descending weight, so that the strong leg is the engine for the descent.

☞

Day 37 – 26 June 2015 – Klösterle to Feldkirch
THE DAY STARTED well enough. Breakfast being unavailable I left the house at seven o'clock and, directed to the baker/café, had a good breakfast of coffee and fresh rolls. To avoid 2

kilometres of road walking I took the post bus to Innerwald and walked on from there in bright, early-morning sun and glorious scenery to reach the outskirts of Dalaas. I have a photograph which shows the glorious scenery. The second half of that walk had led through the *Wald*, which was jewelled with orchids and other wild flowers on the shaded floor. The post bus service 90 was running on an hourly frequency so the 08.13 took me to Innerwald and the 09.28 carried me into and across Dalaas to the stop at Gasthaus Krone. Here the Jakobsweg parts from the main road and rises leftwards towards Muss. It is a lovely walk that would be lovelier did it not at several points cross the trunk road, the local road and the river. Two photographs show how lovely is the walk. It emerges to meet another bus stop at Muhlpass. Here I had the choice of waiting fifteen minutes for a bus or walking on to the next bus stop in Oberradin, at which a later bus was scheduled to stop in seventy-five minutes. I opted for the walk, which more or less followed the left bank of the river. The way was a tarmac byroad and I hammered along in order to reach the next bus stop by 12.40. I did it comfortably and more so because the timetable had been adjusted, for that hour only, to 12.53. The bus came and carried us easily through the suburbs of the substantial town of Bludenz. The train station and the bus station are one in Bludenz and with a wait of only ten minutes I took either a 73 or 76, both of which follow the local main road to or towards Feldkirch.

My destination was Nüziders. The penultimate stage in the Kompass guide is from Dalaas to Nüziders and I had accomplished it by two o'clock, thanks to the ever-useful post bus service. Before the bus ride I had walked four and a half hours at a fast pace and at each step my left leg pained and I winced. I took a long rest at the village café. On my way out of the village I passed an attractive old-fashioned hotel, Bad Sonnenberghof. Shortly after, I collapsed on a wayside bench, ate my muesli bar from the baker and stopped for an hour. I also changed my dressing, and, feeling easier, walked on to Ludesch. This was a road walk through suburban territory. I could see that it would continue for miles to and through Thüringen. So again I awaited the bus and alighted in a prettier place, Bludesch. A pretty *Gasthaus* seemed certain but there was none and the telephone number in the Kompass guide was not in current use. So I settled on the bus and, with the advice of the driver, alighted in Nenzing. At the picturesque heart of this little village stands the picture-postcard Gasthaus Rössle. On the steps stood the landlord. He offered me a room at €76. This being twice the going rate in the country I jibbed, and accordingly he offered to find me a room in a private house. This was quickly fixed and he assured me that it was 200 metres away. Then things started to go wrong. Rather than letting me walk he insisted I waited for a ride with his wife. She came not in ten minutes but in half an hour and then drove me at least a kilometre to the private house. I demurred and said I would rather pay the difference to avoid all the walking. Back at the hotel the room I had been offered had since been let elsewhere and there was no room at the inn. I stuck to my guns, refused the private room and headed for the bus stop.

After a long wait the Feldkirch bus arrived and the driver assured me that there was a good *Gasthaus* in the larger village of Schlins. He set me down with voluble directions which proved to be pure imagination.

After another long wait a bus came that wandered through Satteins and Frastanz before arriving at Feldkirch. I ended up in the Hotel Post at €89. This was a punishment for parsimony.

☞

Day 38– 9 June 2015 – Feldkirch

AT LEAST I had some time the next morning to explore Feldkirch, as the Vienna express did not leave until noon. The old city is confined within a tight ring and is basically Renaissance, an important city in the age of Maximilian I. Now it is an obvious tourist centre with ubiquitous retailers such as Benetton trading with the usual crowds of affluent tourists. The town was having its annual *Weinfest*. Tellingly, the cathedral was shut for the weekend, save during three advertised masses. There must have been seating for near a thousand in the marketplace and I imagined that by the end of the evening Bacchus would be in full command. I was pleased to exit on the Bregenz–Wien express.

☞

Conclusion

I HAD FOR so long set my heart on Feldkirch as a distant yet attainable goal. I had imagined feelings of exultation and triumph, but, as so often, expectation and anticipation were tricksters. My final day was without any doubt my least successful. My error of judgement at Rössle cost me a perfect rest, €13 and the chance of three hours of morning walking. There was much anxiety and frustration. All that I could set off against that long list of negatives was the chance to explore Feldkirch. So I left in low spirits. The weather matched my mood. It even rained.

With hindsight, the true balance of those final days was strongly positive. I walked in glorious sunshine cooled by a bright west wind. Every meadow brimmed with wild flowers and every farmer was in haste to gather in the mown grass. Alpine scenery is incomparably grand and the flowers that go with it would grace any garden. Although the great walk was ended I could now contemplate either the tributary that drops south from Passau or the alternative, which starts in Graz and, after a long stretch in Slovenia, runs through Carinthia, the Osttirol and the Italian Südtirol before entering the North Tyrol to reach Innsbruck. But before attempting either I must do more investigation, preparation and planning than the zero forethought that preceded my plunge from Purkersdorf to Würmla. In retrospect it was the height of irresponsibility to reach Linz before investing in the Kompass guide.

What did I learn from these 38 days? What practical advice would I offer a friend tempted to walk the Jakobsweg?

First, I would not bother to train for the walk. All that is needed is an appetite for walking and the sense not to try to prove anything at the outset, as I so foolishly did. I divided the walk into a series of episodes or excursions as though Vienna were my home. As the Kompass guide suggests, it could alternatively be done in thirty-five consecutive days. I have no idea how I would have coped physically with that regime. I can only say that on a four- or five-day stage, bodily protests are loudest on day two: you are fresh on the first day and fit by day three.

I never went in for much forward planning. But that would not suit many temperaments. For the orderly or the anxious, booking the night or nights ahead would be more comfortable. For them the Kompass guide would be a frail friend. Most of its tips are *Pilgerherbergen* or bed and breakfast houses. These are evanescent: the householder ages, dies, moves or simply decides not to continue. And years intervene between the authors' selections and the pilgrim's reliance. So it is easy to understand why reliance is usually misplaced. Furthermore, the days are long and solitary. It is surprising, given the support that the European Union, the State, the Church, the provinces and the communities give to the Jakobsweg, that so few walk the Weg. As I think I have recorded, over 38 days I encountered only four others, and two of those only as they were quitting. So at the end of the day I always relished the Gasthof, with locals drinking at the bar and a busy dining room with bustling waitresses. Accordingly I have included the telephone numbers of some of the inns that I used. These numbers have an enduring validity. Often the inn continues in the same family for generations.

Remember that whatever you need for the way must fit in your rucksack. That is made easy if you use Vienna as the base for multiple excursions. The five-day weather forecasts in the Austrian press are reliable: you know what to expect before you set out. Even so, the level for entry into the rucksack must be set very high to exclude luxuries or the products of overanxiety.

Ten kilos should be the top end of your scale, for that weighs heavy and the rucksack straps cut into the shoulders. This can be eased by investment in a top-quality rucksack: capacious, designed for comfort and well padded at the chafing points. The best are the Austrian army rucksacks issued to soldiers and reservists. Another ploy is to stock up with old shirts so that one can be discarded at the end of each hot day. I always pack one good shirt into which to change for dinner every evening. It raises morale, and it reassures the innkeeper that you are not a tramp and will be good for the bill the following morning.

One word of advice on the Weg itself: wherever possible, avoid walking on tarmac. It is horribly hard on the feet. It taught me to sympathise with the many racehorses that only go on something the soft side of good. So if you are on the highway, look for the verge. Even if you are on a farm track look for the softer verge or the grass growth in the centre.

Equally, be sure to go the shortest way. That means taking the inside of any bend. The total number of bends on the 850 kilometres is innumerable and you may save 5 metres each time you remember to take the inside of the bend. Then, if you spy out the way ahead, you will often see the chance to take a line that will eliminate the bend, or even several bends, by taking to the fields. Most are pasture and, even when arable, it is advisable to use the land, provided you risk no harm to the crop. It is always pleasant to walk through an Austrian meadow with its rich variety of meadow flowers and grasses.

Finally, in summer always seek out shade. The difference between the temperature in full sun and in shade can be significant. Remember that Austria is given to extremes: very cold winters and very hot summers with not much between the two. Austrian verse and song express great yearning for spring when spring hardly exists there. Certainly not spring as we experience it. The resolution of this puzzle is that in those joyous songs the month of May is the month of spring.

So the ideal is the verge on the inside of the bend and in the shade. These features often do not coincide. Then choices have to be made. I give lowest weight to the inside of the bend, more to the softer verge. Consideration of shade only comes into the reckoning on blistering hot days. Then I would give it the highest weight. Although experience has ruled out midwinter walking, not so for midsummer. For the days are long and it is possible to walk from six until noon and again from four to seven. But in those days a plastic, half-litre water bottle is essential. Which leads me to a related point: especially in summer it is better to stick to two meals a day, one early and one late. In between, a caffè latte works best for me.

Finally, I would emphasise the advantages of walking alone. The solitary walker is never lonely; there is too much to worry about, too much to marvel at, too much to try to take note of, too much to try and remember. On your own you take decisions and risks for yourself alone. If things then go wrong you have only yourself to blame. Fortunately, there has never been anyone who has wanted to join me so I have never had to face the difficulties that would flow from companionship. Of course, these thoughts have no relevance to a couple who closely share their lives, or to a family excursion.

THE SECOND WALK

Graz to Innsbruck: the Southern Tributary

GRAZ

KALSDORF

WILDON

LEIBNITZ

EHRENHAUSEN

GRAZ TO EHRENHAUSEN

Day 1 – 23 July 2015 – Graz to Kalsdorf

ON THURSDAY 23 July I launched an attempt on the Graz–
Innsbruck Jakobsweg tributary. Geanina-Maria and I had
been busy all morning with shopping and the banks and it
was not until two o'clock that I left on the express from the
Hauptbahnhof. The route is uninteresting until the assent of
the Semmering uplands, when the train slows as dramatically
as the foot traveller would. The scenery is magnificent and
continues uninterrupted until a return to sea level just short
of Graz.

Arriving at 4.35 p.m. I had a dash from the station to
find the tourist office, which hides itself discreetly behind the
town hall. Light rain fell as I almost ran to reach this obscure
destination before it closed. What an anxious time! I entered an
almost empty office, where a sympathetic girl grasped my needs
and selected Kalsdorf as marking the boundary between suburbs
and country. She showed me the hotels and booked my choice
of Gasthof Pendl. She directed me to the tram and gave me the
time of the next train out. Thus directed, I arrived at Gasthof
Pendl at about 6.30, was shown to a small room and chose the

dish and the wine said to be most Styerisch. The meal cost €25 and the bed and breakfast €48, comparatively upmarket. Nearby, drinking and laughing heartily, were a bizarre group of four men and one woman whose passion for food and drink had spread their girths and stretched the limits of their Lycra sports gear. The telephone number for Gasthof Pendl is +43 (0)3135 52308.

☞

Day 2 – 24 July 2015 – Kalsdorf to Wildon

THE NEXT MORNING they were no less hearty in the breakfast room as they consumed prodigious quantities before mounting their racing bikes. I felt I suffered from the same illusion as I settled into my rucksack and walked out of the village to find the Jakobsweg at the bridge over the Mur.

Here I made my first mistake of the day, choosing the path on top of the embankment rather than the minor path 10 metres or more below. Nor could I switch, since a swift and full stream ran through the ditch between the two paths. The map told me that I must leave the river but the stream prevented me. Ultimately, however, waterworks, unmarked on the map, gave me the exit from the embankment and, through sandpits, to the main road, where I chanced on a cheerful postman who pointed me to Enzelsdorf and its church dedicated to St Jakob. This was music, since at Enzelsdorf I would be back on the orthodox route. Wherever there is a church dedicated to St Jakob there the pilgrim way is sure to pass.

Just short of the church was an inviting café, particularly so in the extreme heat of that cloudless day. After a litre of mineral water and two cups of coffee I stamped my guidebook in the prettiest of village churches and set out again on the true path. Here I discovered, and had to come to terms with, the fact that there are no waymarks. My only reliance became first the map and then the German text in the Kompass guide for this southern tributary.

Fortunately, once found at the top of the steep bank above the church, the way ahead is easy to follow. Pleasantly undulating, it runs through forest until emerging onto a minor road that skirts Mellach. When it meets the crossroads in Dillach there is the attractive Gasthaus zur Stubn. There I stopped for water and coffee.

The Weg lies straight on, the road running through open country until reaching what the guidebook describes as "an ancient gothic chapel and wonderful rest place". Certainly the rest place is wonderful but I doubt the chapel is more than 150 years old. That is of course a quibble and to reflect the heat of the day I introduced a long lunch break with pickings from the breakfast buffet, wine left over from Vienna and a small cigar, during the smoking of which I repeatedly dozed off. Resuming in excellent good spirits, I proceeded to disaster at Weissenegg. At the confusing crossroads a Jakobsweg waymark is absent where most needed. I saw a road sign for Aue and, foolishly thinking that was what I wanted, I set off for a kilometre at least only to reach a dead end. In the heat of a hot day this is particularly disheartening. Having returned to the crossroads I then consulted and construed the German text, which resulted in another wild goose chase back towards Dillach and then a forest track which brought me to a road and a crucifix. Had I looked at the map as well as the text I would have seen how fallacious my construction of the text was. As a result, of the three choices that the crossroads offered I had rejected the only true one.

From the crucifix I found my way into a village without a name sign and seemingly deserted. I heard voices from a house, and, approaching the open door, found that the voices were only from the television and no human being responded to my knocking. I was approaching desperation when I spied a lady working in her garden. Hurrying to her, I discovered that I was in Kollisch and that I could cut my losses by simply walking to Wildon by road, as she suggested. She gave me a large glass of water and I set off on an easy descent, compensation for the steep climb up to Kollisch, to reach what I thought were the outskirts of Wildon. I would have marched on resolutely in the wrong direction had I not entered a supermarket in search of water. Also at the checkout was an ancient hippy who was curious to discover who I was. When I told him that I was looking for a pilgrim shelter in Wildon he sportingly proposed to drive me to a *Gasthaus* which he could recommend. The *Gasthaus* recommended by Kompass he told me had been closed and on the market for two years. He described Wildon as a dead dump: all the shops were closing, it was being strangled by Leibnitz. Only when we set off did I realise that I had been on the point of walking not into but out of Wildon.

Whatever Wildon's commercial vitality it has a particularly attractive long street of distinguished buildings, particularly the schloss and the parish church. I photographed first the schloss and then the promenade from the schloss to the church. In both photographs the elegant column to the Virgin enhances the scene. The interior of the church is distinguished. My view of the organ gallery does not do it justice. The *Gasthaus* was at the far end and tight against the main road. Nor were its standards of accommodation and cooking any compensation. Best is its sign: Zum Goldenen Löwen. Nevertheless I record its telephone number: +43 (0)3182 2333.

☞

Day 3 – 25 July 2015 – Wildon to Leibnitz

I WAS PARTICULARLY anxious to leave Wildon on the true path. I gave the Kompass guide to the proprietress and asked her to read it and direct me. Either out of carelessness or indifference, she failed to direct me rightly. The consequence was that I took one wrong turn after another and lost the first hour of the day in locating the true exit, which was simply at the other end of the High Street. It is marked *Alte Reichsweg* and leads steeply uphill to reach a forest track through an upland of wild and wooded country. The way ahead is tolerably easy, although there are a number of puzzle points that offer choice without guidance. With reasonable judgement and some luck I was able to reach the church of St Margarethen, which is ancient and calmly commands a wide view over the Mur valley

From the church the walk lies through the village and on a minor road to reach Stangersdorf with its huddle of houses to the north of the Autobahn and the main village to the south. The Jakobsweg crosses first the Autobahn and then the A road. At that second crossing lies the excellent Gashthaus

Zieglerwirt. Here again I stopped for water and coffee, envying a number of families enjoying what looked to be good cooking in the garden.

The guidebook commends the crucifix in the midst of Stangersdorf and suggests it is another good rest place. I found it to be just as described and took another long lunch break at its foot. I felt an irresistible urge to record so charming a scene. The impulse to fumble for the camera is perhaps too easily aroused by what in the moment seems an unusual or exceptional sight. But better too many than too few and this one certainly merits the plate section.

The afternoon journey was dominated by the River Lassnitz. To avoid an oxbow the Weg crosses it shortly after Stangersdorf and crosses it again at Langaberg. Thereafter the Weg hugs the east bank of the river all the way to Tillmitsch. A river walk is always flat, smooth and pleasing. However, on this afternoon something unusual threatened. On the two previous nights there had been massive thunderstorms but then the day had broken as fine and as hot as its predecessor. But now the storm gathered in the mid-afternoon. It roared and flashed about the high ground on the other bank of the river. I knew that had I been there I would have been drenched. Everything told me that it was approaching. There was the rush of contrary wind and the showers of leaves like snow. I turned up the pace to maximum and hoped to heaven for shelter. On the outskirts of Tillmitsch I found it, a sort of bio Wendy house on the edge of both the river and a wide stretch of agricultural land. I got under cover as the rain began. Fortunately I was never in the eye but only on the edge of the storm. After half an hour I was able to walk on and thread my way through Tillmitsch, looking for the bridge that must take me to the other side of the river. Having taken one false turn, which I could have avoided had I looked more closely at the map, I was shown the true bridge by a young man who stopped his car. He was dressed in *Trachten* and no doubt saw me as a potential *Trachten* man because he was particularly kind and solicitous.

Now on the western bank of the Lassnitz I made progress on a pleasant walk which takes some finding but ultimately leads almost into the centre of Leibnitz.

Leibnitz is an unattractive city of considerable dimensions but I was lucky to find the Zur Alten Post at Sparkassenplatz 7, just off the marketplace. This was an upmarket establishment with excellent accommodation, air conditioning and good food. Given its excellence, dinner, bed and breakfast for €106 was a snip. With all that commendation the telephone number is essential: +43 (0)3452 823730.

☞

Day 4 – 26 July 2015 – Leibnitz to Ehrenhausen
THE EXIT FROM Leibnitz is especially pleasant. A short walk on the main street from the marketplace leads to a right turn onto a quieter street which soon gives way to a field walk. The way then lay through thick maize crops and again follows the river valley, although now the Lassnitz seems to have become the Sulm. In the vicinity of Wagna I again took a false trail and landed on the outskirts of a village. This was a Sunday morning at ten or maybe earlier and there was not a human

being in sight. However, the furious barking of a dog at a garden gate brought forth a disgruntled male, overweight and overwhiskered, who, with great persistence, refused to understand my request for guidance to the bridge. Only when I named the pub, the Sulmwirt, did he instantly understand and explain that I was walking in the opposite direction. I soon found the bridge and, on the far side, the Sulmwirt, which looked charming but was staffed by women with off-putting tattoos and lurid hair dye. Nevertheless, I stopped for coffee and then struck on and uphill along a tarmac road, more or less traffic-free, to reach the village of Retznei. If once a pretty hamlet, it is now a grim community overwhelmed by a vast cement works, and all facilities seem to have been designed to satisfy a large and basic workforce. I attempted to hurry on but twice misread the guidebook. Eventually I conceded that I had to climb a steep hill into a housing estate before I gained the country walk that would carry me to my destination. Thereafter I was more or less foot perfect until reaching the outskirts of Ehrenhausen, from where a sharp descent brought me to the main street and the small square facing the parish church.

Since my previous visit with Felicitas in 2009 Ehrenhausen seemed to have become more prosperous and better appreciated, with many well-to-do visitors for the church and the mausoleum. The church is a jewel both outside and within. From the church square there is a short steep climb to reach the Fischer von Erlach Mausoleum, which is a masterpiece of baroque bravura, sadly neglected and in urgent need of sympathetic conservation. The days when the interior could be visited by borrowing the key from the parish priest have long since gone and the door is forever locked. Undulations make it hard to photograph. I took the rear and north facades. I could only manage a detail of the riot of decoration on the principal facade.

Having bought a bottle of local white wine in the *Stube*, I caught the 13.50, which carried me back along my line of route to reach Graz. There I joined the express for Prague, which had me in Vienna two and a half hours later. Since Geanina-Maria had not returned from Croatia I had an evening to myself before she came the following morning.

From Ehrenhausen to the Slovenian border is a walk of about two hours, largely uphill. That I know from a detailed study of the text of the Kompass guide. But I had already decided that my definition was an Austrian pilgrimage. I would not go beyond into Switzerland nor would I deviate into Slovenia. This principle was fortified by previous excursions with Felicitas across the border from Styria into Slovenia. The prosperity and jollity of the locals fades at the border to careworn and straitened folk. The cuisine takes a similar dive. So principle or prejudice led me to the decision to cut out the Slovenian section and resume where the Jakobsweg re-enters Austria at Lavamünd in Kärnten. It made little sense to return to Ehrenhausen to walk to the border and back. This length of the Jakobsweg joins the list of town and city sections that I have cut by riding the post buses. I also had little curiosity since I had walked up the steep hills to the border with Felicitas only a few miles east of Ehrenhausen. No doubt there was sufficient test in the 600 odd kilometres of Austrian Jakobsweg that lie ahead.

Here and elsewhere I asserted two rules: the first that I aspired to cover all the four Jakobsweg walks on Austrian soil and the second that I would bypass cross-border deviations into Slovenia and Germany. I seem to be more a rule breaker than a rule keeper.

First, I have not attempted to fill the gap between Bratislava and Purkersdorf. My defence is only partially plausible. There are four Kompass stages to reach Purkersdorf, the first two, together about 40 kilometres, follow the Danube upstream and the next two, about 48 kilometres, cross Vienna from outer suburbs in the east to outer suburbs in the west. Only a masochist would cross the bounds of a city of 1.8 million inhabitants on foot. But there is no excuse for my failure to walk the first two stages.

Second, how do I explain some five days walking a cross-border deviation into Italy? Well, for me justification is hardly needed, for this is the Sud Tyrol and the Tyrol would still be one but for the reprisals that followed the defeat of Austria-Hungary in the first war.

VIENNA TO KLAGENFURT

Day 5 – 25 April 2016 – Vienna to Lavamünd

ON THIS MONDAY I was undecided. Should I wait to see Geanina-Maria again at the end of the day? What was my destination? How would I get there? The second question was resolved by a close study of the available maps, which suggested that Lavamünd was the point at which the Jakobsweg returned to Austrian soil after a journey of some 100 kilometres through Slovenian territory. The third question was answered by a trip to the ÖBB office at Wien Mitte. The only route after midday was a train to Graz, an intercity bus to Wolfsberg and a regional bus on to Lavamünd. The first question was settled by a telephone call, which confirmed my surmise that Geanina-Maria had another plan.

Accordingly, I packed my rucksack, left my cases at Hotel Opernring and hurried to the Hauptbahnhof and the 13.05 for Graz. Having reached Graz I found that the bus station was in the Bahnhof concourse. There a grumpy woman driver jabbed a finger at the stop at which I later boarded the intercity bus. After crawling out of Graz we sped along the motorway to the very edge of Wolfsberg, but we were five minutes

VIENNA

LAVAMÜND

EDLING

UNTERBURG

KLAGENFURT

VIENNA

behind schedule and I feared that I had missed the local connection. Two locals who had also arrived at Wolfsberg saw my consternation in searching for the post bus stop and took charge. They found it among many bus stops in the station square and waited with me until, almost miraculously and as if at their bidding, the Lavamünd bus appeared. Perhaps it was even further behind schedule. I boarded with fond farewells to kind strangers and, after a good ride through pastures lit by evening sun, we arrived in Lavamünd's main street. I asked the driver if there was a Gasthof in the town. Laughingly he offered five, all within sight. So I asked him which was the best. On his advice I stayed at the Torwirt. Without his advice I would undoubtedly have chosen the Krone.

The Torwirt had aspirations, expressed in a seasonal menu of asparagus dishes. So I had roast river fish with the white asparagus that is preferred in Austria. Everything was overseen by a friendly, attractive woman who joked with all the customers. The noteworthy telephone number is +43 (0)4356 2228.

☞

Day 6 – 26 April 2016 – Lavamünd to Edling

THE NEXT MORNING I had breakfast at six-thirty. I drew money from the bank cashpoint and was frustrated to find the church locked. I was to discover that that is the norm in Carinthia. So it was nearly eight when I put on my rucksack and left the village by the bridge over the Drau. The Kompass guide led me to the point at which the Jakobsweg threw the road aside and took to the woods. Before leaving the highway I took a picture, which captures the very Austrian colour scheme for farmhouses and other residences in the country. Once off the road I noticed that the clover in the pasture had a curious silvery sheen. I was surprised to discover that each leaf had a glaze of ice particles that easily fell off when shaken. Through the day I saw repeated evidence of this heavy ground frost on the early growth of fleshy plants, all limp and blackened. Particularly dramatic was the death of all the new year's growth on an old walnut tree. It hung limp and blackened but still with the characteristic scent which clung to the touching hand.

My first target was the village of Neuhaus. The way was all through the woods and, to my delight, I found it expertly marked. The art of the waymarker is not to be overly helpful. All necessary marks must be in place but none that are unnecessary. Thus the walker knows that he must follow the path and expect no sign unless there is no obvious choice at a given fork. Even so, the walker is always at risk of missing a sign or of a missing sign, lost perhaps to a local thief who had a use for the pole. On this early morning walk I was caught by some strange farm buildings adjoining a small manor house. I assume they were built to dry a crop, perhaps tobacco, but there was no one about to ask. I have included my photograph in the plate section partly in the hope that a reader may know their purpose. I also felt compelled to capture the Drau, which was to be my companion for so much of my walking.

Thus, short of an invisible Neuhaus, I asked the way of an old man at his cottage door who cheerfully confirmed that I was on course and had only to keep going. This I did, ignoring a grassy diversion which rose uphill to the right. Without a waymark it was not to be contemplated. I trudged on the main path for almost 2 kilometres, becoming increasingly anxious at the absence of any waymarks. My path shrank and eventually died at a house under construction. The three workmen were surly Slovenians and showed no interest in my question, nor any desire to help. I retraced my steps until I again found the old man at his gate. With great good humour and voluble conversation that I did not understand, he led me on and pointed me up the grassy track. After a few minutes' climb I emerged in the centre of Neuhaus, on its hilltop.

Neuhaus is dignified by a schloss, a distinguished medieval church and a small supermarket. Again in the village there was no waymark and an old lady could only guide me having read what Kompass had to say. However, she advised me first to collect the church key from the supermarket. This I did to my profit, for the church is dedicated to St Jakob and is a distinguished survival from the Middle Ages with some fine stained glass. With a bottle of water from the shop, I set off on a long slog on the cycle path beside the main road, only relieved by a short stretch of forest walk between Unterdorf and Oberdorf.

After Oberdorf I failed to find the detour to the church of St Georg and held on to leave the main road for the *Hängebrücke*, which proved to be a pedestrian suspension bridge of great length and expert construction. It spanned a ravine, rather than a river, and led to the church of St Luzia. Although Kompass recommended it, I was anxious to press on with what was a field walk to the village of Aich.

Aich is a long straggling village and negotiating an exit was not made easier by the absence of waymarks. In the end the solution lay in the Kompass map, which showed the need to cross a railway line on the edge of the village. Since there was only one way to cross the railway lawfully I knew that I had found my way and settled on the far side of the track to eat my piece.

I resumed a fine field walk through Dobrowa ultimately to reach Rinkenberg. In this border area all signs are given equally in German and in Slovenian. Thus Lavamünd is alternatively Labot. Less obviously, Edling, my destination, is also Kazaze.

Rinkenberg (otherwise Vogrce) boasts a fine medieval church which I was able to see thanks to the fact that a lady of the parish was busy dusting the altar. She gave me a leaflet as I left and set me on the right path to cross the hill that divides Rinkenberg from Rinkolach. The hill is wooded and the gradients, both up and down, gentle. At the top is a shrine and picnic furniture that would have afforded panoramic views had the trees not grown up all round to smother them.

I did not dwell in Rinkolach but pushed on, being anxious to reach Edling and to secure lodging. All day there had been a battle between sun and cloud, sometimes one element prevailing and then the other. But it was always cold and that in part was due to a strong west wind.

Edling is a big, straggling village. Beyond the church at the centre, which was locked, stands the Edlingerhof. This appears to have a monopoly, and to take advantage of the absence of competition. The bar was full of noisy drinkers. Mine was the only occupied bedroom with shower and lavatory down the passage. As to eating, the choice was between something and nothing. Something was chicken fried in batter at six o'clock. It proved to be better than it sounded. The establishment was run by father, mother and daughter. Father was decrepit and surly, mother was faded, and daughter friendly and lively with all the customers. The telephone number for this Hobson's choice is +43 (0)4232 6116.

☞

Day 7 – 27 April 2016 – Edling to Unterburg

AT BREAKFAST THE next morning I had the *Kleine Zeitung*, which confirmed the five-day forecast for a wet Wednesday. It had been a fine dawn but I was hardly surprised to find steady rain from a leaden sky as I dressed to leave. At that point, mother, who had made my breakfast, offered me a lift to Kühnsdorf with her *Mann*. Rather priggishly I declined, saying that, being on the pilgrim way, I must walk on whatever the weather. However, I took precautions. I put on my old jeans and my raincoat with its protective hood. I stowed my cap in the rucksack. At first I walked on with confidence, hitting the track where it left the road by the fire station and walking on through wood and field past Pribelsdorf. I had left at eight o'clock and by nine I was regretting my principled but foolish refusal. The rain cascaded down my coat to drain on to my thighs. Everything below was sodden. My shoes sloshed through puddles and newborn streams. It was about 5°C but colder in the wind. I couldn't stop shivering. The path plunged into the huge forest between Pribelsdorf and Kühnsdorf. The track was rutted by heavy forestry machines. With the heavy rain my approach was muffled and for the first time in so many days of walking I flushed two roe deer across a clearing. The waymarks maintained my spirit until at a crucial junction the direction of the arrow was ambiguous. I took the stronger branch, which after 2 kilometres brought me to a steep ravine running beside a thundering main road. At the road there was no sign and no path on the far side. It had to be wrong. I walked back until reaching the ambiguous sign, there choosing the alternative I had first rejected. This eventually led to a large open space of concrete and tarmac bordering the same highway. Again there was no sign and no path on the other side. I had no choice but to take the cycle path beside the road. At least the Kompass map left no doubt that I must turn not left but right. Hardly had I done a kilometre when with joy I saw the blue and yellow waymark turning me off the main road into a side road that soon brought me to the first house in Kühnsdorf.

At the T-junction with the main street I faced a cheerful old building with the banner "Karlswirt". I was soaked, frozen and in sore need of a *Gasthof* where I could prematurely end this ill-judged day. But first I had the opportunity to pause in the Karslwirt. It proved to be a most cheerful establishment, thronged with people drinking either coffee or beer and of varying degrees of respectability. All were enthralled by the attractive barmaid who flirted with all the men and was pleasant to the few women. She was kind too and I warmed my hands on the hot coffee cup as the liquid warmed my guts. There was nothing more she could do for me. There is no *Gasthof* in Kühnsdorf, she said, and she was not sure if Stein offered more.

As I was considering my options I saw that outside the rain had suddenly turned to heavy snow. The flakes were damp as well as heavy but still it was cold enough for them to settle and swiftly blanket all. After consulting others the barmaid told me that there was a bus to Stein and that it left from the Bahnhof concourse.

As a token I put on my coat, now as wet inside as out, and followed her directions to the station. The timetable at the bus stop negated the idea of a service to Stein. I asked a man at the station, who took me to the stationmaster's office. I explained my predicament and he offered a choice between his next departure for Stein and the area around Klopeiner See, where I was sure to find a *Gasthof*. The See is a popular tourist area and the lakeside is thronged with hotels. But it would mean a walk of some 3 kilometres in the snow, intermittently wind-driven and then falling straight. The choice was finely balanced since no one confirmed that Stein had a *Gasthof*. The waiting room was warm and there would be a train in half an hour. That settled it. When the train arrived I and several others joined the passengers already on board. The electronic noticeboard in the carriage announced imminent departure and timely arrival at Stein on this route to Klagenfurt. Gradually, the electronic board announced delayed departure and delayed projected arrival. It was not a good sign when the driver left the train for a discussion with the stationmaster. On his return we were all put out. Trees overladen with snow had collapsed onto the line and there would be no service.

There was then quite a crowd in the waiting room and a noisy Austrian woman who had emigrated to Australia took charge of everybody's business, including mine, of course, since we could converse in English. The stationmaster had arranged just two buses, one to go east and the other west towards Klagenfurt. The eastbound bus arrived and departed but the bus to go west did not materialise. Then the stationmaster made a general offer of taxis at his expense.

A local lady was firm: the only hotel at Klopeiner See that was open was the Römerhof at Unterburg. A maxi taxi arrived to take a large group who wanted Klagenfurt. After some debate the group agreed that the driver should detour to the Römerhof for my salvation. Thus at about three o'clock I was deposited at the Römerhof. The blackboard outside announced that it was open but in reality it was entirely deserted save for the proprietor's son who was about to lock up and go home. He showed me to a room and suggested that I use the radiators in the bedroom and the bathroom to dry my sodden clothes. He wanted only €33 for bed and breakfast, which he said would be served by his mother. He gave me coffee, a cake from a good selection on display and a huge glass of schnapps before locking and leaving. He said that there would be no charge – that was his hospitality to me.

After he had locked up I saw him clear the blanket of snow from his car and drive off. He had told me where I could find the local pizzeria.

I turned to reparations after a long hot shower. To my dismay I found that the rain had stormed through the rucksack to soak the contents, including my change of clothes and my books. Fortunately, the radiators were hot and over the course of eighteen hours I systematically dried everything. With a new roll of lavatory paper, I interleaved all pages in the Kompass guide and the photograph pages in *The Tears of the Rajas*. The snow was falling unabated and lay more than 15 centimetres deep on any hard surface. What increased the wonder of the storm was that it was falling when the daffodils and tulips were done and the lilac and horse chestnuts in full bloom. The fresh leaf on the deciduous trees captured such a weight of snow that branches snapped off the mature trees and the saplings were bent double. The snow, which had started at eleven in the morning, continued unabated for more than seven hours. I tried, not very successfully, to record this phenomenon with the view from my bedroom window, which is included in the plate section. I decided against the pizzeria and went, exhausted, to sleep. The Römerhof I will always remember with gratitude, and I am sad to report that it has now closed.

☞

Day 8 – 28 April 2016 – Unterburg to Klagenfurt

THE NEXT MORNING the only person in the hotel was the proprietress, who managed a passable breakfast, although the bread was several days old. She was a former beauty with much chat but a cold heart. She could not wait to get rid of me. Fresh snow was falling on yesterday's blanket and I knew that it would be folly to resume the pilgrim path. Under foot, every step would be sloshing wet. Now was a time for discretion. She enthusiastically ordered me a taxi and I was soon back at Kühnsdorf station. My friend the stationmaster cheerfully sold me a ticket and after another snug half an hour in his spacious waiting room I was aboard the Klagenfurt train. Along the track there was ample evidence of the work of the chainsaw that had cleared the line. At the main station in Klagenfurt I took the timetable for Vienna the next morning and set out for the town centre. Since it was still snowing I dived into a bus shelter and rode the considerable distance to reach the tourist information office in the Neuer Platz. There I was well served with advice and leaflets, which only revealed how little Klagenfurt has to offer, considering its not inconsiderable past importance. If it has a leaning, it is towards modern and contemporary art. It has a museum to Robert Musil but a museum can do little to enliven a dead novelist so I simply followed the excellent and informative map of the old town. I started with a long stay in the leading Café Konditorei in the Alter Platz. There I planned the city walk which followed. The snow and slush did the old town no favour. But the clearance of snow in the square created a snow mountain of which the children took full advantage to create this delightful tableau. On a bright sunny day the many rococo facades in the Alter Platz and in the surrounding streets would give up their charm, but for me the only interior of any value was the *Wappensaal* in the *Landhaus*. It was in the charge of a bad-tempered and arrogant custodian but the entry charge is only €1. Neither the parish church nor the cathedral is of any great appeal and the church of the Heiligengeist was locked. In the cathedral there was no one but me and two men tuning the organ. Having no other shelter I ate my sandwiches just inside the west door.

There is an attractive *Naschmarkt* in the Benediktinerplatz which had more or less closed for the day as I headed to the outskirts to find the Gasthof Mack, recommended by the tourist office. They had reserved a room for me, so my arrival was expected, and I was shown to a clean and well-equipped room which reflected the price of €55. I thought that I had agreed dinner at seven and was dismayed to be told that there was no kitchen when I came down. The proprietor suggested a Chinese restaurant down the road or a cold plate of ham and cheese. I took his cold plate which was ample and well presented, a good choice, particularly at €14.30 including wine. The next morning I had an excellent breakfast and caught the 07.39 for Vienna. The telephone number for Mack is +43 (0)463 51119820.

☞

Day 9 – 29 April 2016 – Klagenfurt to Vienna

THE HEADLINES IN this morning's *Österreich* were "*Schnee-Chaos ohne Ende*" and "*Schnee-Rekord für Ende April*". It was reassuring to know that it was not just my private world that had been devastated.

The rail journey from Klagenfurt was new to me until perhaps Bruck an der Mur. But before Bruck the train stops at St Veit an der Glan. An extraordinary sight comes into view immediately to the east of St Veit, from the right-hand windows of the train. It is a fortress surmounting a sharp hill. I was so struck that I took many views from the train. I have selected one that perhaps best captures the drama; see the plate section. Later research in the *Blue Guide to Austria* revealed that it is Hochosterwitz. The castle passed to the Khevenhüller family in the 16th century and is still in their possession. They have made a museum in the castle. One day I must visit this mirage-like wonder. It shines amidst what were beautiful landscapes, particularly as we passed from deep snow to sun-filled spring. Both the Graz and Klagenfurt lines make their slow way through the Semmering mountains, free of snow save on the tops. In the glittering sun, the trees newly in leaf, with the Simmental cattle gently grazing the rich pastures, this was indeed a different world. After Semmering the train picks up speed on the flat run to Wien Hauptbahnhof.

This had been a disastrous return, with only one half of the three planned stages achieved. It proved a salutary lesson on the need to take account of the power of nature and weather, which can unseat the arrogant cavalier even at the threshold of May. What little I have seen of Carinthia only encourages me to return.

GRAFENSTEIN TO MARIA GAIL

Day 10 – 21 June 2016 – Grafenstein to Annabrücke

ON THIS TUESDAY morning I prepared my day. I found a train from Vienna Hauptbahnhof that left at 14.30 and arrived at Stein at 18.48. Gallizien is the end of the stage that at my first attempt had ended in the Kühnsdorf blizzard. My plan was to skip the walk from Kühnsdorf to Stein to give me some chance of reaching Gallizien from such a late start. The lost section would have included a walk along the shore of Klopeiner See. I had touched on the lake area when I found refuge at the Römerhof.

As is too often the case, the settlement at the chosen end of the stage has no *Gasthaus*. I had seen that the only option was some 3 kilometres beyond at Wildenstein. I rang from Vienna only to be told that Tuesday was their day off. They suggested Gasthof Annabrücke, and thank heaven I booked there.

Arriving at Klagenfurt and researching while waiting for the local train, I saw that Annabrücke crossed the Drau northeast of Gallizien and the *Gasthof* was on the west bank. So the map suggested it would be foolish to go so far as Stein; better to alight at the previous station, Grafenstein. So there I alighted

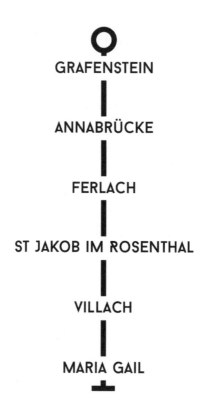

GRAFENSTEIN

ANNABRÜCKE

FERLACH

ST JAKOB IM ROSENTHAL

VILLACH

MARIA GAIL

at quarter to seven with a fair walk from the railway station to the centre of the village. There is a nobility about that centre radiated by the handsome church and the very substantial private house adjoining. In France it would be termed a *château*. A plain pedimented facade united grandeur and simplicity. The adjoining farm buildings were no less grand. There is no sense of isolation, since the surrounding village centre is of the same period and bears the same dignified stamp.

The march on to Annabrücke was not the Jakobsweg route and was on hot, hard tarmac with much traffic in both directions. In all it was some 10 kilometres through a landscape heated by a hot summer sun beginning to sink towards the horizon. As I turned the last corner the *Gasthof* ahead was a welcome sight. It was already 8.30 and I was thankful to have a reservation.

The *Gasthof* on the banks of the Drau is a charming sight nestling beneath the road and the bridge. The landlord and his wife were friendly and looked after me well. Of course I was the only guest, and she cooked me an excellent omelette and an equally good breakfast the next morning.

Isaac Walton would have relished the house and the family. It is a temple to the art of fishing. Every wall of the main room is covered either with stuffed fish or photographs of fish just landed. They are all taken from the Drau and are enormous. Prize specimens are near 40 kilos in weight. Some were catfish, including some enormous creatures which the landlady described as *Wels*. The landlord featured in many of the photographs from early manhood on. Without this stop I would never have imagined that the even-flowing Drau held such monsters lurking in its depths. My bed and breakfast came to €34 and the telephone number is +43 (0)4221 2014.

☞

Day 11 – 22 June 2016 – Annabrücke to Ferlach

THE LANDLADY OBLIGINGLY made breakfast at six and I was on the road before seven. I saw a fox cross the road ahead at speed. It seemed bigger and darker than an English fox, but I cannot see what else it could have been with its flowing tail. The church in Gallizien was locked and I set out on an easy walk through first the village outskirts and then farmland to reach the edge of the forest. The landscape is sublime and I was moved to photograph the scene first looking east and then west. Unusually, I startled first two and then a single roe deer on the fields beside the path. This first stage follows the Drau but within the forest the path rises high above the valley until sweeping down to the riverbank. At the Kraftwerk Annabrücke (not the bridge) the path emerges briefly from the wood. Opposite the Kraftwerk building is an ancient spring piped out of the hill and into a basin. There was a man filling his water bottles and thank heaven I saw his example. I stopped and drank deeply.

These *Kraftwerke* have been constructed all along the Drau, presumably for the generation of electricity. The result is to create a string of lakes as the water is held back and controlled by the *Kraftwerke*. Where the retention is significant the water will be classed a lake, for instance at the day's end the river becomes the Ferlacher Stausee.

Soon after the refreshing spring the path through the forest begins a steep, even relentless, climb to reach Trieblach. This is a pretty upland settlement where I photographed an old farmhouse and some curious electric-green beetles feeding on a plant with white flowers.

This walk from Gallizien to Trieblach is glorious. The wooded way is soft and silent. The wild flowers that abound were so various and strange to me as to be a constant wonder and delight. I recognised the orchids and even a wild lily but the rest were strangers.

From Trieblach the view unfolds of a plateau of farmland gently dipping towards the Drau. On the other side of the plateau stands St Margareten im Rosental. To reach it from Trieblach there is a circular walk and when the circle is half done you are in St Margareten. This is a substantial and prosperous settlement: a large church, a post office, a small Spar supermarket and even a branch of a bank. I bought much-needed water in the shop and rested a while in the porch of the church. I watched, with admiration, a handsome woman as she tended the family grave with minute attention. Although I felt that it was a daily homage, she was lavish with her time. The pride of the village is well expressed in its record totem, the maypole.

In St Margareten I grew careless. I did not bother to look for the shell mark because I thought that there was only one way out of the village. But there were two and I needed not the main road but the side road that descended to the Drau. I walked the main road as far as Dobrowa before I realised my mistake. I contemplated waiting fifteen minutes for the post bus to take me back to where I had erred but in the end decided to take a side road from Dobrowa through Dullach. Before going far I settled in the corner of a hayfield to eat my piece. On a hot summer's day there can be no greater delight than to lie in a shady corner of a hayfield with the scent of a well-dried crop.

As I walked on I met again the welcome sign of the shell, yellow on a deep blue ground. This led me to the bank of the Drau where for the rest of the day the Jakobsweg simply borrows the major bicycle route along the river to Villach.

So the day divided into two halves, the first a great delight and the second an endurance test. Of course the bicycle path has commanding views of the Drau and is fringed on each side by young trees. The surface is compacted gravel and with the sun high in the sky there is no shade. Because of the European clock the full heat of the day falls between two and four in the afternoon. The second day is always the hardest and soon my thighs ached and the shoulder straps of the rucksack cut into my skin. In order to progress I walked forty-five minutes and then rested fifteen. Of course there is consolation in having the river as a companion: I took a shot of passing scullers (they were travelling much faster than I) and a view westward (included in the plate section) of the Drau inflated into a *See*.

At Glainach there is a brief detour to pass the church but then the route traverses a huge and extremely unattractive adventure camp for children. Ferlach is not far ahead and the way signals that. Again I missed a turning which should have brought me into the town centre on the east bank of the Griesbach. I realised my mistake at the *Kraftwerk* and turned sharp left to walk through Ressnig to reach the town centre. It was now almost six o'clock and I hurried to find the tourist information in what is generously described as the schloss (in reality it looked more like a small barracks). The door was being locked for the night but the kind manager reopened and set to to telephone round to find me a room. This did not prove easy but eventually he secured a room at the Gasthaus Meindl on the outskirts of the town. I could have done without the walk to reach it but once there I was kindly received by a couple. I had a room with a balcony and was able to eat both dinner and breakfast out of doors. However, as on the previous night, I was unable to pay by card, which ran my petty cash low. In the bar during my dinner on the terrace the television relayed Austria's despatch from the European Cup, which was not well received by the other customers. Bed and breakfast were €37 and their telephone number is +43 (0)4227 2459.

I had imagined Ferlach to be the perfect Austrian town with a handsome main square lined with rococo townhouses. Of course, the reality was a hard disappointment. Perhaps because of war damage there was nothing to admire, all concrete, and, of course, the church was to match.

☞

Day 12 – 23 June 2016 – Ferlach to St Jakob im Rosental
THIS WAS OF course the day that we voted on the EU referendum. I had cast my postal vote and felt remote from the hullabaloo. Breakfast was not available before 7.30 and when I reached the tourist office again it was just 9 and a polite

man pointed out that the office did not open until 10. That left a finely balanced decision. I chose to wait and filled time by refreshing my petty cash and visiting the unlovely parish church. Still with twenty minutes to wait, I settled in the little park surrounding the office.

I had two reasons to wait: the first was that I needed to plan my return train journey; the second was that there appeared to be no *Gasthaus* in St Jakob im Rosental, the end of the day's journey. When the office opened, however, the girl consulted the local accommodation directory and came up with the Thomashof in Mühlbachstrasse in St Jakob. She booked me in and printed out the train times from Villach. So as I left I thought the wait had been worthwhile.

With the aid of a town map it was not difficult to find the field way. All morning I walked westwards through farmland, parallel with the Drau but well inland from the river. I took two photographs to help me remember the majestic scenery. As the heat built up, the treeless asphalt grew hard and hot, so that wherever possible I took to the grasslands, either cut and drying or awaiting the mower. So it was a pleasure to reach St Johann im Rosental at about one o'clock. This is a marvellous church, which I was disappointed to find locked, but that seems the Kärnten practice. Then came what I would call a churchwarden, who proudly showed me the church, which unusually has two full transepts and is richly decorated throughout. He also produced a pilgrim stamp that we applied lavishly to several surfaces in the Kompass guide.

Shortly after leaving the village I took a picture looking back along my path at the ripening barley. My map warned me that the way would soon return to the Drau so I seized on the opportunity to eat at a lavish shelter built by the local *Gemeinde*. It celebrated some ancient building tradition and there was an illustrated display of the construction and the traditionalists who had fashioned it. I am afraid these special qualities are not evident from my picture.

The return to the punishing Drau bicycle path marked the second half of the day's walk. Here the management of the river has produced the substantial Feistritzer Stausee. So the view from the path is of wide water decorated with many swans and, at one point, a rowing four.

I remember little else of that afternoon. I skirted the church of St Oswald to reach Maria Elend im Rosental. Between the two the way crosses the Dürrenbach by a beautifully constructed wooden footbridge. Maria Elend is a pilgrim church and it was at about six o'clock that I made a small detour to visit it. The entry into the village had been along a busy main road and I contemplated but rejected a post bus short of the village. I seemed to have another chance in the village with a bus due at once. I waited and nothing came. Perhaps it had passed just before I reached the stop. It was the last bus of the day so I had no alternative but to slog it out for St Jakob. This was a long road walk and by the time I reached the outskirts of St Jakob im Rosental I was dehydrated and done. I bought water in the Billa supermarket and sought directions from the fire station. I only half understood what seemed encouraging sounds. I tried again at the café in the main square only to be told that Mühlbachstrasse was not a street in St Jakob but a village some 5 kilometres distant. I despaired. The kind café owner suggested that I stay at the Italian restaurant down the road but when I tried them they said that they did not do rooms. They did, however, summon a taxi and it was nearly nine o'clock when I reached the Thomashof in Mühlbach.

Here again I was kindly received at what is a large and very professional tourist hotel. They cooked me an excellent omelette and gave me a small room overlooking the road. The number for Thomashof is +43 (0)4253 8118. Bed and breakfast cost €46 and supper €16. The cost of supper seems to vary little from place to place.

June walking is tough but after the second day stamina builds up. I had also devised some Heath Robinson padding so that the rucksack no longer ate into my skin and bone. So although tired at the end of the days I was always in good heart.

☞

Day 13 – 24 June 2016 – St Jakob im Rosental to Villach
AT THE THOMASHOF breakfast was not before 7.30. When I made a timely arrival I found the dining room already full of keen tourists regimented by an alarming woman who would have made an excellent sergeant major. I ate breakfast avoiding her control as best I could and set off with two *Brötchen* for my lunch.

In fact the Jakobsweg out of St Jakob skirts Mühlbach so I might have started where I was and cut 5 kilometres from this stage to Villach. However, I felt an urge to pick up where I had left off, so took the post bus back into St Jakob. The church is built on a knoll surmounting the settlement. The pilgrim path was a steep climb to reach the church but I wanted the pilgrim stamp. The day's walk begins from the church and proceeds by most agreeable paths to St Peter, St Johann and then Raun to cross the motorway short of Pirk. I took a photograph of the view from a spot between St Peter and St Johann.

Pirk is the gateway to a long climb through the woods to pass by the summit of St Christof (707 metres). This is quite a climb and probably 40 per cent of the way was in full sun. So sweet is the point at which the gradient shifts from up to down. What a difference that makes! Whereas upwards was a struggle with a rest in each patch of deep shade, down was a delight at a swinging gait to reach Ledenitzen.

This is only a temporary respite since after a few hundred metres on a small road the path swings left into woodland and a comparable climb round the slopes of Bleiberg (772 metres). The map shows this woodland walk reaching Route 84 short of Oberferlach. The forest is thick and there are many tiny junctions. Nowhere is clear waymarking more necessary. Although I am sure I did not miss a sign, I was soon hopelessly lost on a long uphill climb that ended in a substantial forest clearing. Some wit had nailed up a sign: "Joseph Stainz Platz". There was no path out, other than the entry path, save for a narrow and faint track uphill. I knew that I must be wrong since for the previous fifteen minutes the uphill climb had been easterly. This was despair-inducing but as I made to retrace my steps I saw at my feet a thick patch of wild strawberries. It was as though divine providence had seen my need. I knelt and ate my way from one end of the patch to the other. The fruit pointing upwards looked succulent but tasted of nothing. The fruit pointing downwards and overripe provided the sublime taste. So my anxiety was diminished and I retraced my steps until reaching an unmarked diversion that at least pointed westwards.

But this was a false friend, the path steadily narrowing until it died in the middle of nowhere. I could not face a return and scrambled on westward, losing height wherever I could. I knew that this was dangerous and might end in tears but then I saw a roof not more than 15 metres below. I slid downhill, moving from tree to tree and branch to branch until I emerged behind a house adjoining a small church. I knocked on the door and alarmed an elderly woman by asking where was Oberferlach. With evident distrust she told me that this was Oberferlach and smartly shut the door. Her assertion made sense of my map and I decided that I had emerged from the forest only a kilometre or two further west than planned.

By now it was three o'clock and I took an hour off in the pleasant churchyard drinking copiously from the churchyard tap and eating my *Brötchen*. In hot weather, when at least two litres of water a day are needed, the village churchyard is a sure supply. One of the admirable qualities of Austrian tradition is the high standard of maintenance and gardening lavished on each grave. Indeed, in most cases they are more family vaults than individual graves. From enquiry of a lady tending her family grave I discovered that the church is dedicated to St Georg. Beside the church is the mightiest lime tree I have ever seen, and I was pleased to see that it bore the *Denkmal* stamp. It certainly far outmeasures the lime tree in Persenbeug. I took a photograph of its mighty trunk. It is a mark of my wonder and delight that I have three souvenirs of this sacred place:

the last shows its broad location but principally it illustrates the Austrian veneration of the grave. I have included it in the plate section.

Setting off at four o'clock, I had a hard road walk to Neuegg. Here the waymarking was again poor but I picked up a forest walk, often uphill, to reach Egg. Both Neuegg and Egg are on the shore of the attractive Faaker See.

From Egg the onward route is unclear. The official version, which is way-marked, precedes along the lake shore to the south of Drobollach. The Kompass version runs north from the lake. I chose the official route. It showed me for the first time the extraordinary quality of an Austrian lake in high summer. The water is an inviting blue-green and the border between water and land seems so pure and unsoiled. I really envied the few swimmers. Paradise will always be commercialised and the lake shore is no exception. But all these apartment blocks and bathing stations meet a human need and do so in a quiet way.

Having left the lake shore I followed signs and instinct to reach a highway and a waymark pointing westward, but it was now six o'clock and I needed to secure a bed in Villach. If I walked on it might be eight before I reached the city centre so I stopped a man and asked if there was a bus stop. "Oh," he said, "there is one only 100 metres back down the main road." So I joined the main road, found the bus stop and saw that the last bus of the day was due in fifteen minutes. I settled to wait.

The bus arrived on time and as usual I was the only passenger. The bus would take me to the Hauptbahnhof in Villach. The main road ran through attractive country, which led me to think that once again I had abandoned the way prematurely; the city begins only at the bridge after the village of Maria Gail. However, this bus ride was more a necessity than a choice. At the terminus I explored the various options. A short walk from the station along Bahnhofstrasse leads to what is effectively a square adjoining the Drau. I thought that it was the Hauptplaz but I was to discover that the Hauptplaz, with its several hotels, lay across the bridge on the other side of the river. Having cast here and there I decided on the Hotel Mosser, which proved a lucky choice. The hotel was founded in the mid-19th century by the handsome Herr Mosser. I can so describe him having seen a bronze bust in the hall of the first floor beside the single room that I was allotted. The hotel has remained a family business, and there are many illustrations of its history in photographs of successive generations, and of the vicissitudes of the business, which was bombed out in the Second World War. This sense of antiquity and continuity is, for me, attractive and it is continued in the furnishing of the rooms. Another fortuitous discovery was the *Brauhof* across the street. This is the headquarters and shop window of the famous Villacher Bier. Behind and adjoining the parish church of St Nicholas is the extensive *Brauhofgarten*. On a hot summer's evening it was crowded, but there was one table left, and there I had an excellent supper served by a strict but friendly waiter in lederhosen. It was an excellent preparation for a good night's sleep. My night at Mosser's hotel cost €72, but Villach is the second city of Kärnten. The telephone number of the excellent Mosser's is +43 (0)4242 24115.

During my rest hour at the church of St Georg in Oberferlach I had checked my email to find a message from my farm accountant advising on the successful outcome of the EU referendum. So it was in such a place and by such a strange means that I learned of the momentous decision. It seemed fitting to hear of history being made under the shade of the *Denkmal* lime tree.

☞

Day 14 – 25 June 2016 – Villach to Maria Gail

MY RETURN TRAIN to Vienna did not leave until 15.14. The journey time was four hours and twenty-one minutes and I had nearly a day in which to explore Villach or to walk. In the end I decided on a combination of the two, having consulted a kind lady in the tourist office. So, armed with a town map and guide, I looked at the parish church of St Nicholas and the equal church of St Jakob on the other bank of the river and at the head of the main square. These are both medieval churches but St Jakob is by far the more interesting. It has excellent baroque ornament and a wonderful pulpit carved in the 16th century. From there I headed for the baroque church of Heiligengeist, which serves as the parish church for the district of Perau. I photographed the altar in the chapel for the chance to catch both the glory of Austrian wrought iron and, something I had never seen before, an altar adorned not with a painting but with a looking glass. Then came the return to the walk, as I decided to walk back along the Jakobsweg to at least reach Maria Gail. The direct route along the main road is but half an hour. However, the Jakobsweg takes a major diversion to follow a long loop of the river through parkland. This circuit joins the main road immediately before the village of Maria Gail, which lies about a kilometre south of the main road.

To my great surprise, given its proximity to Villach, Maria Gail is a charming and self-contained settlement with no sign of urban development. The pilgrim church of Maria Gail is of great distinction and supplied the postcards I needed to furnish my habit of sending cards from afar. Beside the church is another discovery, the Gasthof Moser. Again, this is a long-established family business with celebration of its history, particularly some great gathering of patriots in the main dining room in November 1918. I took a card and the daily rate of accommodation for the possibility, indeed the expectation, that I would return. The number is +43 (0)4242 34933.

I took the noisy highway back into the city and found the same table and the same waiter for lunch in the *Brauhofgarten*. I took a photograph, which, I think, captures the charm of this very Austrian tradition. I posted my cards at the main post office and comfortably caught the Vienna train. I could not resist more photographs of the romantic Hochosterwitz Castle. When I return it will be either to Mosser or Moser, and I know from the tourist office that I can resume the Jakobsweg comfortably from the main bridge only metres from the tourist office, for the Weg follows the path of the Drau westwards from city centre to city exit in that very Austrian way that makes traversing a city on foot tolerable.

VILLACH TO DELLACH

Day 15 – 20 September 2016 – Villach again

ON 20 SEPTEMBER I travelled much. Geanina-Maria and I left the Wachau Valley in her BMW at just after six o'clock, in an almighty rush to reach Vienna for the doctor's surgery at seven. The rest of the morning was frantic and I did not reach the station until just after two, in good time for the 14.20, the last direct train to Villach.

I had a desire to spend the night not in the city but in the delightful Gasthof Moser beside the pilgrim church of Maria Gail. However, arriving in Villach in the dark at seven o'clock it all seemed fantasy and the reality was once again to check in at the reliable Hotel Mosser within a short walk – 100 metres – from the station. This time the receptionist was disagreeable and the price elevated to reflect demand. So I was in a thoroughly bad mood as I crossed the road to the Villach Brauhof. However, the cheerful atmosphere and the excellent cooking soon had me relaxed and cheerful and I slept well.

☞

VILLACH

WALLNER

SPITTAL AN DER DRAU

VIENNA

SPITTAL AN DER DRAU

LIND

DELLACH

Day 16 – 21 September 2016 – Villach to Wallner

I ATE A large breakfast and shook the dust of the Mosser off my feet. My recent research suggested that I might avoid repeating the long walk out of Villach along the bank of the Drau by taking a bus to reach the *Kraftwerke* river crossing on the outskirts of the city. At the bus station I discovered that there was a bus that would put me down at a complex series of road junctions on the outskirts of Fellach, just past the *Kraftwerke*. The bus driver was helpful and took care to decamp me at the most favourable stop. I was then challenged by the road system – underpass, overpass and triple roundabouts – as the minor road out of the city met the major road travelling westwards along the Drau. I had selected the *Kraftwerke* in part because the Jakobsweg from the city crosses at that point from south to north bank and runs westwards between the river and the railway.

Despite much scrambling and endeavour I made a number of false sallies and still failed to find the *Kraftwerke* crossing. In retrospect I can see that I searched too narrowly and so in the end had to resort to the road bridge, which crossed not only the Drau but also the railway. That left me with no alternative but to take a minor road that ran parallel to the footpath on the other side of the railway. I longed to quit this dusty suburban street and join the pilgrim path on the riverbank but the railway always prevented me. It was not until I had walked a good hour that suddenly I saw that the barrier that protects the railway had ended, and by scrambling through undergrowth and across a ditch I was able to cross the railway and join the path.

Confidence thus restored, I swung along the flowing Drau to reach a road bridge that returned me to the south bank, cutting off two loops formed by the two S-shaped bends in the river's course. So I passed away from the river through the outskirts of Töplitsch and Untergraben. I took the view of the river westwards at about noon.

Shortly after Untergraben the path swung back to the river (again I took the view westwards in mid-afternoon) and there followed a long walk, pleasant enough, to reach a sports complex with adjoining café just short of Feffernitz. This apparition was as welcome as any desert oasis and I settled down to two long cups of coffee in the departing sunshine. This was a necessary restorative as I still had a long walk to reach my goal of Feistritz. It proved to be a pleasing country walk, almost all inland from the Drau through Feffernitz and on to Pobersach. On the road through the latter I noticed a Gasthaus Wallner, which seemed of little promise. Emerging from the village I saw my clear route across a valley to reach the outskirts of Feistriz and I hurried onwards, sure of a comfortable billet in the town.

Crossing the green valley I struggled on through the outskirts of the town and was directed to a grubby self-styled hotel on the main road. Confident that I could do better I headed for the church on the high ground at the other end of the town. The further I went the less encouragement I found. Commerce evaporated and even the houses clustered round the church assumed a forlorn air. Defeated, I returned to the so-called hotel.

I burst into a crowded bar of noisy drinkers. When I asked the barmaid for a room I understood her to say that they did not offer accommodation. So where could I stay? Well the only possibility was Wallner in Pobersach. My heart sank. There is no worse experience at the end of a long day than to be told that you must retrace your steps to some option earlier rejected. But there was nothing for it and my only device was to desert the road and take a line across country through pasture fields in varying states of cultivation. Perfect were the fields recently mowed. Hard were the fields yet to be mowed, as the sward tugged at the feet and guilt bred a sense of unease.

As I approached Wallner I saw a flower-banked backyard and a wide door of general entry. Crossing the threshold I saw what was the nearest approach to an English pub that I had ever seen in Austria. There were locals drinking at the bar, and eating at tables around the walls and under the windows.

I was shown to a tiny room, barely big enough for me and the bed at the same time, by a tough, middle-aged woman who soon switched to voluble English that poured out with a flat East Anglian accent. She revealed that she had lived with an Englishman in Cambridge for more than six years. She was very keen to tell her story of those years before taking my order. That was not complicated since they served only the cold plate of meat and cheese known as a *Jauseplatte*. As soon as she had served me she, chameleon-like, melted into the noisy group at the bar, at least two of whom were plainly drunk. That was the last I saw of her, that evening or the next day.

Morning gave me the opportunity to explore this strange establishment. There was a heavy emphasis on organic produce and self-sufficiency. On the other side of the road was a huge orchard of very old fruit trees and there was much fuss about the home-made apple juice, cider and schnapps. All these angles were aggressively promoted and after breakfast I came across a large school group being shown the wonders of the self-sufficient life. I was half deterred by the marketing but still admired the commitment to beautifying the yard and surroundings with profusions of flowers. I photographed the yard in the morning light. In the orchard I found an old man gathering apples into a square plastic tub which, when filled, would have been beyond the strength of two men to lift. He swept the ground with back bent and tossed the apples up into the container as though he could no longer straighten himself. Below the knee he was wet with the heavy morning dew.

The logs for the winter were stored in circular wire cages about 2.5 metres in height. I could not see how these great vats could be shifted. They were unfamiliar to me, although I was to see them later elsewhere on the walk.

☞

Day 17 – 22 September 2016 – Wallner to Spittal an der Drau

THESE INSPECTIONS AND discoveries were not to be missed or hurried, so I was late back on the path and with the extra 2 kilometres to cover to regain Feistritz, that unlovely town. As I approached the centre I saw a lane on my right marked "Brückgasse". It seemed worth a gamble and it paid off as it led me through back gardens and yards to reach the river and the only bridge over the Drau. Immediately on the far side ran the railway line and the station that serves Feistriz and the neighbouring town of Paternion. Beyond the railway, as the road turned left to follow the Drau westwards, was a daunting blue and yellow arrow pointing me at a footpath that ran steeply uphill. Although conditions were excellent, it was a long, hard climb due north, until a sharp turn westwards brought easier going through glorious country. After perhaps 2 kilometres I reached a road junction marked "Steinbruch". At this junction the local council had erected what appeared to be a piece of modern sculpture of dubious quality, all wood and metal, angular and towering. I had to explore and discovered beneath the pretension the benign purpose, which was to provide a picnic table and benches under cover, with maps and plans to illustrate the source of the donation. Beside the apparition trickled something between a ditch and a stream, over which the council had constructed a footbridge, more for effect than for use. I photographed the view from the picnic table.

Curiosity satisfied, I set off to reach a rarity, namely a house that claimed to offer food and drink to the traveller. It was marked on my map as "Jakelbauer". At the door was a sign that proclaimed it would open at eleven o'clock. Since it was then 10.50 I decided to wait, and not in vain, since at eleven exactly a young mother appeared with a child at her knee and cheerfully made me coffee. I sat outside in bright sun enjoying one of the best views I had seen on this walk. The house faced south and from its height the whole Drau valley spread out for miles to east and to west with the clarity of an aeroplane window seat at about 300 metres, the height that the house stood above the river below.

After this agreeable interlude I had about 2 kilometres on a country road deservedly marked "scenic" on the map. I skirted Sonnwiesen to reach St Jakob in Ferndorf. I stopped at the old church with an equally ancient tree beside it. There was no stamp in the church but a bench at the door where I ate my piece. On from St Jakob lay Innsberg, where I photographed the view of the Drau valley below. Here the Jakobsweg swung right and then immediately left into perhaps 11 kilometres of glorious woods from which I caught occasional glimpses of the famous lake of Millstättersee, which lay long and narrow across the view to the north.

Emerging from the woodland, I reached first the village of Grossegg and then the further village of Winkl. Here I needed guidance and embarked on a long conversation with an extremely friendly and clearly spoken middle-aged man. From my Kompass map I knew I had to reach Molzbichl and he told me how I could do that by road, but I wanted something better. He pointed me on, with a warning that I had to find a left-hand turn. All this confusion resulted from the Kärnten tourist guide taking an entirely different course from the Kompass guide. Instead of dropping down to the river and then along the river into Spittal, the Kärnten map preferred to continue due west from Winkl, following the lake and passing Hochgosch before turning to reach Spittal via Edling. Of course the waymarking was therefore the Kärnten and not the Kompass line. So after about 2 kilometres came a clear blue and yellow arrow pointing me to the right when I knew I should be turning left. Not without anxiety I rejected the waymark and set off on the quest for Molzbichl, knowing that I would have no signs and no guidance.

As often before, I met both success and failure. I had a little more than 6 kilometres to cover and all went well, despite a number of close calls. But then what seemed to be a path petered out when I was in the midst of the woods, leaving me with neither guide nor path. I could only resort to the rule of keeping downhill. Thus I slithered until finding my way into a watercourse that ultimately flowed to the road on the outskirts of Molzbichl.

It is a small town of some charm and in the midst was a substantial *Gasthaus*. As often, the front door led straight into a crowded bar. Since it was late and I was tired, what I sought was not a bed but a bus. A helpful lady behind the bar urged me to walk a short way to the Raffeisen Bank where she thought the bus stop was. She was right, and consulting the timetable I saw to my surprise and delight that I had only ten minutes to wait for the last bus of the day. It arrived on time and I was surprised to see that the driver was the same who had carried me out of Villach on the preceding day. I bought my ticket and was one of two passengers that he sped into the middle of Spittal an der Drau. He was going on to the terminus but as I alighted in the very centre I could not help saying that we had met before and did he not remember. He rather grudgingly admitted that he did.

In the morning I had used the extremely useful website Booking.com to reserve a room at what seemed to be the best hotel in the town. It was in the Hauptplatz, which bizarrely is not a *Platz* but a street of renaissance houses that leads from the Schloss Porcia to the bridge over the Drau. The Erlebnis Post Hotel is an art hotel, which means that all the passages are painted in ugly colours and retrieved objects that can be passed off as works of art decorate or furnish the rooms. However, I found it agreeable. My room was big and commanded a view of the parish church. All the staff were extremely friendly and the cooking was appetising. After the hazards of the day I slept soundly.

☞

Day 18 – 23 September 2016 – Spittal to Vienna

ON THE FOLLOWING morning I saw what I could of Schloss Porcia, which was not much since it was closed for some exhibition. I also saw the parish church, which turned out to be a monster, and walked across what would have been the schloss' park, which has become now a municipal park, to catch the first train to Vienna via Salzburg. This was for me a new line, and the first half from Spittal is through truly mountainous country without habitation or stops. The second half is also through mountainous country but with many famous developments such as Bad Ischl, the favourite summer ground of the Emperor Franz Joseph. Now it looks overgrown and ugly, often from a bird's-eye view as the railway runs high above the valley floor. Also on this line I suddenly saw looming the ill-fated castle of Werfen where Felicitas had broken her ankle. This was for me a nemesis point. I did not remember the castle to be so white as it appeared from the train in the morning sun. I saw the village street and the church where Felicitas and I had joined the wedding throng, I could almost see the famous *Gasthaus* for gastronomes where I had spent that solitary night. These sights stirred such memories that I was quite upset. In Salzburg I changed trains to head on to Vienna where I caught the last flight back to Heathrow.

☞

Day 19 – 8 October 2016 – Return to Spittal an der Drau

IT WAS ON Saturday 8 October that I returned to Vienna on the first flight. From the airport I hastened on, for it is a long train ride to reach Spittal, whether via Salzburg or via Villach. I took the Villach route and it was dark as I walked across the schloss park to reach the Erlebnis Post Hotel. There I found a different receptionist with excellent English and a good deal of pert charm. She seemed to have all the time in the world for me, so I flirted with her and she with me, as she showed me to my room, lingered to explain the lighting system and later sat with me as I ate.

Again I had good dinner and sleep.

☞

Day 20 – 9 October 2016 – Spittal to Lind

THE RECEPTIONIST HAD assured me that there was a mass at eight o'clock in the parish church. I reconnoitred at seven-thirty to find it shut and barred. A woman emerging from the presbytery told me there would be no mass before ten, but there was a service, though not a mass, at eight o'clock in Edling. I had a vague idea of the direction and set off at my best pace through a dark morning of chill drizzle. I found the church minutes before eight and joined the elderly congregation. The priest was young, austere and unsympathetic. The service (was it a matins?) dragged on. After half an hour I bolted for breakfast.

I hoped to get a bus that would carry me out of Spittal to the village of Oberdorf on its edge, but I was soon informed that, being Sunday, it was an hour until the next train and it did not stop before Lendorf. As for buses, there were none. So I had no alternative but to foot it from the centre to the outskirts, which I easily achieved. In Oberdorf I had to find a right turn to carry me into the woods on what should have been a fine stretch to St Peter in Holz. I couldn't find the right turn. There were no signs. I asked a man on a bicycle who gave me confusing and contradictory advice. So in bad humour I had no alternative but to walk the road alongside the railway, which in turn was alongside the Drau, until reaching Feistritz. From there I found my way to St Peter in Holz, and on from there things should have been straightforward but I missed a left turn onto a minor road and so continued on the main road from Spittal, which then became entangled with the motorway. I was lost and defeated. Only in the midst of Lendorf, a good 2 kilometres from where I should have been, did I pick up a clear opportunity to turn south and find my way back to the Jakobsweg.

As I approached the railway I met a spry lady with her dog and she took me under her wing and walked with me until I had sufficient confidence to reject her advice and head to the bank of the Drau, the north bank, and to follow it along until reaching the ancient chapel of St Magdalena am Lurnfeld. From St Magdalena there is an easy walk by road through Möllbrücke and along the river to the *Kraftwerk* where it crosses from the north to the south bank and leads through the midst of an interesting town named Sachsenburg. Why it should be so named I could not discover. After all, it's a long way from Saxony. But there were many signs of its past importance and many buildings along the High Street to admire. This was Sunday afternoon and all was deserted except for a small and rough bar where four determined drinkers were keeping pace with the landlord. At first they treated me with suspicion but then thawed and became very friendly as they set my coffee decorously down at a small table away from the bar.

I needed that coffee to carry me nearly 10 kilometres to my destination at Kleblach-Lind. This long stretch was initially a bicycle path along the banks of the Drau and then through very rich farmland in the comparatively narrow valley between wooded banks on either side of the river. When only halfway along this long stretch, my left leg began to hurt and I knew that I was too far from Lind to press on. So I stopped and took off my shoes and socks and adjusted my support stocking. This did the trick and I was pain-free as I saw Lind in the distance.

Lind is on the right bank and Kleblach on the left bank of the Drau. The official finish was in Kleblach but I decided that Lind was quite far enough for me. According to the map there was the Gasthaus Funder but when I reached it I was told by a man outside that it no longer offered accommodation. He said the only hope was a lady at the other end of the village. I found her house with difficulty and not in vain. For when my knock was unanswered and I had given up and was on my way, the door opened and an elderly lady saw at once that I was on the pilgrim path. Immediately she was friendly and welcoming. Her house was always open to any pilgrim. She showed me to a good room at the top of the house with fine views and confirmed my plan to return to Funder to eat.

Again Funder proved a puzzle. All the doors were locked, although I saw lights and heard voices within. I found a kitchen window and saw a woman inside. I tapped on the window. She signalled me away. I persisted. Eventually one of the doors opened and she asked what my business was. When I said I must eat she beckoned me in and said I could have Wiener Schnitzel or venison stew. I chose the stew and what followed was the best traditional venison goulash I have ever eaten. As was proper, it was accompanied by bread dumplings, red cabbage and *Preiselbeeren*. My gratitude and appreciation made for fellowship and her husband saw me to the door. There he explained that it was his son who was the shot and at that moment a 4x4 drew up and out came the man and the rifle. He had had no luck that night. I returned to the pilgrim house and slept well.

☞

Day 21 – 10 October 2016 – Lind to Dellach
AFTER MY NEAR miss in Lind I decided that I would not risk failure at the end of the next day's walk. So, I reasoned, why not catch the train from one of the little stations ahead back to Spittal, stay the night in the Erlebnis Post Hotel and then take the express to Vienna the next morning? So I planned the day with an eye to the stations ahead. There was a station in

Dellach which was the end of the stage set by Kompass, but there was also a station in Berg if I ran out of time. I had the timetable and there seemed to be an hourly service, certainly until 18.45.

I soon reached Kleblach and thereon a pleasant walk on the very edge of the forest, well above the railway and the river. This lovely walk is signposted as Panoramaweg Oberdrautal and leads one through Lengholz and Gerlamoos to reach and pass through the town of Steinfeld. As it continues it is rather bizarrely named the Beekeepers' Wanderweg. But no matter, it passes through lovely country to reach the substantial town of Greifenburg. Although it was mid-afternoon everything seemed shut. I passed a girl in the street and enquired whether I would find a café in the visible hotel.

"*Ist zu*," she replied.

However, down the street I found a hippy bar where the old hippy gave me a fair cup of coffee. Out of Greifenburg there is no choice but to follow the very main road as far as, or just short of, a *Gasthaus* named Pirker. The left turn onto the side road must not be missed. This leads down to the railway and the river where again the direction is westwards to reach the ancient church of St Athanas. The sensible thing was surely then to walk quietly to Berg station and wait half an hour for the 17.45 but as usual I was rather attracted to the more daring course: go flat out for Dellach where I might with luck catch the last train of the day at 18.45.

I went for it but it was a steep climb from the shrine to reach Berg and from Berg it was a long road walk westwards before the descent into Dellach. Dellach is big and unattractive with no signs to the station, which lies out of town on the edge of the river. I struggled; I could not see my way, and I asked more than once and took little encouragement from the answers until at last I reached the railway line and guessed that the station was left rather than right. I reached the station exhausted and ten minutes too late for the 17.45. That left fifty minutes until the next and last chance. I waited, the train came on time and carried me back through the dusk and into the darkness and Spittal. There I returned to the Erlebnis Post Hotel but without the lively receptionist. I had a quiet evening to be ready for the first train the next day, the 06.30 which got me back to Vienna at 11.35. The day ended in Weissenkirchen but not after much rushing about the city centre and an interesting introduction to Geanina-Maria's new friend Birgitte and her historic family home in the nineteenth district.

A BREAK FROM THE JAKOBSWEG

Winter Interlude – December 2016

HERE AGAIN I am in the winter season when it is futile with the shortness of days to advance further on the snail's trail of the Jakobsweg. But this is the season when Kremsmünster calls and not to deaf ears. I had the Austrian Airlines 06.00 flight for the second of December provided by the Bratislava Conference and I had Roger Kinnerley's farewell party on the evening of the first. It all fitted almost too neatly. So fate hit back with the crash at the Marlborough College gates and the consequences which only the quickest thought and action could prevent from chaos or disaster. That I seemed to achieve until waking in Anthony Hunter's spare room at two-thirty in the morning when I realised that I had carried only two cases onto the train and had not perceived until that moment separation from my passport case. I spent the next hour in furious thought before resolving to pursue salvation at the airport. The driver of the car to Heathrow was Polish and he was certain I would get by with my driving licence. It might work for a Pole but not for a Briton. The kind ladies at check-in and sales did their best for me but I was soon on a doleful train to Paddington and on to

Chippenham. No joy in Andy's van but at last the wreck was traced to Bristol, and what relief when the wallet was confirmed in the back. Although I had been under pressure, it was gross carelessness to have left it when transferring my luggage to the van when Andy rescued me. The outcome was twenty-four hours' delay after frustrating negotiation with the shockingly incompetent Austrian Airlines sales office in Innsbruck.

So it was that I arrived at Kremsmünster at 1.13p.m., not on Friday but on Saturday afternoon, to a warm welcome from Pater Franz. Partly because the three-day Adventmarkt was in mid-course I was much more within the community. My room was in the heart of the abbey and I ate with the monks. I was invited to Mittagshore in the church and complet in the internal chapel, a long room barely lit by four small windows. For the night office, with the dark punctuated by occasional stall lights, it was more theatrical than any opera set, although at the same time entirely authentic and real. The community was admitting a novice in the following week and he, Anselmo, a young man from Munich, was spending Advent with the community to enable him to decide his future in January. I hope to see him there next year having taken the plunge.

The Adventmarkt was all fun with bands, concerts in the church and crowds enjoying the bright cold weather. Schwester Lydia was as sweet-souled as ever, possibly a mite more frail. The school development was completed and the garden works for the 2017 *Fest* were well underway. I felt more and more the strength of the Christian faith, and the vitality as the crowds thronged the court and the monthly youth mass on Saturday evening drew Felix and friends from the law school at Vienna

University. I was going straight on to Bratislava on Monday afternoon and was able to write my paper and prepare Geanina-Maria's accounts in the generous hours between offices.

☞

Spring Mishaps

I HAVE ALWAYS valued the spring and autumn seasons for walking. In winter the days are too short and the weather too uncertain. In summer the heat reduces the walking day to early and late. So any assumptions I had nurtured for 2017 were false. First, I did not return to Austria in the spring. Why? Because on 30 March I attempted the extreme. After a rackety time with Geanina-Maria in Bucharest I had risen before five for the 08.25 flight to London. Then I had kept my two o'clock dentist appointment at Sapford. Thence to Chippenham for a return fare to London to attend the Hare Court silks' party. Back at the station the Syrian had failed to leave my key on the wheel arch. Only through the Sainsbury's manager and Edward Heard was I able to locate him and thunder till he appeared. So it was past ten when I reached Henmarsh and got to bed. As I was about to settle, I remembered my water mug and skipped out to get it. My next recall is the pain as I sagged over the chair at the head of the kitchen table. There was blood everywhere and it was flowing from a head wound. It was four in the morning. The drama gradually unfolded to reveal eventually, on a repeat examination ten days later, two fractured bones in my neck. So this mishap prevented my return to the Jakobsweg that spring.

☞

Kremsmünster, Durnstein and Kremsmünster again – July 2017

I HAD, HOWEVER, carefully planned nine summer days in Austria. I had three targets: to spend some days with Geanina-Maria; to manage the *Country Life* visit to Kremsmünster; and to give Andrea Ciserova what time she wanted. In only the first was I frustrated.

I left on the first flight on 6 July, arriving in Vienna at ten in the morning. No Geanina in the waiting crowd. She did not answer her mobile. I settled in the café to wait and opened my iPad. There was her email sent just before midnight telling me that her grandmother in Transylvania was on her deathbed and she had had to go. The disaster was magnified because the news was so unexpected and I was so unprepared. She said she would be back on Saturday so I had forty-eight hours to fill. I soon decided that I must make the best of a bad job and the best was the Hotel Richard Löwenherz in Dürnstein. I could catch a train from the airport to St Pölten, there changing onto a local train for Krems. In twenty minutes the Budapest–Zurich train would stop at the airport. It all looked so simple but the express never picked up speed. It dawdled into Vienna and there halted. There were problems at Meidling. After a long diversion we quit the city but then ground to a halt, unexplained, at Tullnerfeld. We were one and a half hours late by the time we reached St Pölten. Happily, I had only a five-minute wait for a local train to Krems. There arrived I waited in sweltering heat for the Dürnstein bus. My luggage was heavy and by the time I reached the hotel I was in a sweat.

After that my fortunes soared. I was given Room 6 overlooking the Danube and it was in every way charming. I had a bath and dozed until dinner. On my way to the usual *Heuriger* across the main road, I investigated what I had thought was a tourist restaurant that I had often passed, thinking it might be worth a try. In reality it proved to be an upmarket *Heuriger* with excellent cooking and, of course, excellent Dürnstein wine. I was lucky to get the last of the outside tables on such a lovely summer's evening.

The next morning I had an early, decent breakfast, although not peaceful. Then, advised by the proprietoress, I took the ferry across the Danube to Rossatz. A bell at the riverside summons the boatman, who, for a modest fare, ferries the passenger to the other side. From there my destination was St Lorenz, about 5 kilometres distant. On the low ground the fruit trees were laden. It was the apricot season and ripe fruit was everywhere; there was no need to pick as windfalls were abundant. But then came the climb, stiff uphill to a viewpoint with the town below, a mosaic of jumbled rooftops. From there onwards the path constantly dipped and then rose to test the walker's stamina. It is designated a world heritage trail, marked, I discovered, with a white stencilled sign applied to rocks and trees, so that once understood the waymarking is excellent. The descent into what I expected to be St Lorenz was from a piece of artwork that commemorates the victims of Nazi atrocity in the Balkans (I could not understand why it was placed there). The path down is narrow and steep. The walk ends at the main road rather than at St Lorenz, and as I had to find a drink I took the side road, which meant a 1-kilometre hike to the village. There I found a busy and very commercial café. On the return I filled my rucksack with windfalls from a super-abundant apricot tree.

I had to be back by six, when the ferry would close. I went a good pace and it was only five o'clock when I reached the ferry point and struck the bell to summon the boat. By the ferry station there is a caravan park and a sandy beach with many bathers. An attractive woman in a bikini caught my eye as I waited for the ferryman.

Dinner at the same *Heuriger* was not so good: too crowded and not the same attentive waitress. Before dinner I heard from Geanina-Maria that she would not be back until Monday so after dinner I walked to the bus stop and saw that there would be an 08.36 bus to Krems on Saturday morning. On both these two summer nights I smoked in the hotel garden and watched the moon rise across the Danube. It was almost full.

The next morning I had a trouble-free journey to Kremsmünster. Pater Franz was soon there to meet me and drive me up the hill. I was at once into the rhythm of the community: midday service, lunch in the refectory, vespers, breakfast with Schwester Lydia. In the afternoon I walked round the garden show in the abbey grounds, marvelling at so much expense attracting so many people.

On Sunday I extended my exploration, walking to Kirchberg and taking the shuttle bus to the schloss. At Kirchberg there was a Filipino baptism in progress in the large church. The schloss is ancient but much restored. The garden show was contrived and the museum of musical instruments extensive but unimpressive. I also climbed to the top of the *Sternwarte* (observatory), which was truly impressive, but I saw only the stairs and the terraces.

On Monday I thought there would be less of a crowd but not so. Bus tours run seven days a week and had taken the visitor tally to more than one hundred thousand since the opening of the show in April. At ten o'clock I was able to join the full *Sternwarte* tour, which opened the doors into the various extraordinary collections: natural history, minerals, gemstones and shells. So by the time the *Country Life* team arrived, at about three that afternoon, I was fully prepared.

The *Country Life* crew could not have been more delightful. John Goodall, all boyish enthusiasm and charm; Will Pryce, silent, exacting and commanding in anything that concerned his art.

On what remained of Monday I conducted a general tour of the abbey and its surroundings. While Will was photographing the school chapel it was my job to keep others out, and I was aided by Alexandra, manager of the abbey's office for public relations. I was surprised when she allowed a group of three to go in. She explained that she could not stop Pater Claudius as he was her boss. This proved to be the best of luck, since when the group emerged, the man kissed the older woman goodbye and walked over to Alexandra. It was thus that I met Pater Claudius, the Father in charge of the abbey treasures. He explained that he had been showing Princess Loewenstein the chapel. When John and Will emerged we were soon an animated group being led to photograph the fish ponds and then on to the old pond which I had never seen, although Pater Franz had mentioned it. It lies perhaps a hundred metres to the west of the abbey and is enclosed within a 16th-century building. It is a very beautiful secret and was obviously the inspiration for the later fish ponds within the abbey walls. It is the first manifestation of a flow of hill water which enters the old fish pond, flows into the adjoining lake, then serves the new fish ponds, the canal and the second lake. When we parted from Pater Claudius we agreed to meet him at ten o'clock the next morning to view the treasures. I went to vespers and John and Will continued to make use of the evening light.

The next day was a very full one encompassing the treasures, the library, the *Kaisersaal*, the *Sternwarte* terraces, the abbot's private rooms and the chapel within the *Clausur*. We had intended to host a supper in the *Schank* but none of the invitees materialised and furthermore it was the *Schank* kitchen's rest day. As we left the *Schank* I said to the pretty waitress: "Du bist so schön. Du musst eine sehr gute Hochzeit machen." She was delighted. Fortunately Gasthof König was open and the three of us made a good supper.

The next morning I said my farewells and Pater Franz took me to the station for the 08.36 which got me to Vienna at 10.30. Throughout this stay the weather had been remarkable. Each day started cloudy but then became increasingly glorious and sun-drenched. The temperature would rise to create a thunderstorm in the early evening or during the night. The next day the pattern was repeated.

Saturday was clear and the great moon was riding towards the west.

Lambach Abbey from Stadl-Paura (page 41)

Stift Göttweig sails into view (page 9)

Left: Frau Hollerweg's family (page 50)
Right: The stairs in Schloss Heiligenkreuz (page 8)

The open waters of the Saalach (page 58)

Above left: Schloss Werfen
(page 55)

Above right: The Altdorfer
larches (page 103)

Right: The shrine outside
Voldöpp (page 77)

Below left: The
Wallfahrtskapelle at
Stampfanger (page 73)

Below right: The hidden
window at Weitau (page 69)

Right: The first sight of Kartause Aggsbach (page 12)

Middle: Haymaking approaching Oberellbögen (page 270)

Below left: The tree peony at Franzensfeste (page 246)

Below right: The flower meadow near Pontigl (page 254)

Left: The source of the Drau (page 226)
Right: The house at Pflügen (page 212)

Left: The Corpus Christi on the ancient bridge at Heinfels (page 223)
Right: A hollowed-log drain on the descent to Kiens (page 233)

Top: A view westwards of the Drau, between St Margareten and Glainach (page 172)

Middle: The Olanger Stausee (page 229)

Bottom: The Drau downstream, taken from the bridge near Dölsach (page 215)

Farm buildings near Lavamünd (page 156)

Left: The graveyard at St Georg's church in Oberferlach (page 178)
Right: A good rest place at Stangersdorf (page 148)

The blizzard from my hotel room at Unterburg (page 163)

The Wilder Kaiser as the clouds dissolve (page 71)

The Kloster der Englischen Fraülein (page 301)

The dramatic position of Hochosterwitz (page 165)

The Inn between Passau and Schärding (page 298)

Left: The temple in "das barocke Prunkgärtl" at Schloss Neuburg (page 302)
Right: The *Wallfahrtskirche* at Mariastein (page 320)

Glancing back at Passau (page 299)

The view of the Inn from the outskirts of Kleinsöll (page 323)

Left: My poor old shoes at the Wilder Mann (page 298)

Right: A milepost for Santiago de Compostela, only 2,214 kilometers away (page 325)

Below: Schärding, dominated by its *Pfarrkirche* (page 282)

Left: The witch's house near Kirchdorf (page 345)

Right: A stretch of the *Radweg* between Obernberg and Kirchdorf (page 345)

Below: The farm outside Sarleinsbach (page 286)

Above: The Franciscan monastery and garden in Maria Schmolln (page 354)
Below: The flying altar in the *Filialkirche* at Gebertsham (page 364)

My lengthening shadow in the Rossbach forest (page 350)

The *Wirtshaus* in Thannstrass (page 353)

Above: Approaching Mattsee (page 365)

Right: Journey's end: celebrating at the Steirische Bodensee (page 378)

Sunday was a full moon and the night was cloudy but it must have cleared because there she was again on her journey westward at 2.40 a.m.

My return to Vienna was more frustration with Geanina-Maria but at least it culminated in a successful meeting at Schwechat with Andrea Cisarova.

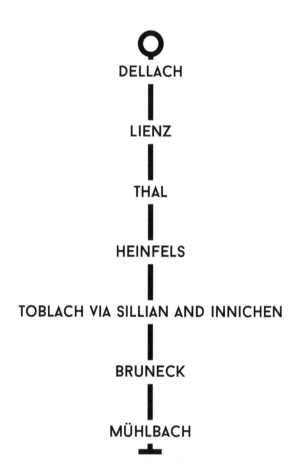

DELLACH

LIENZ

THAL

HEINFELS

TOBLACH VIA SILLIAN AND INNICHEN

BRUNECK

MÜHLBACH

DELLACH TO MÜHLBACH

Day 22 – 24 October 2017 – Dellach to Lienz

IT WAS A full year since I had ended my autumn walk in
Dellach. A prolonged autumn stretch was imperative and I
had left it almost too late. So it was in Dellach that I had to
resume. On the previous day I had taken a midday train to
Spittal. I had chosen the Villach rather than the Salzburg route:
I wanted to see again the spectacular climb to Semmering and
the descent across the plain to Klagenfurt, past the spectacular
citadel of Hochosterwitz.

The Semmering climb was through murk and mist with
the impact of autumn dominant. As we left St Veit an der
Glan the train shuddered to a halt in a tunnel and, after a long
wait, shunted back into the station to proceed on an alternative
route. Accordingly, we were half an hour late into Klagenfurt,
time lost and never recovered. So it was dark when I reached
Spittal and pursued the familiar path through Schloss Porcia
park to reach the High Street and the Erlebnis Post Hotel
(+43 (0)4762 2217).

Having supped, slept and had an early breakfast I returned
to the station to catch the 07.37 bound for Lienz, which put

me down in Dellach at 8.14 a.m. As I surveyed the deserted platform I felt the unreality of what I was attempting; only by persistence and good fortune could I achieve my desire to reach the Südtirol.

My first impression was of the chill. It was either freezing or close to it and I was glad to have a new alpaca jersey between my waterproof jacket and my cotton polo neck. I had had the straps of my rucksack padded by the upholsterer in Devizes and had cut its contents to a minimum. By these devices I hardly felt its weight as I joined the westbound way. But the staff that had been with me since Melk had gone – I should never have entrusted it to Geanina-Maria – and I only successfully replaced it on the third attempt, upgrading with each replacement. The third selection was a fine dry hazel, the end of a line of sticks marking a verge. Once I had tested it and not found it wanting, I felt that at last my journey had begun.

A curious relationship develops between the Jakobsweg pilgrim and his staff or stick. My first was a second-rate hazel, the best I could cut in Felicitas' garden. I had lost it through exhaustion in the ticket office at Melk station. Its replacement was a hazel chosen from a bunch cut at home for moving cattle or controlling them in the yard. It was a fine stick, decorated with a Jakobsweg sticker given me by the girl in the Melk tourist office. That became a casualty when lodged with Geanina-Maria between my visits. The Dellach stick is now lodging safely with Aleksandra. When on the path my stick is my most precious possession. We are together every moment of the day. At night we share a room. The stick hauls me up the steeps and saves me when I lose my balance. The stick becomes the guarantor of my well-being. Its loss would portend trouble ahead. That there has always been this special relationship is evidenced by Wilhelm Müller's poem "Das Wirtshaus", immortalised by Schubert's setting in *Winterreise*. The hero, denied a place even in the graveyard, turns to defiance:

> "Nun weiter denn, nur weiter,
> Mein treuer Wanderstab!"

My target was Lienz, a distance of 35 kilometres, with a ten-hour time estimate. I was full of confidence as it was a glorious day of bright sunshine and majestic scenery. The morning's walk was through forest paths above the valley floor. Below ran the mighty Drau and, beyond that, the railway and the main road, but high on the left bank all was peace and quiet.

My stick, which I had acquired outside Rassnig, carried me on to the next settlement, Stein, achieved after more than an hour of steady walking. Another steady hour through the woods took me to the point on the map marked Schloss Stein. This schloss proved a mystery. Although the map marks it as being directly on the way, I never had even a glimpse. At one point, outside a farm, there was a finger arrow to the schloss but I rejected what was an immediate uphill climb since the downward path was the dominant one and was endorsed by the familiar shell sign. My subsequent sense of failure was reinforced by a wayside shrine erected as a memorial to Princess Orsini und Rosenberg (née Gräfin von Goëss) and her husband the Prince, who had soon followed her to the grave, one dying in 2004 and the other in 2005. Since my return to Stein I have checked the Internet, which confirms the existence of Schloss Stein and that it is the seat of the family and has been so since the 17th century. The accompanying photograph shows that the schloss is perched like an eagle's nest on top of a pinnacle and thus easy to miss in a wooded landscape.

Unfortunately, I had not thought to photograph the shrine. Indeed, my camera was still deep in my rucksack. When I realised the missed opportunity I set to to capture my surroundings. As I walked on from the shrine I recorded the Drau Valley running between snow-capped alpine mountains on each side. There was a brisk west wind blowing cold off the high snow slopes of the mountain. The blue skies were reflected in the rushing waters of the Drau. The house, sitting below the towering mountain in the photograph included in the plate section, is in Pflügen.

After three hours of glorious walking in the forest or along its edge I reached Waidach. This is the only substantial settlement between Dellach and Lavant. I photographed the church spire to show its substance.

The morning had shown that hereabouts the Jakobsweg is very poorly way-marked and sometimes waymarks are more crucial in townships than in the wilds. My path descended towards the town but then required a U-turn to find an exit to the west of the town. I only accomplished this thanks to a *Gasthof* marked on the map and named as Stöcklmühl. My heart rejoiced at the sight. Not only had I orientated but I had the prospect of a drink. Commonly a walk on forest paths at best leads you through one or two villages but they might as well not be there for all that they offer the pilgrim. Thus I was in need of liquid as the day had warmed. I tried the door of Stöcklmühl but a grumpy girl refused to sell me either coffee or water. As I walked away a woman, obviously the owner, drew up in a smart car. When I complained to her at the lack of any waymark she proudly showed me the *Jakobsmuschel* nailed in complete obscurity to a fence behind bushes. I left her without much gratitude and found both sun and shelter from the biting wind in a timberyard where I ate the piece that I had prepared at breakfast.

On from Waidach the terrain did not much alter. An hour and a half of easy walking along the forest edge brought me to Flaschberg. I took a photograph which shows the approach to the village. All over Austria those who shoot – and it is mainly roe deer that they shoot – construct hides elevated about three metres and commanding a good field of fire over pasture or woodland glades into which the deer are likely to emerge to feed at dawn or dusk. The pasture approaching Flaschberg is covered by such a hide.

Thereon the path diverged from the course of the Drau to traverse first Unter- and then Oberpirkach. Soon thereafter my route returned to the river and for a long two-hour slog followed the course of the *Radweg*. These cycle paths are very popular and generally follow the course of a great river, such as the Danube through central Austria and the Drau the length of Austria's southern border. The *Radwege* are impeccably signposted in contrast to their poorer relation, the footpath. They break my heart and spirit. They are invariably some 2 metres in width and tarmacked. Often they run straight as a die for 2 kilometres or more and their prospects are unforgiving.

Of course this is only the debit account. On the credit side you never doubt or question the direction of travel. They are close companions to the beautiful rivers and they surge through magnificent scenery. Moreover, it is often possible to avoid the tarmac by walking what is usually a narrow verge to one side or the other.

So this was the nature of the long walk from Oberpirkach to a bridge that crossed the river and the railway to carry a minor road to Lengberg. At the Lengberg bridge the Jakobsweg veered left away from the river to reach and encircle Lavant until rejoining the Drau *Radweg* opposite Dölsach. From that point there was a walk of perhaps two hours' duration along the *Radweg* and the river to the very centre of Lienz.

Consulting my map I saw the opportunity to avoid the detour around Lavant and its outskirts by simply continuing the riverside walk from the point of departure to the point of return. Indeed, shortly before the point of return I could see that there was the road from Lavant to Dölsach which crossed both the river and the railway en route to Dölsach. Any departure from the orthodox route carries a risk which must be justified. The justification for this deviation was twofold. First, I had no time left to reach Lienz by the orthodox route. Second, I had not the stamina to achieve it either. By taking the Dölsach road I could soon reach a side turning that led to Dölsach station. I had a timetable which suggested there would be a train for Lienz at half past the hour.

This manoeuvre worked as I had hoped. Taking the main road I was able to cross river and railway. After a while I found the station road. On the platform was one other traveller, which encouraged my belief in the timetable. Sure enough, on the half hour the train came, and six minutes later we reached the terminus at Lienz.

I had booked into the Hotel Sonne in the Südtiroler Platz (+43 (0)4852 63311). A friendly taxi driver gave me directions, but even with his aid I wandered the town in the evening light before discovering my goal. The hotel is large and reasonably well appointed. I was given an excellent room with, oh joy, a bath and not a shower. I had walked nine hours and it was my first day so a long hot bath was a necessity. Back at the reception I discovered that I could not eat in but was directed to an ambitious modern restaurant in the square called, for some reason, "The Garage". Extreme exertion destroys appetite and I had only a soup and a vegetable starter. It was the mineral water and wine that I was really after. And so soon to bed.

I had taken some photographs just before and just after four o'clock. First as I crossed the river towards Dölsach I photographed the Drau both upstream and downstream; the latter is in the plate section. Next, approaching the bridge, I was very taken with the mountain tops to the south. For suddenly I noticed that we had left alpine mountains and were now meeting for the first time the strange jagged dental peaks of the Dolomites.

☞

Day 23 – 25 October 2017 – Lienz to Thal
THE NEXT DAY, Wednesday 25 October, should have seen me another 30 kilometres west in Strassen but I was tired after

such a long first day and Lienz is the principal, and perhaps the oldest, town of the Östtirol. I could not simply walk on. The breakfast room was busy at its opening with businessmen preparing for a day's work. I took my time and as ever prepared a piece to carry on the way. After breakfast I located the tourist office and the conveniently adjacent post office. Behind the counter in the tourist office I found a lady of intelligence and experience who provided reassuring information, including rail services from Südtirol to Vienna. It seems that there is at least an hourly service from Spittal to Innichen, also known as San Candido. From there the line runs westward to reach Brenner and then north to Innsbruck. However, there seems to be a separate service and timetable west from Innichen. For when the river valley of the Drau terminates just west of Innichen, the river valley of the Rienz, westward flowing, takes over.

This same efficient and determined lady then tackled my immediate need, arranging for me to stay overnight at a private house in Thal, an achievable target even if I lingered in Lienz until early afternoon.

Tourism in East and South Tyrol is intense through the high summer and then from Christmas for winter sports. In the dead months between, the tourist offices, still well staffed, are there to give undivided and generous time to the needy.

Having bought my stamps at the post office I had only to tour the churches for postcards. In Lienz there is no shortage of medieval churches. Just off the main square, on Muchargasse, I visited the convent church, Franziskanerkirche. At the end of the street there was a second medieval church, Klösterle, the Convent Church of the Dominican Sisters, with an ancient house and blacksmith's forge on the other side. West of the convent church is the Pfarrbrücke, the bridge that leads across the river to the 14th-century parish church of St Andrä, which holds an elevated position. Its graveyard is enhanced by a chapel decorated by a famous, local, late-19th century painter, Albin Egger-Lienz. It was shut. The church itself provided the necessary postcards, a view of its bold spire against the backdrop of the Dolomites. Thence is a good walk to St Michael's and, returning to the centre, Spitalskirche. St Michael's is the most distinguished architecturally, with its intricate Gothic rib-vaulted ceiling. The little Spitalskirche east of the main square has been given over to the Russian orthodox community. Why there should be such a community in Lienz I do not know.

Overall, Lienz is a truly charming town: there is very little that grates and very little modern development. So the overall impression is of old-fashioned provincialism. It would make a good base from which to explore the wonderful country that surrounds it.

It was nearly two o'clock before I found my way out of town, crossing the Drau, which, in the middle of town, had picked up water from its confluence with the River Insel. I could see from my map that in navigating the suburbs I needed to pass the town sports centre. That I achieved but I followed the road rather than the footpath to reach Amlach. That was pure carelessness on my part. The footpath would have been much more pleasant and would have avoided the disaster to come.

As I came into the village I settled in the bus shelter to eat my piece. Then, walking on, I came upon the village *Gasthof* facing the square. Either I turned left or right. The left turn looked right and felt right. Had I consulted the map I would have seen that these attractions were false. Only when I reached the next village of Ulrichsbichl did I realise that if I continued I would end in Lavant. This 100 per cent error cost me 2 wasted kilometres and much frustration. Even when I returned to the point of error the unappealing right turn offered miles of doubt and uncertainty, unresolved by frequent enquiry and voluble advice, until I reached the essential bridge that would carry me across the Drau into Leisach.

The Drau Valley has many different aspects. Sometimes it is ample with water meadows and crops on either side, but here, immediately west of Lienz, it narrows to little more than a defile with plunging cliffs on either side and scarcely room for road, rail and cycle paths. Standing on the bridge and looking westwards the prospect takes on a dramatic tension as the walk ahead offers nothing but the penetration of the lowering Galitzenklamm Gorge.

But first Leisach: a pleasant village and from it easy to discern the side road running westward along the slopes above the main transits below. As I reached the outskirts I saw a remarkable barn of some antiquity and quality. At each of the four corners rose a pillar in which local stone is roughly jointed. But the real artistry lies in the facade, with two lancets surmounted by a star and above the star a delicate Corpus Christi. This I was pleased to photograph and in my excitement I left the spot with my guidebook sitting safe on the wall opposite. I walked on a mile or so climbing uphill all the way until I stopped to check the route. Dawning disaster! Where had I lost the guidebook? Fortunately I knew I had needed it to navigate Leisach. Then came a more refined memory. I had put it on the wall to take the photograph. There was nothing for it but to go back. I had stuck the Post-it with the details of my overnight stay on the flyleaf. I dropped my rucksack and jogged downhill to the village. There it was waiting for me. By way of celebration I took a photograph of this wonderful barn to give context to the photographs of the embellishments on the facade.

These blunders had cost me time I could ill afford. It was now past three o'clock and I was little more than 3 kilometres out of Lienz. I had a long field walk, spurning the farm roads where I could. Wherever the farm road curved into an arc I took to the fields and created the bowstring between the two points of the bent bow. With my eyes I followed the path of any passing vehicle, which fixed for me the distant point for which I should aim. This method is not without risk since the dead ground may conceal a parting of the way. The state of the land was most favourable. The grazing season had passed and there was therefore no sward on the pasture. Almost every piece of land had been plastered either with farmyard manure or farmyard slurry. This made for an easy, if pungent, surface. Not only did I benefit from the shortcuts but I was also relieving the soreness that prolonged walking on tarmac causes.

So, making the best pace I could, I reached Lienzer Klause at about four o'clock. This was once the summer residence of a bishop and has a most noble gatehouse which provides entry to within the extensive walls of the fort. However, most that is visible is ruin and the way passes straight through the domain.

Thereafter the going became tough, with two marked climbs and descents. In Glöre I asked for help and was reassured that I could not fail to find my destination, Thal-Römerweg 13 (+43 (0)4855 8551). Suddenly it was easy to get within shouting distance of my destination – but which of the several houses in Thal and then of those on the Römerweg? It was dusk and I was baffled, when coming fast downhill from behind I heard thundering footsteps and much shouting. I assumed it was the local lunatic and paid no heed. It was in fact Herr Unterweger and his son who had deduced that I must be the wanderer sent by the tourist office. They ushered me into a house that I would not have myself selected. Their continued shouting did not please the lady of the house who gave them, and me, a grumpy reception. Clearly the lady of the house was an antique collector: every corner, every surface was adorned with some precious find. No doubt these were the fruits of her B&B business. Although she had a forbidding manner, she was not hostile and agreed to make me a soup, accompanied by dark bread and brown beer. That was all I needed since I was dehydrated by the two climbs and descents. She sat with me as I ate and I was surprised to find how easily I kept up my conversational end. I slept well and the next morning found a minimal breakfast before bidding them farewell at about nine. While she was granite, he was warm and friendly, a delightful eccentric. There could be no doubt as to who was boss in that household. The weather on this second day had been grey but at least dry. A consequence was that I took photographs only of the two points of interest and none of the surroundings.

☞

Day 24 – 26 October 2017 – Thal to Heinfels

THE NEXT DAY (Thursday) I set off after an early breakfast and immediately encountered Thal railway station. That made me realise that I was on the wrong side of the track and needed to get to the river. Given the steep embankment this was no easy task but, guided by a friendly local, I found my way to a good path along the Drau. This whole day could be dedicated to the Drau. Nowhere was I more than a few metres from the river. Sometimes I was on green fields, sometimes on the *Radweg*. Sometimes the way lay on the right bank, sometimes on the left. Almost at once there was a bridge carrying me from the right to the left bank and I took a picture both upstream and downstream, illustrating that what had been once such a mighty river was now no more than a river to fish; indeed it might have been a scene in the Scottish Highlands. I encountered two men in an expensive estate car and discovered that one was the fishing manager and the other a journalist from a German fly-fishing magazine. An hour further on the river looked smaller but then towards mid-morning it had a placid air.

So I progressed to eat my piece in a timber yard at Fontnell. I reclined in the sun and watched a myriad of bees feeding off ox-eye daisies and a flutter of goldcrests pecking at teasel heads. I photographed both. Here the country was less dramatic. Hills had replaced mountains, between which stretched a broad valley with the Drau reduced to little more than a wide ditch. The autumn colours were special. Everywhere the golden larch was intermingled with the sombre pines. None of my photographs caught the brilliance of the golden larch. I skirted Abfaltersbach and then passed Geselhaus where I was too shy to take a proper portrait of an old farm woman off to feed her stock and passing the time of day with a neighbour, both leaning on bicycles.

Thereafter the Jakobsweg took a long half circle to reveal the delights of Strassen. Again I declined the circular walk, seeing that there was the dependable river route, this time on the left bank while the railway ran on the right bank. Having rejoined the official route I made on until reaching the railway station in Tassenbach. Here the map was plainly misleading. It marked a path to the left of the railway line. The path to the left of the railway led only to a camping site, Lienzer Dolomiten, which I certainly did not want. I was lucky to encounter a gentle Italian, who in his own tongue urged me to the right bank of the railway and to the left bank of the river.

That simple solution bought me soon to Rabland. I had been walking for some eight hours. The weather had improved and it was brilliant sun and warmth. I was very dehydrated. Oh, what simple pleasures there are for the weary walker! Here I reached a track crossing the railway and the river and leading to the most bustling, cheerful café I ever saw. The outside tables were thronged with families and couples enjoying the sunshine and the fact that it was some sort of national holiday. The lady swiftly bought me a mineral water and a caffè latte. Beyond that she reassured me that I would find the Sporthotel at the crossroads in Panzendorf about 2 kilometres distant. This crossroads lay in the shadow of Heinfels Castle. The castle was dominated by a huge crane to aid the restoration but it made a romantic sight, which I photographed as I swung up the side road to reach my destination.

The Sporthotel was enormous and unappetising. Fortunately opposite was a bustling *Gasthof*, Der Brückenwirt (+43 (0)4842 6336). It was catering for a large coach party but the kind lady owner was quick to offer me a very nice bedroom. I smoked a cigar on the balcony in the rays of the setting sun. On her recommendation, since only the coach party would get a meal, I walked downhill to an exceptional kitchen where I was lucky to get the last table (Ansitz Burg Heimfels: +43 (0)4842 20094). It was the best meal of the week: a very Austrian dish of rösti with much venison stirred in. It was their week for all things wild, or at least all wild mammals. I returned to my bed and slept very sound.

☞

Day 25 – 27 October 2017 – Heinfels to Toblach via Sillian and Innichen

THE NEXT MORNING (Friday), I found that the *Gasthof* stands by the ancient bridge over the river. It is a wondrous construction, all in wood, roofed and embellished within with sacred images. Without there are scarlet splashes from the window boxes. This tradition of a covered bridge seems to be particularly Austrian and this is the best that I have seen. I photographed the inside and out together with the Corpus Christi and the St John Nepomuk sculpted in wood. On the Corpus the gilding of the loincloth was a striking feature; see the plate section.

Uplifted by the bridge, I walked the main road from Heinfels to Sillian, where in the parish church I found the mummified corpse of St Fermo. How he had ended in such a comparatively obscure place I could not explain. Indeed, the claim seems to me dubious. St Fermo is particularly venerated in Verona and his remains are believed to lie in the church there which is also dedicated to him. Nearby I found a typically reassuring Austrian chemist who armed me for the fight against my cold and cough. I easily found the side road that led south to cross the river to join the Weg, which swung sometimes on one side of the river and sometimes on the other. I captured the landscape and the rich farmhouses. I also caught the sacred Drau as it ran through the forest with the Dolomites raising their craggy heads to the sky. This was only twenty minutes from the border, which I crossed at 11.24 a.m. There was a board mounted on a pole marking the border but nothing more momentous to mark the passage from Austria into Italy, nor was there anything thereafter to put Austria behind. Culture, tradition and language remained steadfastly Austrian or Tyrolian. As I walked on I took photographs to show the valley overshadowed to the south by the Dolomites, past Obervierschach (in Italian, Versciaco di Sopra) with its bold church. Across the fields I went to enter Innichen (San Candido) at the north end of the town.

Innichen is an ancient settlement of comparative importance. It would be easy to pass through the length of the town without chancing on anything of much note. So I stumbled about, failing to find the museum, the church or the information office. The last was particularly obscure since it was located in an ancient building heavily shrouded in scaffolding. A local clearly thought I was mentally defective as I repeatedly failed to find it and repeatedly returned to him for further directions. When I did find it I was pleased to see that it would apparently reopen at three o'clock. Sylvia's Café across the square looked most inviting and I spent a pleasant twenty minutes waiting there. In the tourist office I had the undivided attention of a bright, intelligent girl who told me about her town and did excellent research into trains from Mühlbach in Südtirol to Vienna. Finally she gave a thoughtful answer to my question: would the Südtirol ever return to Austria? "No," she said, "we have the best of both worlds and anyway it is all too long ago." She kindly offered to guide me from her office through the town to the westbound way. I arrogantly said that I had my map and therefore had no need. Of course, I soon got hopelessly lost and only recovered from half an hour of frustration and hopeless approaches to strangers when a boy on a building site urged me to climb higher. I didn't believe him but I did what he said and, without faith or hope, caught sight of the Monet blue and yellow colours of the Jakobsweg badge. I was so relieved and moved that I photographed it at 3.23 p.m. I had left the tourist office at 2.16 p.m. That was the cost of my arrogance. I took a photograph of one of the squares in Innichen with the Dolomites rising dramatically above.

The way from Innichen to Toblach is a fair one, along the valley and through a forest of pine and larch. Indeed, on the map it is marked "Larchwald". But along this stretch I was preparing for a momentous sight, Drau-Ursprung: the source of the Drau. It is hard for me to convey what this meant to me. The Jakobsweg had first met the Drau in Maribor, and I myself had first met it in Lavamünd. The river flows for perhaps a thousand kilometres before it meets the Danube and marches on with that greater river to reach the Black Sea, ever flowing eastward. At Klagenfurt, or more precisely at Annabrücke, I had seen the vast *Wels*, or catfish, that had been fished from its depths. I had seen the great *Kraftwerk*, which had turned great stretches of the river into Stausee. I had seen it gradually dwindle to the dimensions of a Scottish salmon river and then ultimately to little more than a broad ditch dividing two pastures. Now here on my very own pilgrim way, equally between Innichen and Toblach, I would bow my head before its very source. Approaching the spot with the sun breaking through the clouds, I tried to catch the brilliant gold of the larches. Then I was there. It looked like any one of a million brooks trickling down the hillside, surely like all the others about to join some greater stream? But no, this was no commonplace brook. This was the source and origin of one of Europe's mighty rivers, which would grow as it travelled through Italy, Austria, Slovenia, Croatia and Hungary. I photographed it from on high as it reached the Jakobsweg. I chased it up the hill at 4.03 p.m. and further up at 4.04 p.m. until it became plain that it was almost from heaven. Returning to the path I photographed it as it flowed away downhill at 4.06 p.m. That was for me the highlight of the day, indeed the highlight of the week, the highlight of the walk. I have chosen one of these for the plate section.

As I walked on I noticed very strange earthworks in what is, after all, a national forest. White boulders are spread over considerable distances and without apparent gain for so much effort, and there are nearby huge earthworks perhaps from which the scattered stone was lifted. It remains a mystery.

As I approached Toblach the sun was breaking through and touching the Dolomite fangs. I took a general view and then the enlargement. My final photograph on reaching the huge youth hostel on the outskirts of Toblach was of two trees intertwined, a pine and a larch.

Just as Innichen is uplifting, so Toblach is deeply depressing. It is now a massive holiday resort thriving on both a summer and a winter season. The main street flows north–south and stretches more than a kilometre from the youth hostel to the church square. On both sides of the street, and tightly packed, are huge hotels. Towards the centre I found the tourist office, still open, but clearly not pleased to get a late customer. To my amazement I was told that of all these hotels only one was open: Nocker (+39 (0)474 972242). I made them book me a room, although it was less than 50 metres to walk. Beside the hotel was a butcher's shop, also Nockers, and out of curiosity I went in. The businesslike elderly shopkeeper had the advantage since she at once perceived that I was the overnight guest from the tourist office, for she owned both the butcher's and the hotel. So there was much confusion on my part before I finally found myself ensconced in a comfortable room with a balcony. In a practical way she suggested that I must buy provisions in the shop to eat in my room. Back in the shop she supplied me with half a bottle of red wine, some rolls and some cheese. So although solitary I was comfortable and on the next morning there was a passable breakfast.

☞

Day 26 – 28 October 2017 – Toblach to Bruneck

IT WAS SATURDAY, and before leaving Toblach I explored the town. Its development is extraordinary. To the ancient town centre the 20th century has attached a heavy, straight tail running perhaps a mile south from the town. As the tail depressed me, so the town, once I reached it, uplifted me. It is dominated by a great church, not so much beautiful as classic mid-18th century and therefore impressive. The facing square and surrounding streets are fit neighbours, creating a dignified provincial township. The post office that I sought out for stamps was buried in the bowels of an ancient town house of the early 17th or late 16th century. The buildings were so huddled that the town was hard to photograph. Having done my best I set out down the tail until I met the start of the departing Jakobsweg near the station.

The morning walk ran through the valley with wooded slopes rising to my left. Here, from 1908 to 1910, Mahler rented a farmhouse for each summer season. Here he composed two symphonies (the ninth and the unfinished tenth) and *Das Lied von der Erde*. I photographed the house and the slopes of pine and larch beyond. Another photograph looking westward illustrates how abruptly the Dolomites ended at Toblach to be replaced by wooded hills.

It was past midday when I skirted Niederdorf. There I was taken by a stand of trees in rich autumn colours. As I skirted the edge of Welsberg I photographed my new friend, the River Rienz. I was now about halfway to the day's destination and soon reached the Olanger Stausee. I suspect that this attractive lake was formed by damming the Rienz. In the afternoon sunshine the water was a vivid blue and I photographed my first sight of the lake, then a mid-view and finally a backward glance. In the plate section is the last of these. As I walked the lakeside I had a call from Geanina-Maria to say that she had had to cancel her return and would not be in Vienna with me on Monday. Once again I was in turmoil and crisis.

At the end of the water there were no signs and little choice but to follow the road or climb a steep bank to reach the edge of Oberolang. This was the prelude to a very unattractive section of the route. There was a road sign for the panoramic route to Bruneck from Oberolang but I couldn't risk it; my map showed plainly that I had to traverse Ober-, Mitter- and Niederolang. Once again there was a complete absence of waymarking, but at least plenty of people in the streets on this Saturday afternoon. Somewhere in Mitterolang I went wrong and eventually found myself by a railway station. At least I was able to orientate myself and see the need for a long loop to get back to achieve the outskirts of Niederolang. From there I walked on with ever increasing urgency and uncertainty. It was getting late and I dared not make another mistake. I was almost in despair when I came upon a man with the kindest face, who listened, understood and reassured me that I had only to continue on. That I did, following the river and knowing that I had about an hour and a half of daylight which should suffice to reach Bruneck. My last photograph of the day showed the valley of the Olangs and the re-emergence of distant mountains.

I had passed Percha in the distance for I was on the footpath well south of the town, the river and the railway. According to my map the path would lead me on forwards to the south until, avoiding all suburbs, I arrived in the heart of Bruneck straight out of the *Wald*. But it was not to be. Suddenly there was a sign closing the footpath and signalling a deviation. I could ignore the sign and hope for the best. But surely if I followed the deviation there would be signs? I had time neither for error nor for a circuitous deviation. In the end I chose the deviation. Just when I needed luck none came my way. There were no signs. I found a tarmac track but it led uphill and seemingly north-easterly. As I hurried on I saw in the dusk a huge farmhouse surmounted by a castellated cupola. In other circumstances it would have demanded closer inspection. It was surrounded by equally impressive farm buildings. As I approached I heard what I thought were the sounds of men working and I hurried for help. It was an auditory mirage. The only sounds came from animals clanking about in the building or in the yard. I forged on past the farm buildings and as I pressed on and up the hill there was just the last glow of light on the western horizon. I was lost and without prospect of reprieve. As the night fell pitch dark my road bore right and joined the E66. The great house I had passed was something like Perland. It was an ideal distance from Bruneck, close but remote. The main road had no footpaths, traffic was hurtling by and I could only press tight against the metal barrier as I went forward. After a dangerous kilometre I reached the road junction for Bruneck. Here again there was nowhere for the walker but at least less traffic. It was a long mile to reach the roundabout that brought me the welcome sign "*Zentrum*".

Even then the walk to the centre was long but at least straight, all the way along Dantestrasse. Arriving at the bridge over the Rienz I asked for the Goldene Rose (+39 (0)474 537780) only to find it was staring at me from the other side. This was a happy choice. It had been the grandest hotel in Bruneck for a hundred years and was full of nice old things, including an erotic painting of a nude on a bed hanging in the hall. I was shown to a palatial suite with a huge balcony, more a deck than a balcony. After a long soak in the huge bath, I descended to enquire for dinner. I was directed to the Weisses Lamm, fully booked, alas, and moved on to the second choice, the Goldenen Löwen. Even here I had to wait half an hour but then made a decent dinner.

☞

Day 27 – 29 October 2017 – Bruneck to Mühlbach

SUNDAY. I HAD arrived too late in Bruneck to catch a vigil mass. There are four churches in Bruneck and the times of mass at all four appear on a notice in the hotel lift. Overnight the clocks had changed to winter time so dawn came at six o'clock and the first mass was at six-thirty in the Capuchin church. I arrived on the dot to find a characteristically plain church, with bare walls and altars raised in dark wood. Mass was taken by two monks. It was comforting and a good start to the day. I ate a good breakfast and set out to tour the town. Bruneck is ancient and extremely attractive. It would be an excellent place from which to explore the surroundings. Not far from the Capuchin church is a baroque church of modest proportions. Walking up the river on either bank eventually leads to the top of the town and the parish church, large, circa 1840 and to my eye unpleasing. At the foot of the castle there is a church with an impressive double onion spire but it is no longer consecrated. Then down the hill you come to the Ursuline convent church. This is perhaps the oldest church in Bruneck. After spending an hour and more locating the churches and admiring the two handsome main streets I had to get on.

Having taken advice from the hotel receptionist I crossed the river and then turned to follow the Rienz on its westward journey. Crossing at the third bridge I headed north to reach the church at Stegen and thence westward through lovely wooded country to reach Fassing. This was just a hamlet in deep farming country. The farms looked very prosperous, one especially with a field full of pedigree Grau heifers. At the farmyard there was a noble black Labrador, big of body and broad of head, just like my dear old Tiber. We made firm friends as I moved through the hamlet, contemplating the route shown on my map, which descended rapidly to half-circle Sonnenburg and then amble up to reach St Nikolaus. Being unsure I asked help from a family of four who were walking down towards me. Having consulted my map and seen the recommended route the father of the family emphatically rejected the orthodox and persuaded me that I should walk up to the head of the village and take the footpath through to Lothen and thence on to St Nikolaus. There could be no doubt that what he recommended was a great deal shorter than the official route and so I took it. Again it was a very pretty way and in Lothen I had to spurn an alternative that led up to Pfalzen. In Lothen there was a farm selling cheese at €9 a kilo. I was very tempted, despite my rule against packing anything unnecessary in my rucksack. I was spared temptation since I could make no one in the farm buildings answer my call. And so on with what was to be a long walk through St Nikolaus and then on for perhaps an hour and a half to reach Kiens. It was a lovely, lonely walk and towards its end I cut a huge corner, walking straight across a pasture. As soon as I completed the manoeuvre I felt anxious. The onward path seemed to be clearly heading north-east. I retraced my steps and it was fortunate I did so as I found that, concealed from view, the footpath had continued straight through a wood leaving the road behind.

Further on I saw below me a huge and beautifully maintained farm with two young people walking rapidly down to join my path. They walked faster than me, but I do not always follow the road and by cutting the hairpins sometimes I led until again overtaken. We continued thus until I stopped to photograph Kiens lying below and picturesque in the distance. I also photographed the utterly traditional tool for draining a forest track, a hollowed log laid across the path; see the plate section. I photographed this one because I had never seen a clearer example. I suspect that it had been freshly laid and had not yet bedded in.

So it was that I reached the edge of Kiens at about half past one. The track simply dropped me between two factories on the main road leading to St Sigmund. St Sigmund was my destination but the main road was not an acceptable medium. I could see from my map that I needed to be well north of the main road and up in the woods. As I surveyed the higher ground

I saw a large church standing prominently on the hillside. I seemed to have no alternative but to try it out. It proved to be a much longer walk than the sight of it had suggested. When I reached the church I found that I was embraced by a deserted village scene. I cast left and right and then saw an attractively dressed lady but with orange hair and past her prime. More important, she was kind and took great pains to set me right. In the event I did not do as she suggested but walked a little higher and suddenly there was the blue and yellow waymark. What a joy after such uncertainty! I set off on a long woodland walk which suddenly died at the far side of a farmyard. The cause of death was a new made *Forststrasse* which was firmly closed with many "entry forbidden" signs. I walked back to the farmyard and fortunately the wildly barking dog brought the farmer. What could I do? "Oh, take the new road, ignore the signs." I did just that and fared well until, at a junction, the new road suddenly and inexplicably ended in a thicket. I had to climb back laboriously to the junction and then cast off on an old footpath which ultimately brought me down to the E66. I declined another half-circle deviation on my map and headed straight along the E66 to reach the point at Sigmunderhof where the half-circle deviation returned to the main road, which I crossed and headed off for Ilstern. Thereafter was a long walk beside the railway, beside the Rienz, beside the E66, but always in pleasant woods away from these arteries to reach Vintl and on along the shores of the Mühlbacher Stausee to Mühlbach.

I had started late and the day was fading, so I doubted I could do better than Vintl. It was with high spirits, therefore, that I reached a bridge which would lead to Obervintl. Just before the bridge I met a kind man and asked for reassurance. He assured me that I was almost at journey's end: I could be in Obervintl in five minutes and in Niedervintl in twenty. I took him at his word, not looking at my map, but in reality it was a long walk from the bridge to reach Obervintl and a very long walk to reach the bridge that would lead into Niedervintl. I walked on and on in the gathering dusk. After an hour I assumed that I must have missed the bridge into Niedervintl. I further assumed that I must be approaching Mühlbach. Neither of these assumptions would have been tenable if I had made a proper study of the map. In the end my folly was revealed when what I had taken to be Mühlbach proved to be just Niedervintl. I crossed the Rienz by the bridge but the way suddenly died and I had to cross the railway and trespass to get into the town. I saw a girl outside a house and asked for a *Gasthof*. She waved me on with many a smile. I then found a man who was running a pizzeria. I asked him for a *Gasthof* and he said, "Come in here." "But I want a bed," I said. "Oh, you won't find a bed here in Vintl," he replied, "you must get on to Mühlbach." It was now dark and I was exhausted. I headed for the railway station. Unfortunately it was the Sunday service and there was only one train an hour. I then found the bus stop and consulted the timetable. The expected bus did not appear. I returned to the railway station. There was a man on the platform talking volubly to his telephone. That seemed a good omen and at 5.55 p.m. in came a train, which within four minutes of rapid running put me into Mühlbach. While waiting at the station in Vintl I had smartly booked a room through Booking.com at Gasthof Seppi (+39 (0)47284 9701).

Searching up from the station I found the hotel in Richtergasse, overlooking the Kirche Platz. So fifteen minutes after making the online booking I was at reception. A disorganised man showed me a room. I asked for food and he waved me casually to a pizzeria, as though it were next door.

When I eventually found the pizzeria it proved to be a most jolly place. It was having a Mexican week but I managed to get a Tyrolian dish of three different dumplings followed by an affogato.

When I returned to the hotel at five to eight everything was locked, shut, barred and dark. I shouted, I bellowed. Eventually the blowsy proprietor stuck his head out of an upper window and rather testily agreed to come down to let me in. He then disappeared and I went to my room. Horror: it was one of those doors that automatically locked itself and could only be opened by the key. Since I had not needed to lock I had left the key inside. I hurried to the door through which the proprietor had disappeared and thundered on it to no avail. I went back to the street and bellowed, to no avail. I was facing the prospect of shelter but no bed. In desperation I went outside, collected handfuls of gravel and flung them at the window from which he had previously appeared. After the third cannonade he appeared again and with an extremely ill grace admitted me to my room.

The next morning I did not linger. After a quick cup of coffee I headed for the station, which I found not without difficulty. At least I was in time to catch the 08.00, which took me on to Franzensfeste, where I changed and managed a train which took me all the way to Innsbruck. There I had only fifteen minutes to wait for the Vienna express. So I was back in Opernring by three o'clock with time to see the wonderful Raphael Exhibition at the Albertina. Thereafter I was on my own. Geanina-Maria was in Bucharest and Felicitas was in Bavaria! I had even tried Geanina-Maria's friend Aura, who had been sent to pick me up at Schwechat the previous weekend, but she was in Milan.

On the following morning I headed for Schechwat. I missed the Stadtbahn by one minute, waited thirty minutes for the next and that was then fifteen minutes late into the airport. So I had little time to spare to catch the 11.25 flight home.

In these six days of walking I had covered some 152 kilometres. I had seldom walked six days consecutively before. All in all I managed well. My weakness is midday optimism leading to afternoon crisis. By that I mean that if the morning goes well I then assume that I have time in hand and that the afternoon will be trouble-free. But often it is in the afternoon that I lose my way or encounter testing going. As optimism fades, the spirit fails. What should be uplifting becomes a penance. My body stiffens with the tiredness. I lose my balance. My only fluency is the monotonous left, right onward motion. I must learn to keep time in reserve to provide for the unexpected and to avoid risks that come with the dark.

I was very lucky with the weather; most days sunny and no days of rain. It was cold – frosty, even – at eight in the morning, but by two o'clock I was shedding my alpaca. Some days I badly needed my sunglasses. This last week of October was as late as is wise. The days were already short enough. The deciduous leaf was largely fallen. It was mainly the larch that made the autumn colour. The maize crop was entirely in. The pastures were smooth as a golf-course fairway. Either they had been grazed down or they had been mown and then every field had been enriched either by dung or slurry, whether it was pasture or ploughland, so at no time of year would the walking surface be better. My only reservation concerns the molehills. I have never in my life seen such a proliferation of molehills. Perhaps they are uncontrolled but I wonder how the farmers can make silage with so much soil bound to be gathered into the baler.

So often I have said to myself: "This is the finest country I have seen anywhere on my walk." I would not hesitate to say that of the Ost- and Südtirol.

☞

ALL IN ALL, however, 2017 was a year of setbacks and disappointment. My fall reduced an average of seventeen walking days to six. The support I received from Geanina-Maria was reduced to zero. I still had a long way to go to reach my goal.

VIENNA TO STEINACH

It was not until May 2018 that I returned to the Jakobsweg. The crossing from South to North Tyrol ascends to the Brenner Pass and I did not want to be again caught in a snowstorm. I had spent 8 May at the Judicial Academy outside Bratislava presenting an offer to train Slovak judges in international family law. Before leaving Bratislava I had spent an hour or more with Andrea perfecting a new contract covering twelve months from May 2018 and meeting again my excellent interpreter, Henrietta. I also met for the first time Katerina, with whom I had been exchanging somewhat testy emails for the previous twelve months.

After meeting the board and the director of the Judicial Academy we had returned to Bratislava and discussed our future programme of work. After parting from Andrea I walked to the station, via Hotel Tatra, to catch the 14.38 to Vienna. You might think that between two capital cities there would be an express train connection. But Bratislava is still treated by ÖBB as some provincial town to which a purely local train service suffices.

Aura had elected to keep faith with some office party and so I found a six o'clock mass in the Michaelskirche, it being the

239

VIENNA

MÜHLBACH

STERZING

GRIES

STEINACH

Ascension Day vigil. I had supper at Albertina and an early bed at Opernring.

☞

Day 28 – 10 May 2018 – Vienna to Mühlbach

ASCENSION DAY IS a public holiday in Austria and I offered to defer my departure for the Südtirol. But Aura was content to spend her free day at Oberlaa. Accordingly I left Opernring in good time to catch the 08.25 Lienzerdolomiten, as the daily through train to the capital of the Östtirol is grandiosely marketed. For it is, albeit a through train, a very ordinary service stopping at many stations en route. As I left the hotel it was a glorious May morning and, it being early on a public holiday, there was an empty city offering the subtle and indefinable scents of a late spring day, this being the habitual Austrian plunge from winter into summer with spring acknowledged only by the poets. The train journey was uneventful and we duly arrived in Lienz at 14.01. The local train that would cross the border into South Tyrol did not leave until 14.50 and I used the time to plan in the information office a return journey from Steinach, on the Austrian side of the Brenner Pass. The cross-border train did not go further than Franzensfeste and stopped at every small station en route. The duration of each stop was at the discretion of a lady guard who frequently consulted her watch to avoid early departure and sometimes cancelled her instruction to proceed if she detected a latecomer entering the station. The instruction was given by a blast on her whistle and the flap of a square of green cloth, which, between flaps, she rolled up and pocketed.

Of course I had walked every metre of the way and followed the rail route on my Kompass guide. This exercise I had started in Klagenfurt with many views of the Wörthersee before reaching Villach. From Villach there were many memories before Spittal and then onwards past Kleblach-Lind until we reached Dellach. In the guide, Dellach to Lienz is a one-day stage and to my delight I saw from the train the castle of Stein which I had so foolishly missed on foot. It is a white fortress crowning a rocky crag, and so tightly is it built that an external circumambulation appears impossible.

It is at Lienz that Dolomite crags first appear and they last not much beyond Innichen. As we left Innichen I could see the dwindling of the Drau and then the point of its source clearly revealed even from the train by the extensive earthworks in the forest. Many other memories were awakened as we made our slow way on from Toblach to Bruneck and finally to Vintl. Here, supervised by the lady guard, I was the only passenger to alight. Had I not been here before I doubt I would so easily have found my way from the railway station to resume the Jakobsweg. We had reached Vintl at five o'clock and I reckoned that it was about 10 kilometres all along the Rienz to reach Mühlbach. It was a fine evening and I soon found my stride. It was a good walk, although in the forest there were a number of sharp ascents and descents. I was high in the forest when I caught sight of Mühlbach below. At that moment my mobile rang, an Austrian number that I did not recognise. It was the receptionist at the Hotel Ansitz Kandelburg, anxious to know where I was. He struggled to comprehend that I was approaching on foot. Again, thanks to my previous stay, I found my way past the station and up to the parish church of St Helena and the surrounding square. The Internet had found me a hotel only two doors from its previous choice and its comparative expense was explained by its antiquity and the kitsch with which it was furnished.

The receptionist turned out to be in charge of all departments and was an artist in making his own life easy. I had a good dinner in the restaurant I had used before; indeed, as far as I could see there is no other. My attic bedroom was huge and the adjoining bathroom was well fitted with both bidet and bath.

☞

Day 29 – 11 May 2018 – Mühlbach to Sterzing

I HAD PLANNED an early start, given that I had to make 35 kilometres to reach Sterzing. But it was seven o'clock before I was ready. I knew that there was no breakfast before eight but still I was surprised to find the ground floor dark and deserted. I switched on a few lights and was about to quit when the man of all work sauntered in with supplies from the baker. In a friendly way he made me a passable caffè latte and pressed on me two small croissants weighing not much more than a gram each. They went well with the coffee and I surreptitiously gathered up two aniseed rolls before leaving.

Finding the right exit from a town is crucial to success: it is the first challenge of every day on the Jakobsweg. The hotelier had given me voluble instructions but I had understood not much. I got more from the Kompass guide, which had me leave St Helena to the right and to cross the Valserbrücke. The crossing was a wooden bridge over the noisy torrent of the Vals and I soon found the long deceased Restaurant Bichler. Then I knew for certain that I was on the right path, which made a half circle, dictated by the confluence of the rivers Rienz and Eisack, to reach Aicha. This is a lovely woodland walk, particularly on a May morning. The forest floor was carpeted with wood anemones and other delights including cowslips and wild strawberries. I passed two forest shrines, almost chapels. Between the two were fourteen Stations of the Cross, each carved on a hemisphere of pine, the images proud rather than incised. The cuckoo rang out, not a solitary bird but several, just as in England in my childhood. As I neared Aicha there were many ravens in and above the pine trees with their unmistakable croaking.

On the approach to Aicha there was a grove of Spanish chestnuts, so old that the majority were either dying or dead. But they were marked with the heritage Denkmal badge, which increased their memorability and ensured their continuing preservation.

In the heart of the village I saw an inviting café with tables outside under the awning. Already installed were three young mothers with their offspring, one being in charge of the café. She made me a good cup of coffee, which I felt I had earned after two hours of walking. When I asked for her help she directed me to what should have been a straightforward route on to Franzensfeste.

My walk in and out of Aicha showed that every inch of land was given to fruit: either apples or pears, I was not sure which, or strawberries. The onward walk from Aicha proved problematic. There was of course no marker for the Jakobsweg and the markers for local options gave no clue as to which would favour Franzensfeste as the destination. I chose one option without optimism and with no resulting reward. Despairing, I diverted to a second option, despite its seeming intention to lead me back to Aicha. Then I had the good fortune to see two ladies of a certain age, tanned and fit, rapidly approaching. I appealed to them to rescue me but their response was only to offer to share their map of the regional walking routes. Then a man with a dog appeared, but separated from us by the railway tracks. The two ladies in whom I had put my trust skipped across the tracks, spoke briefly to the man with the dog, then set off at a brisk pace. By the time I had negotiated the crossing they had disappeared. So I turned to the man with the dog and explained my need as best I could. As well as the dog, he had at his feet a substantial cardboard box filled with what looked like the product of a successful visit to the local Lidl. The situation appeared unpromising. I contemplated simply following the railway tracks, which offered the certainty of a direct line to Franzensfeste. However, he took care to understand my bad German, grasped my need and confidently advised a path descending steeply to a junction at which he said I must turn right.

As I followed his instructions my confidence increased. I knew I was heading in the right general direction and after half an hour or more I glimpsed the surface of calm water through the trees below. I dallied with the Kompass map and concluded it must be the Stausee that filled the southern end of Franzensfeste, meeting the last dwellings at a bridge.

I guessed that the lake was not a natural feature but a hydroelectric scheme created by damming the valley, and one of some antiquity since along the edge of the *See* substantial holiday villas had been built. At the head of the *See* was the bridge which carried me across into the town. I followed the main road up to the parish church and opposite it was a most inviting café where I stopped for another latte, more out of necessity than indulgence. My eye was drawn to the garden of the café by the sight of the elderly proprietor returning to the kitchen with a basket full of lettuce but this was nothing to the enormous pink tree peony in fullest bloom on the edge of the café car park. Its importance was clearly not overlooked since a wide silver ribbon had been tied round its extending branches; see the plate section. Having lavished on it the admiration it deserved I left the car park only to see another wonder, a lizard in full flight pursued by a brown rat. Death was hovering until the rat saw me and broke off the chase.

A few metres on and I was tempted by the regular sign for pedestrians and bicycles bound for Brenner. I took this option and walked on through the station yard until the path faltered. When I consulted the Kompass guide I at once saw that I was on the wrong side of the tracks. I should not have been on the town side but above the town at the forest edge. At first I walked through the booking hall and contemplated crossing to the far platform in the hope of finding a way out of the station on the far side. However, the platforms were too well staffed and the risks clearly outweighed the potential reward. So I retraced my steps thinking that at least I had only wasted less than a kilometre. I remembered that immediately ahead, at the point where I had turned onto the cycle route, was a tunnel under the railway. This I now took and shortly found what was clearly the legitimate route arching right and rising. After I had made perhaps a kilometre I saw a man raking newly mown grass off the steep bank. I might have walked on but something prompted me to seek reassurance. First he confirmed that I was indeed on the Jakobsweg but then he gave me the bad news. Ahead lay a massive construction programme, something about a new railway line into Austria. The forest path was now completely closed. Why were there no warning notices, I asked. Indeed, he said, it was a disgrace. So, cursing, I turned again, reinvested in the *Fahrrad* route and ploughed on beyond the station yard. At the far end of the town the segregation of bicyclists was abandoned and all shared the Bundesstrasse. It would have been even worse if the Autobahn above and beyond had not been carrying the ceaseless stream of heavy goods vehicles, motor homes and motorbike clubs out for a weekend jaunt.

Then the rain started, not gentle drizzle, but real, high-mountain rain. Its drops were isolated but huge. When one hit the target of my balding head it exploded on contact like a schoolboy's water bomb. Eventually I succumbed and too late pulled on my waterproof and cotton hat. As the main road swung upwards I saw to the left a bridge over the racing river. I knew it was mad but I could not resist the temptation. Over the bridge I found a faint path following the river upstream. Again I knew that it was risk-laden but the rain had washed away the remains of caution. The path dwindled and then died. However, there was a stone embankment to contain the river and I was able to use this as a path until it also died. Two hundred metres ahead lay the beginnings of the construction works for the new railway line: boulders and massive heaps of soil. Around this a stout wire mesh fence, perhaps 1.5 metres high, prevented trespass. I followed the fence left-handed until its beginning, lashed to the girders above the railway embankment. With the strength of the desperate adventurer I started to unleash the wire fixings as best I could. I succeeded partially, creating an opening through which I could have squeezed had it not been at least a metre from ground level. But then I saw that with the advantage of the fence I could clamber up to reach the girders that projected from the embankment to prevent trespass. Again with a surge of strength I was up, over the girders and on the main railway carrying the traffic – goods and passenger – between northern and southern Europe. Of course it would carry me straight as a die to where I wanted to be. But would I get away with it? I had to cross the construction site, which was teeming with workers, and I fancied that there would be train drivers and guards raising the alarm. But I had no choice. Immediately inside the girders ran the metal box containing many strands of covered electric wire. On top of the box rested cement slabs simply laid loose, each touching the other. But they formed a path which rocked and rattled to my footsteps. The further I went the less anxious I became. In forty-five minutes of rapid walking only one train passed, heading south. I pulled down the brim of my cotton hat and pretended a legitimacy which I completely lacked. Once well past the construction site I saw a forest path to the left that ran parallel with the railway. It was easy to cross the tracks where there was no embankment and to drop onto a meadow with an entry onto the track. In no time I was back on the Jakobsweg and heading north.

The path that I had rejoined quickly turned into a bicycle route and, asphalted and tarmacked as it was, it proved hard on the feet as I proceeded steadily to reach Mittewald and then on. This was a long, monotonous walk only relieved by the occasional village. Furthermore it was the turn of the bicycle brigade to be warned off for closure due to some other construction works. Of course for them there were abundant warning notices placed at regular intervals, all advising them to desist from their ride and to entrain their bicycles from Franzensfeste to Freienfeld. I doubt whether any of them followed the advice or instruction. I, of course, ignored all warning and proceeded. At the point of "closure" there was simply an end to the tarmac and a diversion over a dirt track which many cars and perhaps bicycles had been taking. So I carried on.

I do not now remember the villages of Grasstein and Niederried, perhaps because the path skirted rather than penetrated them. However, I hold the clearest memory of Stilfes, which I approached on the forest track from Niederried. The wonder of Stilfes is its church, which is unusually large and very prominently sited. Although enclosed by the village on three sides, its south aspect has nothing more than gravestones dividing the church from the farmland. Thus the traveller approaching from the south sees this triumphant church rising out of emptiness and immediately its impact is complete. The church is ancient and so is the village. I entered the church and found a large assembly of mothers and children just under the altar in the charge of the priest. I did not wish to intrude and I was unable to see what they were doing but it was some sort of instruction or maybe tradition with which the children were clearly much taken. After a photograph from below the organ loft I crept out to find a rainbow almost in the graveyard. I headed on, seeing that my next goal had to be the village of Elzenbaum. This was a lovely field walk and I regretted that the hour was growing late and I could not linger. It took me perhaps an hour to reach Elzenbaum, a village of curious isolation. It felt as though nothing in the second half of the 20th century had made any mark or effected any change on either the buildings or the way of life of their inhabitants. At either end of the village was a freestanding oven, or so it seemed to be, perhaps for communal baking or communal roasting. Across the valley rose the castle of Sprechenstein, dramatic against the evening sky.

It was 6.30 when I quit Elzenbaum and I still had at least an hour to reach my journey's end. I pressed on as hard as I could until the footpath decanted me onto the Bundesstrasse. I was fearful of not finding a bed, and furthermore I was footsore. So as soon as I reached the Bundesstrasse I resorted to appeals to passing cars for a lift. Although rejection was humiliating I had nothing to lose. If a car stopped I was blessed and if they all swept by I was none the worse off. A few cars passed but none was minded to stop and so it was that I arrived on foot on the outskirts of Sterzing at about 7.30.

Sterzing is a highly important and ancient town. The curiosity is that the wonderful parish church lies about a kilometre from the old town and its only historic companion is a large, almost fortified house built by the Teutonic knights, whose headquarters in Vienna I had long admired. Now it houses the town museum. Since I was clearly far from the town centre I ignored the modern hotel opposite the church, Zum Engel, and pressed on, uncertain of the true direction, there being no signs to the *Zentrum*. Approaching a small chapel at an intersection of roads I encountered a strange procession of about seventy people snaking for 50 metres or so along the pavement. It was led by children in what may have been choir dress and was followed by neat, elderly parishioners. There were many nuns in the procession and the priest dominated from the centre of the group. I had no idea who they were, what they were doing or where they were going, nor was there anyone to ask. I could hardly halt the procession. Then I saw a lady pushing a bicycle and I questioned her as to how to find the centre of town and where I could find a good hotel. We became quite friendly and she took a keen interest in what I was doing, dressed as I was and clearly on some purposeful long-distance walk. I showed her my Kompass guide and explained the Jakobsweg from Graz to Innsbruck. She in turn explained that the historic town centre was off on the other road and was probably not worth my accessing since she said I would not find a hotel there as good as Zum Engel. Accordingly, we walked together, she pushing her bike, until we reached Zum Engel, at which stage we bid a fond farewell.

Zum Engel undoubtedly lived up to her recommendation. Its speciality was wellness, with an adjacent spa and sauna, but the room I was given was excellent and I had a carefully cooked dinner. The breakfast the next morning was at the very top end of luxury. Of course it took me to the top end of my budget,

€120 all in. It made a very satisfying end to twelve hours of walking and many hazards encountered and overcome.

☞

Day 30 – 12 May 2018 – Sterzing to Gries

MY DESTINATION, SET by the Kompass guide, was Steinach. It was 35 kilometres from Sterzing and demanded an early start, but I squandered time. First I was loath to miss what I knew would be a first-class breakfast, which did not begin until 7.30. Nor could I walk away without exploring Sterzing. First there was the parish church opposite the hotel. The austere exterior concealed a magnificent space: a long nave with a splendour of columns soaring to a high roof. My camera clicked away as I aimed it at the remarkable pews, the whole interior from beneath the organ and the capitals of the nave columns.

The town centre was about a kilometre distant and I approached it by cutting across open fields to reach the mouth of the long street dominated by the medieval tower. Again, I had my camera out. This street is divided, like Bond Street, into the old and the new. Between them is a marketplace. Here I found the tourist information run by an efficient girl to whom I complained at length about the complete absence of waymarking for the Jakobsweg, particularly culpable in Franzensfeste, where there was nothing to warn of the closure ahead. She agreed that this was all quite unacceptable and assured me that major works were planned both to create proper forest walks and to mark up the way. She helpfully recommended a shop, where I stocked up with local postcards, and directed me to the post office, where I shot up to the counter when all in the long queue ahead of me seemed paralysed. By now it was ten o'clock and I had to get going. I was feeling the effect of the previous day's struggle and the weight of the indulgent breakfast, too much and too rich. Finding the right exit from a substantial town like Sterzing is always problematic. Luckily I had a town map from the hotel which marked up both a footpath and a bicycle path to Brenner. The girl in the information office had recommended the bicycle path but the footpath was nearer and surely preferable. I plunged into the cul de sac indicated by the map but I could see no way out until a man playing football with some children showed me a gap between two houses which led uphill to a tunnel under the railway. Once through the tunnel I was on my way, following a forest path that led on through Unterried to Oberried. Although I had hardly earned it, I stopped there at a café and wrote my postcards as I enjoyed my coffee and the pleasant view. The road from Oberried rises to pass the castle of Strassberg, a romantic ruin which I photographed, as well as the view behind. A very attractive forest walk followed until the path dropped down into the valley to reach the considerable town of Gossensass. The Bundesstrasse for Brenner thunders through the town and I was very doubtful of finding my way out. I saw the "I" for information but it was already past noon. Fortunately the post office next door was open and there I was assured that my postcards would go out on Monday morning. The lady also offered me advice as to my onward path. I soon saw that she was not herself a walker since she had simply advised me to take the main road. Thanks to the Kompass map I was able to see that I should be west of the parish church and that saved me from the main road, which ran east of the parish church. But west of the church there were no signs other than to the H. Ibsenweg. This Weg was marked on my map and, although not what I wanted, it lay well north of the town. So whenever in doubt I chose Ibsen. He served me well and eventually after an upward climb on a very narrow track I emerged on a minor road which carried me on to the hamlet of Pontigl. I saw from the map that my side road was about to join the main road, along which traffic roared in unceasing convoy. It was mainly composed of heavy goods lorries, camper vans and motorbikes – the latter not singly but in large groups and associations. It was a daunting prospect. I retreated to the edge of a field ablaze with dandelions (see the plate section) and ate the piece which I had prepared not at Zum Engel but in Mühlbach. Somehow I was always a day behind.

Beside the junction was a house and a good lady working in the garden. I asked her for some footpath to carry me to Brenner. She said there was nothing but a bicycle route much higher up and I would be better to take the main road. So I set out walking uphill as steadily as I could, with the traffic deafening and threatening me all the way. I was able to follow the route on the map. First we crossed underneath the motorway and then crossed back again, at which point I saw that I should be able to find again a quiet way to the west of the main road. Soon I saw the track to the left and, close by between the road and the track, was a fast-flowing stream. But there was a footbridge, gated at both ends. As I approached the footbridge I saw that the gate was padlocked and in support were stern notices forbidding all but authorised persons to make use of the bridge. Nothing more ludicrous, nothing more unconvincing could have been contrived. I clambered over the gate, crossed the bridge and clambered over the gate at the far end. I was on a path that ran alongside the stream and skirted the village of Brennerbad. There I was returned to the main road, which I had to follow to reach the huge transport depots on either side of the border. There was a café in the main marshalling yard and here a friendly waitress made me a good cup of coffee and recommended a home-made *Torte* which was just as good as she had said; there were ground almonds in the sponge and tart, red berries between its layers.

As I set off I saw that it was half past four and I still had probably 17 kilometres to Steinach. My map showed a footpath, running west of the town and west of the Brennersee, lying about a kilometre ahead. I found a forest path that seemed promising but which proved to be only for local dog walkers and soon I was back on the main road and still in Brenner. I made on until caught in a spaghetti maze of junctions between the motorway and the main roads, at which in desperation I took a chance and headed for the forest edge. I guessed that there must be a path to the west of the Brennersee. I followed a stream which seemed to be gushing raw sewage into the lake, which no doubt diluted it effectively before the water flowed out at the other end. It was at that other end that the footpath died despite its clear continuation shown on my map. I had no alternative but to climb up the bank to reach the edge of the road where a military vehicle was parked with what appeared to be three soldiers. I am only uncertain because their cap badges were a large red cross on a white ground. They were friendly and helpful and clear in directing me to walk down to join the main road. I did not entirely understand why they rejected my plea for some alternative until the leader enquired whether I spoke English. Smiles all round and then he explained that there was some sort of track through the forest but that it was extremely dangerous, with falling rocks and the like. I could only walk on safely on the main road.

Time was now short and I set out at a fast pace which I could easily achieve. All the way from Mülhbach to Brenner I had been climbing, sometimes gently, sometimes steeply. But from the marshalling yard in Brenner I not only re-entered Austria but on a gradient that was always descending, sometimes gently, sometimes steeply. So I made a good pace on downhill through Lueg until reaching the more substantial village of Gries with a railway station and several streets.

I forgot to mention that on the outskirts of Brenner I had encountered the familiar Austrian footpath sign, black on a yellow ground. I read Jakobsweg and my heart soared. I was back in Austria and I would be looked after. The sign pointed me uphill on a good shingle track and I hurried on until suddenly and inexplicably the track stopped dead. I could only think that it was newly made and incomplete but why, oh why, put up the new sign until the job was done? I could not face going back so clambered rather perilously down a steep bank until regaining the main road.

The entry into Gries was encouraging, with a bold sign advertising the Hotel Rossl. As I reached the main street I saw on the left a *Gasthaus* and went for it. I got to the kitchen where the patron was making a wonderful strawberry cake. Unfortunately he was fully booked, for he only had three rooms, and he directed me to the far end of the town where he said I would be safe. He explained that the Rossl had not offered rooms but only meals for a long time. So I set off. At least the street led on towards Steinach and after maybe a kilometre at the very end of the village I came to the hotel of his recommendation. It was getting late and I was anxious and my anxiety was enhanced when the lady in the kitchen did not immediately assent but went to speak to her boss in the dining room. However, he immediately agreed and I was shown to a clean room and came down to a cheerful dining room. The proprietor proved to be a very friendly and delightful man. He applauded my choice of *Gröstl*, a very Tyrolean dish, and with it a large measure of Grüner Veltliner. I also had a litre of sparking water, which I badly needed after my pounding walk on the main road.

At the end of dinner he explained that breakfast was available from seven o'clock. I asked at what hour would be the first mass at the village church. He went to enquire and returned saying the first mass was at ten. When I rejected the option he explained that since the old priest had died the young priest was in charge of six villages and could not offer more than one Sunday mass in each. I took a schnapps and slept soundly.

☞

Day 31 –13 May 2018 – Gries to Steinach

THE LADY I had met on entry the previous evening was in charge of breakfast and there was no sign of the patron. She asked whether I would like an egg and when I said yes, she offered an omelette. When it came it was plain but perfect, about an inch thick; probably three eggs had gone to make its girth. I asked her advice on my best route to Steinach, having my eye on the 10.50 to Innsbruck. She was very clear and very forceful in saying that I must walk the main road until I reached Stafflach. Only there could I pick up a footpath which would take me not only to Steinach but to the station itself.

So at about eight o'clock I set off, making a good pace down the main road which ran always beside a fast-flowing river, sometimes one side and sometimes the other. In Stafflach there was a church but it looked as if it was seldom open. I had some difficulty in accessing the footpath but in the end found it to the right of the main road and the railway, with an entry through a farmyard. Once found, it was a good forest walk up above the valley until it dropped down to a very modern pilgrim church, constructed alongside a major earthworks or hydro scheme capturing the waters from the valley flowing in from the east. Beyond that, I walked through suburban streets until I saw the station immediately to the left. I climbed the fence into the railway and explored the options, which included two platforms and a ticket machine. I had time in hand and bought a ticket that suggested that I could reach Vienna by 2.30 if I changed not only in Innsbruck but also in Salzburg. As I wandered about waiting for the train, I found that there was a much advertised exit from the second platform directly onto the footpath, which I would have discovered for myself had I not prematurely climbed the fence.

The return journey went well. From the main station I took the U-Bahn to Karlsplatz for Opernring, where I changed and rearranged my luggage in readiness for the huge evening meal that Aura was cooking for me.

GRIES

STEINACH

PATSCH

GRIES TO PATSCH

Day 32 – 30 June 2018 – Return to Gries and Steinach

THE ANGLO-GERMAN CONFERENCE concluded on Friday afternoon but I had taken advantage of the invitation to remain in the judicial college until the following day. On Friday evening Aura and I met Felicitas for an early supper in the Naschmarkt. The next day I attempted to find an afternoon mass in the cathedral, it being a day of obligation for St Peter and St Paul. Disappointed that there was nothing before the high mass at six, I turned to the taxing task of purchasing some jeans, as I had left mine behind when packing. I knew Zara in the square and Aura had told me that they also sold men's clothes. At the shop I found the summer sale in full swing and the ground floor stifling; things were only marginally easier in the men's department. Clearly they trade with midgets and I bought the only pair in the shop that I had any chance of getting into. Such was the struggle that I was five minutes late for our table at five o'clock.

Aura took me back to the schloss in her magnificent Range Rover. I had to pack for the Tyrol and she for her holiday in Istanbul so we did not linger.

The next morning I was prompt at the main gate to meet my taxi. Horror: someone had double-locked the pedestrian gate, my only means of exit. I had left my key in my room and could not reach it as I was also locked out of the *Gasthaus*. The driver appeared and between us we planned a successful climb over the gate, by no means easy. The driver was Pakistani and of course spoke excellent English. Thanks to his aid I was in good time for the 07.33 from the airport to Innsbruck. There I changed onto a local train which set me down in Gries at 14.20. That gave me five hours to reach my destination, the Aktiv Hotel zur Rose, in Steinach. My plan was to attempt the further stretch of the Jakobsweg that lay well west of the main road and ran up to Nösslach and then on to St Jodok before circling back to Stafflach. Although I had already followed the Jakobsweg from Stafflach to Steinach I could either do it again or pick up the local train which stopped at St Jodok, the station before Steinach.

Gries station lies high above the village to the east and the Jakobsweg leaves the village at the south-west corner beyond the *Gasthof* and uphill towards Vinaders. Immediately short of the Bäckerei Springer (no longer trading) is the obscure exit. I missed it and walked on uphill until doubts beset me. As I returned I met a local on foot with a moustache made up of the thickest grey bristles. He put me right: although there was no sign this was the path for Nösslach. His authority dispelled all doubt and only the gradient lowered my spirits, for the rough path climbed steeply in a series of zigzags. It was a hot afternoon, I was out of practice and soon I was ascending only by resting after every fifty paces. At least this technique carried me up to the most picturesque pond, created by damming the descending stream. Imagine a circular double bed for two and you have its dimensions. All around was green meadow. On the water dabbled two ducks, a domestic breed attached to the farm, which also kept hens. This pretty scene gave me an excuse for a prolonged pause as I tried to capture the charm of the scene with my camera, and failed.

I had just set off when a woman came up the path from below. She had a hat against the sun, Norwegian walking sticks, a pack on her back and, totally revealing, the Kompass guide in her hand. After greetings in German we found English our common language. I explained my wonder at meeting a fellow pilgrim almost for the first time in 1,600 kilometres of Austrian walking, and she explained that she was from Graz and was approaching journey's end in Innsbruck. However, she planned to return after a week at home and then to set off from Innsbruck for Feldkirch.

We started walking together up the hill and I soon realised that she was fitter and swifter than me and that I was holding her back, a dilemma resolved when we reached the little chapel of St Jakob. When I said that I would visit the chapel, which lies on a crest above the path, she declined and so we parted. I should have given her my card and offered my account of the journey on from Innsbruck but at the time I did not think of it and only afterwards regretted this failure to help a fellow pilgrim.

The chapel was simple but carried the traditional stamp with which I inked my guide. I also photographed the chapel before walking on along a tarmac path shared with occasional passing traffic. I took a photograph of the view from the chapel.

It was from here on that the complete absence of waymarking proved so costly. Nösslach was marked on the map, as was a motorway service station to the north-east of the village. With hindsight I believe that at this point I diverged onto a road that would lead to Steinach when I should have found a path more or less following the motorway for upwards of two kilometres before crossing the motorway and descending to Stafflach in the valley below. As it was I stopped on this false route at a busy hostelry, the Humlerhof. My map marked a path which would take me back to where I should be and the waiter confirmed its existence. I am doubtful if the path that I took was the path he intended as it plunged steeply across farmland to reach the motorway. Without any sign or encouragement I found a track that led under the motorway and, again with hindsight, I believe that this was the true way. But, I should say, true at the date when the guide was published. For on that afternoon as I emerged from under the motorway I entered a vast construction site. The forest had been cleared and the hillside transformed into a flat plain about the size of three football pitches. Perhaps it was the beginning of some motorway works unit but, although I carefully surveyed its circumference, there was no sign of any path leading onwards. It was an early disaster. I could not face retracing my steps to what was in any event little better. If I had to gamble, the best option seemed to be a descent on a swathe through the forest which had been clear felled and at the end of which I could see a red roof and beyond it a highway with cars creeping along like occasional beetles. It was hard to judge the distance but, from above, it appeared to be about 200 metres below where I stood. The way between where I was and the red roof was invisible, however; I could only see that it was vertiginous. It might be dangerous, although escape seemed so near. I might encounter a precipice that could not be crossed. Despite the risks I hardly hesitated. First upright with the aid of my stick, then more slowly with two sticks and finally on my bottom, like a child tobogganing on a kitchen tray. The difficulties were compounded by the fact that the clear felling had removed any handholds and had left a litter of thinnings and brushwood thick on the ground. Progress was very slow and it took me an hour before I merged from the forest onto a pasture bank. This too was too steep to descend on foot and so it was that I continued to the barn beside the farmhouse on my bottom. Although I had made it I was thoroughly shaken and had to rest for five minutes before surveying the scene and recognising that I was within yards of the chapel in Stafflach. Thus orientated, I had a choice. Either I could repeat the Jakobsweg from Stafflach to Steinach that I had tested in May or I could head on for St Jodok. In St Jodok is a railway station and I could then reach Steinach by train. I had checked the timetable in Gries and seen that there was an hourly service from Brenner to Innsbruck which would stop at St Jodok at about fifteen minutes before the hour. The girl that I had met above Gries had told me that she intended to stay the night in St Jodok and maybe that encouraged me to investigate. Furthermore, the circular diversion from Stafflach to St Jodok was the official Jakobsweg route.

Although of course there was no waymark it was easy to find the path to St Jodok as the map showed it ran between the river and the railway. It was an almost idyllic stroll across fields of pasture on a footpath which must for centuries have been used by the local inhabitants travelling between the two villages. This sense was emphasised by two local girls ahead of me on the path also walking at my slow pace. As we travelled on there was always about a hundred metres between us and by the time I reached St Jodok they were no longer to be seen.

In the village the footpath was distinct and to the left of the road, charmingly fenced on both sides. However, it was hard to see the relationship between the village and the railway station, which was clearly well above the valley floor. I mistakenly thought that the station was ahead when in fact it was already behind me. I had seen a sign but, although clear, it seemed to suggest a ski station rather than a railway station. By the church I met a man who was setting out on a run. He was extremely helpful and emphatically sent me back to the sign I had rejected. It was a short, steep climb to reach the station and as I approached I sensed the arrival of a train. I was too exhausted to accelerate and as I reached the platform level I saw the Innsbruck train pull out of the station. The other contributor to this setback was my rough appreciation, as I left Stafflach, that I had no chance of catching the 18.45. So there I was at an empty station with an hour to wait for the next train and as the sun went down so did the temperature. To pass the time I settled down to read and send emails with occasional entertainment as goods trains passed through the station.

I am sure that the traffic of goods on Austrian railways is of infinitely greater volume than in England. Goods trains are not only frequent but of enormous length. They carry timber, they carry shipping containers. They even carry huge lorries loaded for the cross-border journey. Why lorries are moved by rail rather than by their own power on the motorway I have no idea. The railway track to Brenner from St Jodok on leaving the station takes a huge circle up and round the valley. Shortly after leaving the station the trains enter a tunnel from which they emerge on the other side of the valley. Thereon their progress is very visible as they labour up the slope before entering another tunnel on the straight uphill run to Gries.

The 19.45 arrived on time and four minutes later I alighted in Steinach. The Zur Rose is in the High Street and three very Austrian-looking blondes directed me to it across the bridge. I recognised the hotel from the online photograph and was soon negotiating with the friendly manager. The hotel specialises in healthy living and I was just in time for the formal set menu of some five courses. I took a shortcut through the menu, aided by an extremely appealing elderly waiter. I had a small but comfortable room and knew that I could get breakfast from seven o'clock. If I had not been so late I could have looked for an evening mass. If I had not had so far to go the following day I could have looked for a morning mass.

☞

Day 33 – 1 July 2018 – Steinach to Patsch

As IT WAS, I was up at six o'clock and at breakfast on the dot of seven. The same delightful waiter was on duty and superintending a group of at least twenty men who were perhaps on some bicycle tour. They occupied a long table at the back and there were only a few others independently breakfasting. I made myself a good piece and resisted the temptation of an egg dish cooked by the kindly waiter. So it was that I set off at 7.55 and heard the church bell strike the hour as I left the railway station on the dedicated footpath that led from platform two to the Wipptaler Wanderweg, which the Jakobsweg had naturally adopted. It seems to run all the way from Brenner to Mühltal and so it was to be my companion all day. Absent any signs for the Jakobsweg, at least the signs for the Wipptaler Wanderweg were reassuring.

As I had finished in Steinach in May I had thought that that was good enough performance and that it would not be worth such a long return for only one day's walking. However, with time dissatisfaction grew and I knew I could not claim that Steinach was good enough. Furthermore, I had thought that the final day of 32 kilometres would be all gently downhill following the river. As I left the station in Steinach I encountered a very different reality. I had a stiff uphill climb to reach the village of Mauern and thereafter the whole day was one of ascent and descent as the Wanderweg made its way northwards high above and always to the east of the river. The test is magnified by the terrain. There is not a yard of forest walking, nor a metre, or hardly a metre, that is not on tarmac. What would have been an ancient footpath has become a minor road shared with motor traffic and often with ribbon development on either side. I took this photograph which shows what I mean. When the Wanderweg passes through pastureland the road is cut into the steep bank so there is no verge between the tarmac and the adjoining fields.

Thus I gradually progressed like an ant across the page of the map to Tienzens then past Matrei to reach Pfons. I liked this rose bush entering Pfons so took its picture. In these small villages there were no cafés. I survived by drinking from the pipes that fed the cattle troughs until in the middle of the day I mixed the little wine in my rucksack with a little water to make a spritzer. This I needed when challenged by the route from Pfons to Oberpfons. In Pfons itself, when faced with yet another Y-junction with no indication as to whether to take the left or right fork, I asked a rather unfriendly local. He urged me to take the right fork. I suppose he saw me as a soul in need of torment. Before coming to a dead end I had passed a laden cherry tree in a garden beside the road and had unhesitatingly helped myself to a good handful. The only compensation of having to retrace my steps from the dead end was that I bagged a further handful on the way down. Cherries do relieve drought in the mouth and sinuses. Once back at the Y-junction I took the lower path and found my way to the hamlet of Oberpfons. Here, at another Y-junction, I was astonished to see at last a sign for the Jakobsweg pointing right. I took it and after climbing slowly for 100 metres found another Y-junction but without mark. The right hand looked the better choice but it proved to be only the entry into a recent development of three houses. I returned and attempted the left hand but it carried me only into what looked like a recently developed quarry. I cast on a faint path uphill out of the quarry but it led nowhere. I simply had no option. I dropped back into the village and sat down in the hope that someone would emerge on a Sunday afternoon. In a small Austrian village this is a forlorn hope. Where are the inhabitants? Are they away? Are they in bed? Are they eating a long lunch? So when I saw a woman walking purposefully uphill towards me it was as if I was in the presence of an angel. I thought that perhaps it was my chance encounter of the previous afternoon. After all, if she had slept in St Jodok and had left the village at about 8 it was plausible that she would have caught me up about where I was. I soon saw, however, that this was a local rather than a long-distance walker. I explained my problem and she laughingly understood and showed me that the quarry had effectively concealed the path. Not only could she direct me but she could guide me since she was going the same way. Again we set out together uphill on the narrow track between banks on both sides. It soon became clear that she had no intention of going my pace and that I had no chance of going hers. After she had pulled ahead she paused and warned me that ahead I would meet a bank at which I must bear left. When I reached the bank I was done and stopped to drink most of my spritzer, just keeping a reserve for the way ahead.

The way ahead led through open country until it reached Oberellbögen. This was a long slog relieved by pleasurable encounters with families haymaking on the steep banks. The banks were mown by a small machine designed for a 45-degree gradient but thereafter the swathes were raked by hand and then pitchforked onto a trailer. Gathering the hay seemed to be a family task, usually two women raking, two men pitching and one man on top treading down the mountainous load. I photographed two separate teams in action, the second is in the plate section.

I found the villages of Oberellbögen and Ellbögen thoroughly confusing. I couldn't distinguish one from the other or where Ellbögen ended and Mühltal began. However, I knew that I had reached Mühltal when I found a bus stop beside the bridge and a timetable for the service that ran through Patsch as far as Innsbruck main station. As I inspected the timetable, a lady came and asked if I too was awaiting the bus. Before I could answer the bus arrived and she skipped on. Should I do the same? I was tempted but it was only three o'clock and it seemed premature to admit defeat. This rejected opportunity distracted me from checking the Kompass map, which would have shown that at that point I had to leave the road and find a valley walk that meandered to Patsch and beyond. So it was that I made uphill on the main road, a long slog in the heat, to reach the village of St Peter. Beside the church was a *Gasthof* restaurant swarming with people, walkers, holidaymakers and bicycle groups. I had finished the spritzer and abandoned the bottle as I left Mühltal and I was in sore need of a cup of coffee. As I walked down to the hubbub I saw a bar and what looked like a crowd of men in *Trachten*. Ah, I thought, these are the waiters, I will soon be served. Alas, they were not waiters but part of a dense crowd of customers eating, drinking and enjoying the hot afternoon. I pushed through the crowd to reach the bar at the heart of the house. There the crowd was equally dense. I guessed that I would waste half an hour in pursuit of a desirable but not vital investment. I pushed my way out and trudged on, up and down hot tarmac slopes with the aim of catching the bus as it stopped in Patsch. As I drew near the village I saw the Brenner bus pull into a layby on the other side of the road. The bus was empty and the driver had dismounted to smoke in the shade. He was friendly and quick to grasp my plan. Yes, the Innsbruck bus would pass in five minutes. In that time I could not reach the stop in Patsch. He advised me to walk back to the house on the corner. I did what he advised, although I had seen no stop at the corner. Nor did I get a second chance to look as the bus swept up before I reached the corner. I hailed the bus with a confidence that I did not feel and was rewarded. The driver stopped in the middle of the road, waited for me to clamber on and sold me a ticket to the Innsbruck Hauptbahnhof, his final destination. I was the only passenger on board.

Other passengers boarded in Patsch and also in Igls and Vill. Extraordinarily, the road from Patsch to the banks of the Inn in the city is all downhill: sometimes steep, sometimes gentle, but always a downhill gradient so that bicyclists from Patsch to Innsbruck city centre would not have to use the pedals once. The Jakobsweg took a different line from Patsch to Igls and on through Vill: perhaps a pleasant off-road walk but surely not an easy one. When I eventually explore Innsbruck I may take the bus to Patsch and walk the way back.

As it was, I arrived at the station at half past four having missed the 16.16 on which I held a reservation. I caught the crowded 17.14 and arrived at the Hauptbahnhof in Vienna at 21.45, fifteen minutes behind schedule. I received a warm welcome at the Hotel Opernring and settled in there until leaving at two o'clock the following afternoon.

Thus an inglorious end to a very long walk.

THE THIRD WALK

The Austro-German Northern Tributary

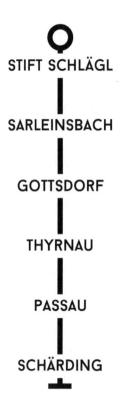

STIFT SCHLÄGL

SARLEINSBACH

GOTTSDORF

THYRNAU

PASSAU

SCHÄRDING

STIFT SCHLÄGL TO SCHÄRDING

Prelude

WHEN I REACHED Innsbruck in July 2018 I completed the Jakobsweg tributary that had risen in Graz. With the Jakobsweg main river and main tributary completed, was that to be an end? I was aware of the Jakobsweg second tributary running from the north through to meet the main stream somewhere before Salzburg, as I thought. I knew it was covered by a Kompass guide which had been out of print since 2008 and which was seemingly unobtainable. But I felt that I had to investigate further. First, in a specialist bookseller in Vienna a helpful assistant suggested an alternative publisher, Outdoor. From that I saw that this second tributary was only briefly Austrian and was mainly through South Bavaria before re-entering Austria north of Kufstein. I was both disappointed and intrigued. Thanks to eBay, I was able to acquire a second-hand copy of the Kompass guide, which told the same story. I saw that the Weg crossed the Czech border into Austria very close to St Oswald. It was an area of upper Austria that I had never visited and I was curious to see what it was like. Aura offered to leave me at St Oswald on a Sunday evening before herself returning to Vienna. But I then saw that Stift Schlägl is only a few kilometres from St Oswald, and I was keen to sleep at the Stift. So the simple solution was to target the Stift rather than St Oswald, which lacked overnight accommodation.

With hindsight, this plan was late conceived and ill executed. It was only when we stopped in St Pölten that I asked Aura to telephone the Stift. The receptionist was hardly accommodating and said that if we were not there by five o'clock there would be no possibility of entry. We flew easily along the motorway to Linz but thereafter we struggled on an A road, eventually reaching the Stift with only twelve minutes to spare. It is fully described as Prämonstratenser Chorherrenstift. I know nothing of the Pramonstratensian Order and had little opportunity to understand it. Music and choral singing were obviously important, as I discovered when I attended the vespers on arrival and the mass at 6.30 the following morning. The abbot officiated at both services and all the monks were dressed in white, some with capes above their surpluses. I counted nearly forty brothers and a few nuns who were clearly affiliated. There was a large local congregation at the vespers, which I surmised was a special celebration, and after which all ascended to what I supposed was a special meal. I only watched the brothers and the congregation filing up the staircase and I did not presume to follow.

The abbey seems to be run on quite commercial lines. As well as providing accommodation and board in the neighbouring *Stiftskeller* it seems to offer an almost continuous stream of courses, teaching everything from faith to healthy exercise, each led by a specialist brother within the congregation.

The receptionist was a lady in early middle age of much Christian goodness but not much worldly determination or decisiveness. The overnight rate for a pilgrim of €60 is, in my experience, unprecedented, particularly given the basic nature of the accommodation. The *Stiftskeller* was lifeless but the cooking and service thoroughly professional. When I came to pay the next morning the receptionist was worried by my question as to how I might find the Jakobsweg on its way through the village. The abbot happened to pass and she turned to him with the problem. He was forthright and clear in his description but was clearly irritated at being involved. He had come for a paper that he needed from the receptionist and was quite rude to her in saying that she must hurry or he would be late for his meeting. Irritation is a common human reaction and seems to affect even the abbot. However, I was struck by his seeming lack of charity. I was grateful for my stay there but I would not choose to return. It is perhaps their misfortune that I have Kremsmünster as my ideal. Stift Schlägl is famous for its brewery; it seems to be big business, supplying not just the Stift and the vicinity but the whole of Austria. For example, both the bottled and the draught beer at Kremsmünster come from Schlägl.

☞

Day 1 – 1 October 2018 – Stift Schlägl to Sarleinsbach
I LEFT THE monastery at 9.15. The day was grey with a light rain and a cold wind. I was using for the first time the Outdoor guide to the Jakobsweg (number 294 in the Outdoor series), which covers the route from Bohemia into Austria, on

into South Bavaria and finally returns to Austria for the last stretch from Kufstein to Innsbruck. As I was to discover, the guide is weak on maps but strong on text. So it is ideal for the intended German audience but of limited use to me, a poor German speaker.

The abbot had given me a start point by the Shell garage and I set off up the hill in search of St Wolfgang. I could see that only the existence of a *Wallfahrtskirche* had led to the inclusion of St Wolfgang, which was by no means on any direct route to Geiselreith. So when I was offered a choice between St Wolfgang and Geiselreith I took the easier course. It did me little good, for as soon as the St Jakob waymarks petered out I got mildly lost.

The country is a land of rolling hills, often forested. Although there is little flat land it is still rich farmland with arable crops grown everywhere on the gentle slopes. So I was constantly either on an ascent or a descent, passing substantial farms, either isolated or in groups of three or four comprising the hamlets for which I was aiming. I was able to orientate from an unmanned railway crossing and then the main highway from Schlägl to Rohrbach.

I have very little memory of that first morning through the drear drizzle. Both Geiselreith and Kartzing have faded from my memory, as has the long walk on to Fürling. However, I remember the long descent into Fürling. It is a straggling village without centre or much coherence. I was irritated to find that this year's growth on a lush magnolia had obscured the marker for a crucial left turn. I did what I could to prune the growth and set off on a sharp descent. After only 100 metres there was a wide junction without anything to suggest a right fork leading into a farmyard. I didn't hesitate; I had no doubt as I swung leftwards on the more prominent arm. My confidence ebbed as I covered more than a kilometre without a sign. The onward path was strong but there were many junctions to left and right and then a descent into woodland with multiple choices and no guide. It could not be right. However reluctant, I had to return to Fürling. Was it a punishment for my meddling with the magnolia? Standing under the affronted shrub I applied orthodox thinking. The only option was the right-hand fork into and beyond the farm, a choice that was confirmed by the welcome sight of the yellow shell marker on the outskirts of the next village, Berg.

My map and guide called for an elaborate diversion to pass a plague column and then the church of Maria Trost to the east of Rohrbach. But what was plain on the plan was unfathomable on the ground. Clear waymarks might have convinced me but there were none. As I dropped towards the railway line a flurry of what I would swear were partridges got up about 100 metres ahead and swooped swiftly out of view. Were they partridges? It seems most unlikely given that in all my years of walking in Austria I had never seen a game bird, except perhaps once a pheasant. But if not partridges, then what? They had the unmistakeable flight of a game bird and the covey was about ten strong. I will never know.

I was soon at the unmanned rail crossing alongside Berg station. Immediately in front was a T-junction. To my dismay there was not the vestige of a sign to go either left or right or for a footpath that carried on downhill. I was lost, abandoned by the waymarker and behind schedule. My only security was that the parish church in the substantial town of Rohrbach was dedicated to St Jakob. So if I could find the church I would be reunited with the way. But how to find the church? The town was out of sight. Should I turn left or right? Left seemed the more plausible but I badly needed reassurance. After some fast walking I was encouraged to see shops and small businesses on both sides of the road. I then saw two pedestrians. The first was an old man who responded with amazement and incomprehension to my request for the road to the church. I next tried a grumpy middle-aged woman who was not disposed to be either helpful or friendly. I ploughed on. Rounding a right-hand bend I was rewarded by the sight of the town dominated by its *Pfarrkirche* (parish church).

Once I had located the church the incomprehension of the two locals was even more extraordinary since the church was large, high-standing and had been very recently reroofed, so that the shining copper sheets gleamed like jewels even in the grey light. The church is of considerable importance, setting aside its dedication to St Jakob. It owes its late 17th-century interior to Carlo Carlone, and a host of craftsmen working with him achieved the stucco, statues and high altar. Despite this distinction I found the church dark and gloomy, perhaps because of the sunless day. So I did not linger, even for a cup of coffee, but followed the directions in the guide and clear *Wegweiser* that pointed me to Götzendorf. But once again the zeal to guide the pilgrim did not extend much beyond the edge of the town. I did my best to go cross country but without waymarkers I lost any sort of confidence. Emerging from a wood I saw to the left and above what I assumed to be Götzendorf and its schloss, I plodded up a steep incline to reach the huddle of houses on the summit. Surely signs would resume there? There was no sign, but I saw a lady at the door of a smart house loading her child into a smart car. She tried to help but all she could tell me was that I was not in Götzendorf. That was the next village. To her relief a walker approached from the other direction, wielding his Nordic sticks purposefully. He would know everything, she said. When he arrived, however, he only confirmed what I had already learned and stared with incomprehension at my map marking the way ahead.

So I descended from the heights to a timber mill by a bridge in the valley below. As I started the next climb Götzendorf gradually came into view. Each ascent was probably only 60 to 90 metres but they always take the stuffing out of me. At the edge of the village I met an old man who did not recognise either of the next two villages on my route. His advice was to follow on through his village. This I did and, passing the last house, already on the descent from on high, I noticed a lady cleaning the inside of her living room window. I called to her and she generously emerged and offered to help. Fortunately, she was authoritative. She advised me to cut out the walk to Rutzersdorf and Auerbach and to head straight for Mairhof. This suggestion tallied with what I could see from the map and made even greater sense when she pointed out Mairhof, a hamlet almost directly across the valley from where we stood. She explained, however, that I would have to make two sides of a triangle in order to gain the only bridge across the river below.

As I descended, crossed the river and started the ascent, I never lost sight of my destination, so never lost heart on the third climb to reach a village. Although Mairhof is on the Jakobsweg, again there were no signs for the onward progress to Meising, the last village before journey's end at Sarleinsbach. As I hesitated at the edge of the village I saw a man in a farmyard starting up a digger. As I headed towards him he switched off the engine and climbed out of the cab. This kindness was manifest in his looks and demeanour. I showed him the map and explained what I had to do. Having grasped my intention he advised me to forsake Meising and simply take the high road into town. That, he explained, would save me probably half an hour. Since it was already late and I was tired (this was a 29 kilometre stage), I gratefully accepted his advice. The road down from Mairhof filtered into a relatively main road and Sarleinsbach lay some 2 kilometres ahead. I covered the distance mechanically, pushing one foot in front of the other until arriving in the small town that is Sarleinsbach. There were said to be two or three possibilities for an overnight rest. The first, Zum Kirchenwirt, was clearly closed. The second, Jagawirt, was garishly painted and had a crowded bar. But when I enquired for a bed the elderly woman at the bar shook her head and directed me to Kräutermandl, which was clearly the leading light. Without much enthusiasm I left her and rejoined the main road walking uphill. I was stopped by a shout and looking back saw a man leaning out of a window at pavement level. "No need to go on," he cried, "I will have a room ready for you in half an hour." So I returned to the crowded bar and amid all the shouts and laughter ate a poor meal before going up to an adequate room. I was in bed by eight and slept until six the next morning to be ready for the seven o'clock breakfast served by the old woman. All had been adequate and the bill was modest.

☞

Day 2 – 2 October 2018 – Sarleinsbach to Gottsdorf
THIS DAY STAGE was shorter, only 20 kilometres. My destination was Neustift im Mühlkreis and my first target was Putzleinsdorf. Again, the signs out of Sarleinsbach were excellent and I found myself following two identically dressed ladies, each carrying a shopping bag. Although the way was downhill from Sarleinsbach they were ahead of me and always extending their lead until they branched left, obviously heading for a substantial property beside what I took to be a stream at the bottom of the valley. There being no sign, I followed the tarmac to the right and ended up at the bottom of a valley some distance ahead with a well-maintained footpath following the stream to what looked like a livery yard beyond. A car approached the turning into the yard and the kind man at the wheel stopped to help me. I showed him my map and my desire for Eilmannsberg, Wulln and a pilgrim church, Maria Bründl. He shook his head regretfully and explained that I was already well off route. The way to Eilmannsberg lay well back. Given that I was where I was, he advised me to take my own line and to head for Putzleinsdorf. I must climb out of the valley and my first point must be a substantial farm, to which he pointed above on the skyline. When I reached the

farm it was big, even by local standards, and painted daffodil yellow. Attached to the main facade was a huge crucifix. I photographed this partly to capture the colour; see the plate section. (This was the first time I had taken out the camera, which reflects the dreary weather on the previous day.) I wanted as many variations of the Austrian yellow to help me choose the repainting of Henmarsh, which Ptolemy Dean had advised. Although there was abundant evidence of family life, there was no one in view and I descended to the barn door. No one there, but the milking herd, all chained and recumbent, jumped up in fright and I quickly retraced my steps. Since I could not ask, I set out on the obvious track leading away from the farm towards the forest. It was about three hours before I approached Putzleinsdorf. I took a photograph which gives a sense of the improving weather and the terrain. In the town I stopped for a cup of coffee and chose a slice of excellent cheesecake to make up for the poor breakfast. I recorded the view, a backward glance as I left.

From Putzleinsdorf to Pfarrkirchen im Mühlkreis was a stiff climb of some 250 metres and I arrived there at about two o'clock. The village is aptly named since it has a distinguished church designed and decorated by the Carlone brothers and various of their contempories. Although highly praised in the guidebook, the interior disappointed me. I was about half an hour in Pfarrkirchen and set off for the next village of Wehrbach by what was a downhill path. However, again I got lost in the woods and, without signs, finally reached a settlement of a few houses with two young mothers on the village street. Fortunately one of them was quick to understand and advised me to abandon Wehrbach and head for Altenhof, which was her neighbouring village. I had no difficulty in reaching Altenhof, which boasts a schloss that has been developed for tourism. From the schloss I followed the guidebook directions closely. They were invaluable, as the route descended across open pasture and the trace of earlier feet was at best faint. Just under a kilometre further on I came to the bottom end of a heavily wooded gorge. At the head of the gorge lay a dam enclosing a substantial reservoir, Rannastausee. The distance from the mouth of the gorge to the reservoir is perhaps 3 kilometres long and it is a spectacular, steady ascent, the well-made path running high up along the right-hand side of the gorge. Beside the path is a complicated pumping system carrying water through a black fibreglass pipe with intermittent water-pumping stations. Sometimes the rocky sides of the gorge emerge and sometimes the path is carried across a ravine by a standard-construction metal footbridge.

Emerging at the dam, the reservoir unfolds, long and sinuous but never wide. It was four o'clock before I reached this point and I had some thirty minutes of fast walking on a forest road to reach the only pedestrian crossing over the reservoir. I photographed the view of distant Konsing from the bridge. I reached the other side at about 4.45 and was faced by a very stiff climb from the water's edge to exit the gorge near my destination, Neustift. My heart hammered, my lungs pumped and frequently I paused to relieve these systems. At the head of the gorge was first a forest path and then a metal road leading into the small town. Here I was to spend the night. There were two guesthouses, the first closed and the second enjoying its

Tuesday *Ruhetag*. My guidebook made that plain and I kicked myself for having missed the warning.

What to do? The next bed was available in Gottsdorf but it was already 6.15 and Gottsdorf lay 3 kilometres along the road. Might there be a bus? I saw an old man approaching with a milk can and I asked his help. Would there be a bus? No, they ran through the town on the other road to the Danube. Might there be a taxi? He didn't know. He proceeded on his way and five minutes later after I had been racking my brains for some solution I saw him returning, presumably with a full can. He stopped and said that he had been thinking and knew how I might get a taxi, would I follow him? So I walked beside him until we reached a café off the main road where he said that the proprietor or the proprietor's brother operated a taxi. We went in and he explained my predicament and the café owner made a quick telephone call and told me to wait outside for the taxi. That I did and five minutes later it arrived, driven by a young man. I again explained my predicament and he said that he would gladly take me to the *Gasthof* in the next village. So off we set and only five minutes later I was at the door of Zum Lang in Gottsdorf. I kept him waiting while I made sure of my bed and then, much encouraged, gladly paid him the €10 fare.

Zum Lang (+43 (0)7285 6470) was a golden find. The husband and wife team, young and ambitious, provide the highest standards of service and comfort. The room was excellent. Even better was the wife's cooking and I enjoyed an outstanding meal, a hearty sleep and an excellent breakfast. I was sad to leave such a haven.

☞

Day 3 – 3 October 2018 – Gottsdorf to Thyrnau

FROM NEUSTIFT TO Thyrnau is a walk of some 29 kilometres. Of course, I benefited by starting from Gottsdorf but the weather continued grey, damp and with a cold north-westerly wind. I hardly remember any detail of the morning walk through poor weather and small settlements – Hitzing, Stollberg, Dürrmühle, Diendorf and finally Tabakstampf (a curious name for a village) – to reach the town of Untergriesbach. I do remember that there were long stretches of road walking and occasional farmland passages. I took only one photograph all morning and that was of the distant landscape.

Untergriesbach was for me a fair disaster. I had approached through a prosperous farm with a large herd of milking cows to reach a left turn and a long climb through the suburbs to reach the marketplace. This entry is at the high end of the marketplace and its whole length down to the parish church is immediately exposed. What I saw were massive works of road improvement. Not only was the highway up but so were all the pavements. This had clearly had a profound effect on local trade. Most of the shops were inaccessible and all were closed for business. Several were taking advantage of this hiatus to undertake external decoration or internal revolutions. It was a depressing descent to the parish church. Here I found a young woman and child planting the family grave plot for winter. I asked her where I could get the coffee I so badly needed. She said, almost with satisfaction, that there was nowhere in town open. I rested for a while in the fine church, which, however, gets no mention in the guidebook, then, climbing back to the head of the Marktplatz, I saw on the left an ice-cream shop. It was open and sold not only ices but also fair coffee, unexpected but welcome relief since it was now just after one. I was not yet halfway and wondered whether I would ever get to Thyrnau. I left town through a long suburb and photographed a chapel with a curious filigree wrought-iron turret. The way ahead was largely road walking, skirting Rampersdorf and Ziering.

Then at Schaibing there was a dramatic change. We left the asphalt and dropped through a woodland *Forststrasse* to reach a bridge over a substantial stream. The road ran straight on but there was a clear left turn following the path of the stream. This was blocked, however, by substantial earth-moving equipment and excavations that almost closed the road. There were clear waymarks for this lower road but I was hesitant. Fortunately, an old man on a bicycle came by and was pleased to help. He confirmed that I should follow the waymarking and not hesitate, so I embarked on what was at least an hour following the Aubach until it reached Schmölz. This was a heavenly interlude. As seemed to be the daily pattern, the afternoon sun had broken through and flooded the forest with light. Plainly there had been very substantial waterworks all the way through, with a newly made road of light gravel, level and ideal for walking. The drainage had all been expertly designed and executed so that the gravel was always dry and where necessary under-piped. Towards the end of this woodland river walk there was a clearing with two substantial houses. A newly planted quince bore familiar fruit but with a leaf that I had never seen before. I took a photograph of the sunlit scene and one of a monument to some historic rail route.

Schmölz is a village of mills, taking advantage of the junction of two streams, and there is a pretty chapel dedicated to St Martin. I knew from my guidebook that Schmölz was the low point to which I had been descending ever since Untergriesbach. To reach the next village of Zwölfing I would have to gain 150 metres of height. The track from Schmölz ran through forest recently clear-felled and the path was strewn with debris. At times it was almost vertical and again I puffed and panted my way up until I reached first the edge of the forest, then the end of the forest track and the beginning of the tarmac, which led into the highway and, ever upwards, to Zwölfling. At least the tarmac gradient had been gentle.

By now it was already evening and my destination lay still 3 kilometres ahead. I could see from the guidebook that it would be a switchback with ups and downs to reach the substantial town of Thyrnau. The guide said that there was a bed to be had in Zwölfling but I was determined to make on, partly because I had seen from the guidebook that there was accommodation at an abbey in Thyrnau. So I called on my last reserves of strength and stamina and pressed on, hammering along the tarmac road, which after Zwölfling flowed into a larger highway that ran through the town of Thyrnau. As I approached the town ahead, the main road became engineered for crossings and entries and exits that gave scant consideration to the pedestrian. So to traverse the road system was an adventure in order to reach the relative tranquillity of the local road up into the town.

On the outskirts there was something that appeared to be a religious house, but it proved to be the former community of St Christopher. There was perhaps three-quarters of a kilometre to reach the centre of the town, where I met a boy smoking outside a pub. I asked for his help. Could he direct me to the abbey or at least to No. 1 Abteistrasse? He looked perplexed and pulled out his telephone to access his satnav. He showed me the picture. "We are here and the abbey must be somewhere over there," he said. I thanked him and followed the direction he had waved. I had only crossed the road from where he stood when I saw a bold road sign to the abbey and, 100 metres on, the huge mass of the abbey building looming in the dusk! It was a forbidding sight, dark and brooding. But straight ahead lay the main portal. I tried the door and to my surprise found it unlocked. I entered the hall, divided by a wrought-iron screen. On my side of the screen was a bell marked "*Pforte*". I rang. After perhaps two minutes I was answered by an approaching sister all in white, bespectacled and in late middle age. She looked at me with considerable surprise but not unkindly. I said that I was a pilgrim and would like to rest the night. She left to make enquiries. When she returned she was clearly still uncertain. However, she opened the screen to admit me to the inner hall. She was still using her internal phone to seek directions or confirmation of her instinct to take me in. Eventually she seemed to decide to act on her own initiative, and led me along a passage, pausing to hand me bottled water and, further on, a bottle of beer. Then she showed me to a room and pointed out other rooms for shower and lavatory. When I asked if there was a morning mass she showed me the route to access the chapel by a door that led into the chancel. Mass would be at six-thirty and breakfast at seven. After I had settled in my room the door opened slightly and a hand slid a packet of biscuits along the floor before swiftly closing the door. What kindness. I did not need the biscuits since I had the pastries that Aura had brought from her grandmother and a cheese sandwich which I had made at breakfast at Stift Schlägel and had never had occasion to eat. So I was content with these and my half litre of beer.

☞

Day 4 – 4 October 2018 – *Thyrnau to Passau*

THERE WERE SEVEN sisters at mass, which was conducted by a robust old priest. When I went to breakfast there was an old man at the table dressed in *Trachten*. I had no idea who he was and only as time passed did I begin to think that he was perhaps the priest, not immediately recognisable without his vestments. We were then joined by two ladies who engaged him in lively conversation, to which I occasionally contributed when addressed. It was a good breakfast with a carefully boiled egg and excellent home-made raspberry jam. I discovered that my friend from the previous night was Sister Elizabeth, who was summoned to deal with my account. I chose eight postcards but when I endeavoured to pay she whispered conspiratorially to the effect that I should simply pocket them. There seemed to be a conflict between generous instinct and rectitude but I did what I was told. Sister Elizabeth wrote a little bill: room €20, breakfast €5. I had that in two notes and settlement was therefore straightforward. She led me to the door and warned me against the weather. I must take care and I must keep warm. I understood why as the thick freezing fog enveloped me. I could not see 50 metres ahead.

The parish church was closed and under heavy restoration. Nearby is a famous Loretto house. I find these Loretto houses singularly unconvincing. Only because of the weather I went to find the Landgasthof Grinninger. After Zum Lang it was a disappointment. I had missed nothing there. I then passed time by seeking the tourist office. I knew that the *Gemeindehaus* was at 18 Hofmarkstrasse. I had passed it twice without noticing, but it dealt only with local administration and the information office was some 5 kilometres distant at Kellberg. However, they were most helpful and printed off a map of the Jakobsweg route through their parish and proudly produced a Jakobsweg stamp, which they applied to the page of my book. Sister Elizabeth had herself applied a stamp to my book, which records that the abbey is the Abbey of the Cistercian Sisters of St Joseph.

☞

I NEED TO rectify two omissions from my record of the previous day.

The first is that my taxi ride had robbed me of the experience of crossing the border between Austria and Germany, which runs between Neustift and Gottsdorf. According to my guidebook there is a border stone there dating back to the reign of Maria Theresa. There is also, close by, a memorial to the fact that this is the historic Schmugglerweg. So had I walked I would have encountered two points of history that might have been of exceptional interest. The border runs north–south between Neustift and Gottsdorf until it shortly reaches the Danube. The border then follows the river north-westwards until it reaches Passau, where it switches at the confluence to the Inn, thereafter travelling southwards with the river. So from Gottsdorf to Passau I was strictly on German soil, although never more than a short step from Austria. In my mind it was all Austria from Schlägl to Schärding.

The second omission is that the parish church in Gottsdorf is dedicated to St Jakob and in the porch I found the proper ink box and stamp with which I have adorned my book.

My way out of Thyrnau led me past the abbey and what would have been its substantial outbuildings. Soon I was on a field path with almost no visibility and grass wet from the fog. This was full autumn season and, although there had been little leaf fall, everywhere the ground was strewn with apples, pears, beech mast, acorns and sycamore seeds. There were no pheasants so the acorns lay thick under foot. On this field path I saw a particularly heavy fall and, looking up, saw an oak with extraordinarily prolific acorn cover. I picked a sprig and put it in my coat. As I walked on, the field path led into the local byroad, which descended to Schwarzmühl. There the Jakobsweg leaves the tarmac and runs at once into a forest walk. Gradually the sun prevailed and filtered through the dispersing mist and forest trees.

My experience of waymarking in Germany, although limited, leads to the conclusion that it is excellent everywhere except where most needed, namely in thick forest. So again on this occasion, after I had confidently chosen the stronger path, suddenly it began to diminish until it had completely disappeared. So there I was, in the middle of the forest, facing a deep gulley which, even if successfully crossed, would offer no way ahead. Like a huntsman whose hounds have suddenly checked, I opted for a wide cast. To my left lay only the stream, the Satzbach, bubbling happily on towards the Donau. So I cast right-handed and uphill, thinking that I had erred in refusing the right fork at the previous junction. My cast revealed nothing and I was truly lost. My only option was to find the path as it had been before it died its death and work my way back for a fresh start. I recognised the path below, where it skirted a dank black pond. Having reached it I retraced my steps. Then on my left I noticed a strong forest path which had been covered with broken red roof tiles for traction. It stretched uphill invitingly and I reasoned that it must have a significant beginning. So I clambered uphill in the increasing heat of a perfect autumn morning. What a contrast was this weather to the proceeding three days. I had to completely change dress to keep step with the weather. This necessitated an increase in the weight of the rucksack and a reduction of the padding under the shoulder straps, but that was better than drowning in my own sweat.

The tile path proved a lucky chance as it led to a tarmac road and a triple junction. The third path was also a forest path but bore the emblem of the golden shell on the blue ground. What joy, what triumph! I walked on in perfect bliss and photographed the forest scene just after ten o'clock and again at eleven-thirty. I passed through Witzmannsberg and then Zieglreuth. The latter village was clearly a dormitory for the city of Passau. After an unattractive transit, on leaving the last house the path crossed the main road and continued down a highway until turning right sharply into the forest. I then had three quarters of an hour of glorious woodland walking to emerge at a big field of pasture on the outskirts of Grubweg. Between this pasture and the substantial town of Grubweg there was no borderland. One foot was on the grass, the next was on the pavement opposite a substantial discount supermarket and other hallmarks of town life. Fortunately these included bus stops only 20 metres down the road. It was 12.30. I was exhausted from the excesses of the previous day and my adventures in the forest. I checked the bus stops. On my side was a timetable suggesting a route into the centre of Passau with a half-hourly service next due in three minutes. It was irresistible. I and two other passengers boarded and the driver confirmed that he stopped in the Rathausplatz. Although I had completed only half that day's stage to Schärding, common sense cried out to make it the first half of a two-day stage.

In the tourist office in the Rathausplatz adjacent to the bus stop the young girl spoke moderate English but was curiously unhelpful, even hostile. I surmised that she was not happy in her work. However, she booked me into the Hotel Wilder Mann next door and confidently advised that the Jakobsweg went out from Passau on the Austrian bank of the Inn.

I left my rucksack in the curious Wilder Mann, which no doubt once hosted the nobility of Europe but now attracts only elderly guests of modest means. I then spent the afternoon searching out the sights. The Neue Residenz, the episcopal palace, has a staircase of imperial grandeur. The cathedral is the work of Carlo Carlone and is too grand and florid to attract me. The best thing I found in Passau was the Confiserie Simon near St Paul's church. I will not expand on its virtues, beyond recording that I never had a better cream cake in Vienna and would have filled my luggage with its home-made chocolates and *Lebkuchen* had I not had to carry them on my back. I had supper at the Brauhaus, choosing one of my favourite dishes, *Pfifferlinge* in a sauce with *Knödel*. It was only a moderate success.

☞

Day 5 – 5 October 2018 – Passau to Schärding

BREAKFAST AT THE Wilder Mann was on the sixth floor in a spacious roof room accessed only by lift. The assembled company hardly matched the grandeur of the room. But I made a fair breakfast when the eggs arrived lightly boiled to perfection. Without much enthusiasm I prepared some bread with ham and cheese to take on the way. I had paid on arrival but, seeing the city enshrouded in another thick fog, I delayed my departure until ten o'clock. I set my poor old shoes on the windowsill for a portrait photograph; see the plate section. The signs said that I had 19 kilometres to reach Schärding. Having no sense of urgency I spent time testing the confident advice of the girl in the tourist office, but having tried the start from both banks it was quite clear that she was wrong and that the way was always on the west bank of the Inn. The early passages through the city are as pleasant as could be devised, close to the river and artistically landscaped. This phase ends approximately one kilometre on at Ingling where major hydroelectric works have been constructed.

Once past Ingling lies a heavenly walk close to the bank of the wide flowing river, along a valley which is forested on both its sides. So this is a forest walk following a great river. It reminded me of the way along the Traun out of Linz and the way along the Salzach out of Salzburg. But here there is no motorway and only the railway running on the east bank shares the valley. Between a photograph glancing back at Passau (in the plate section) and a photograph of an idyllic house on the outskirts of Neuburg was a passage of three and a half hours' steady walking. Between the two I took many photographs to capture the grandeur of the river (one of which is in the plate section) and the beauty of the forest. My indolence is plain from the fact that in three and a half hours I had covered only 9 kilometres but I will probably never pass this way again and it takes time to absorb so much beauty.

Neuberg and its schloss lie about 1 kilometre inland from the river path and I did not make the detour, thinking that I might visit Neuberg with Aura on the following Sunday. So I hastened on through a landscape that never diminished in grandeur until I emerged from the forest with startling suddenness. Bends in the path removed any foresight. One moment I was in deep forest, the next I was on the edge of an extensive meadow in full sunlight. Ahead in full view rose a fine church, which I immediately photographed. Consulting my guidebook I discovered that it was the Church of Mariä Himmelfahrt at Vornbach. My guidebook informed me that it was a church of great beauty and importance. Its gothic form had been eclipsed in a major rebuild in the seventeenth and eighteenth centuries. It contains many trophies, including gothic madonnas, and an organ of historic importance. As I understand it, attached to the church is the former Benedictine monastery to which the church owes its grandeur. There is apparently a chapel in the cemetery which was the former parish church but I did not seek it out. Vornbach church is simply the most graceful and sunlit beauty. As I inhaled its spirit three ladies were separately preparing the chancel and some side altars for harvest festival. English tributes to the bountiful goodness of the growing seasons are negligible by comparison.

From the church the way leads through the village and needs careful attention, but once you find Mühlenweg all flows serenely back into the Inntal-Radweg, which the parish of Vornbach interrupts. From Passau the pilgrim has shared the way with the *Radfahrerer*. They are numerous, some cycling north to Passau and some, like me, heading south. Sometimes they are elderly, the men in lycra and with short grey beards. Sometimes they are professionals moving at great speed and with great determination. It does not pay to get in their way. Such is the flow that I must have said "Grüss Gott" a thousand times between Passau and Neustift. After Vornbach there is only Nieder Schärding, through which it is easy to pass. Pressing on with weary legs I saw ahead the main road bridge over the river and thought that I would take it and drop down into Schärding, but that is not designed. This modern bridge sweeps loftily above the way and I had no choice but to continue to the old bridge at the south end of Neuhaus am Inn.

Before the old bridge is the remarkable sight of a *Kloster* built on a small island close to the west bank of the river. The *Kloster* occupies the entire island so that its walls on every side seem to fall into the river. My guidebook informed me that it was the Kloster der Englischen Fräulein, built in the Middle Ages and then rebuilt for the baroque age. I had encountered this order's convent in the centre of St Polten, an equally attractive exterior of the same period. The order was founded by an English Catholic, Mary Ward, in 1609, she being inspired by St Ignatius of Loyola. The order seems to have taken root in Bavaria and Austria where it acquired its label of "the English girls". I took a number of close-ups and then a distant view as I crossed the old bridge; see plate section. The delight at stumbling on this island *Kloster* is immediately magnified manyfold as Schärding comes into view. It too rises sheer from the waters of the Inn and is crowned by not a citadel but the dominant, high-standing *Pfarrkirche*. It is an unearthly moment. Revealed is the celestial city. Truly, this is how the city of Zion must appear. Perhaps the photograph in the plate section does not bear out this hyperbole.

I had pre-booked a room at the Biedermeier Hof, which is modest in price and also in amenities. The friendly son of the proprietor tolerated my German and recommended the Brauhaus for supper. This was a good recommendation. Here the chanterelles were described as *Eierschwämme* and served with gnocchi rather than dumplings – altogether a better dish. So ended this autumn stretch more or less from the Czech border across the Austrian promontory to run south on one side or other of the German border. At its end the walker may choose Neuhaus am Inn in Germany or, across the bridge, Schärding in Austria. Of course, Austria was my choice and Schärding is almost too good to be true. I suspect its presentation as a pure baroque town is superficial and much of its effect is the result of scrupulous planning and conservation, creating an environment that attracts tourism, trade and investment. On the following morning I moved to the superior Hotel Forstinger in the lower marketplace to await Aura's arrival from Vienna. I enjoyed the exterior of the parish church more than its interior. I relished the farmers' market in the expanded upper market and I found an *Abendmesse*, only after great perseverance, at the church attached to the *Kurhaus*, which is in the hands of the Barmherzige Brüder. The priest was a powerful old man, but eccentric, I thought.

On Sunday, with the advantage of Aura's Range Rover, we drove across the old bridge to Neuhaus am Inn and thence on through Vornbach to Neuburg. Not only does Neuburg lie a kilometre west of the Jakobsweg as it hugs the Inn, but it also stands probably 300 metres above the riverbank. Neuburg is dominated by its castle, which commands a long stretch of the river and has done for a thousand years. So, although a hefty diversion, it would be justifiable given the historic importance of the castle and it would also offer the option of an overnight stay in the Hoftaferne adjoining the castle. In one of the Jakobsweg guides I had read that at Schloss Neuburg there was "das barocke Prunkgärtl". It was those words that compelled me. And what I found exceeded all my expectations. This small formal garden lies outside the schloss and so flaunts itself that it is impossible to enter the schloss gate without surveying it all laid out and exposed on ground that falls away towards the distant Inn. Its dimensions are perhaps forty metres square within its four walls and its triumphant crescendo is the grotto pavilion at the end of the garden, symmetrically placed against the far wall. Even to the most fastidious critic it is a masterpiece. It was commissioned from Carlone when he was engaged on the embellishment of Passau's cathedral. The decoration is achieved with stone, shell and mirror glass, all very fragile, particularly when exposed to high-summer heat and mid-winter cold. We were lucky to see it in perfect order, perhaps thanks to recent restoration. All in all, it seemed to me perfect in its proportions, decorated with fantasy and wit and achieved with the highest standards of craftsmanship. I took many photographs, of which I have selected one for the plate section. The castle is a wonderful fortress commanding not only the Inn valley to the east but also all other approaches. But after the garden I had eyes for little else.

☞

OVER THE COURSE of approximately a hundred kilometres from Schlägl to Schärding I had been in pursuit of my goal of covering all the Jakobsweg on Austrian soil. But from Schärding the way immediately turns sharp west into Germany and remains in Germany for ten long days of walking. So, what was the solution for me? The Jakobsweg re-enters Austria at Brannenburg for a full day's walk to reach Kufstein. From Kufstein there are four full stages to reach Innsbruck. I had found the last five days taxing. I had not the zest or zeal that once I had. The rucksack had become a burden when once I hardly felt its weight. Just as I eschewed Slovenia so I would eschew Germany. Therefore next spring I hoped to pick up the way at Brannenburg as it re-enters Austria and follow it to Kufstein and at least on to Breitenbach. Just before Breitenbach this Bohemian tributary meets the main stream of the Jakobsweg flowing from Bratislava to Feldkirch. Thus for two more days and 40 kilometres I could say that I had completed the Jakobsweg on Austrian soil, for I had already walked the stretch from Breitenbach to Innsbruck.

BRANNENBURG TO STRASS IM ZILLERTAL

Day 6 – 14 May 2019 – Brannenburg

WHEN I REACHED Schärding the previous autumn I was convinced that I would resume at the border point where this pilgrim way re-entered Austrian territory. I had no desire, and perhaps no reserves, to undertake the many days of walking in South Bavaria that connect the Austrian passage in the north to the Austrian passage in the south. If Schärding marked the point at which the Jakobsweg leaves Austrian soil in the north, Brannenburg is the point at which the Jakobsweg returns to Austrian soil in the south.

So, at half past ten in the morning on 14 May the Budapest express bound for Munich pulled out of Vienna's main station. It would carry me to Rosenheim, where I had to change onto the local service to reach Brannenburg. Aura had made sandwiches for me and I saved them until the train pulled out of Salzburg. I reached Rosenheim just before two o'clock and I had half an hour to wait for the local train. In the station concourse I passed the time by buying postcards from the newsagent and a nail file from the chemist. I was not killing time in the shops: these were urgent needs.

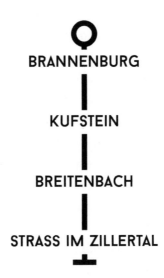

BRANNENBURG

KUFSTEIN

BREITENBACH

STRASS IM ZILLERTAL

The local train was crowded with schoolchildren and I had hardly time to look out of the window before we drew into Brannenburg. The station yard was deserted and offered little clue as to whether to take the road to the left or to the right. I chose to turn left and in just under a kilometre approached the town centre.

The tourist industry is important to Austria and Germany and a high-quality tourist information service has consequently developed. Offices are marked by the letter "I" in white on a green background and they are not to be missed. Even when not in need, it is wise to pop in for reassurance. Being a civic service it is usually in the town hall, and so it was in Brannenburg. Freshly arrived on the new route, I had plenty of questions for the kindly lady at the counter. Surprisingly, she spoke no English and conversation was reduced to the extent of my German. As soon as I explained my presence she gave me a good map covering the Jakobsweg from Salzburg to Kufstein. Breaking a long day to Kufstein into two days, she suggested staying overnight in Reisach. There was a monastery there dedicated to St Theresa. In low cloud and rain a short day seemed attractive and I asked her to book my next night there but her call to the monastery was not answered. Thinking ahead I asked her to research what there was in Breitenbach and I easily recognised the Rappold as the *Gasthaus* that I had in my memory. I asked her to book two nights but only the first was available. With her help I had thus mapped out the three walking days that lay ahead. She also gave me a town map, marking the parish church and my immediate destination, Hotel zur Post, which I had pre-booked with Booking.com. I am in no doubt that we both enjoyed the fifteen minutes we spent together, she as the giver of advice and me as the grateful recipient.

The parish church was a disappointment, the grey stone blocks of its construction visible inside as well as out. I was surprised by this austerity until I remembered this was not an Austrian church. The zur Post had an equally austere, even neglected, exterior heightened by the notice on the door saying that it did not open until 17.00. Fittingly, the post office was next door, and I was able to buy stamps and to learn that the box would be cleared at 16.50.

Reaching the crossroads at the heart of the town I found a cheerful ice-cream café and settled there to write my cards in the happy atmosphere created by many fellow ice-cream eaters.

Trying to cut the difference I saw the post van clear the box and drive away when I still had five minutes to wait for the hotel door to open. I am inclined to pre-judge a hotel by its name. Names that suggest continuity, such as The Golden Lion, The Black Eagle or The Post are automatic choices for advance booking. Of course, sometimes they disappoint and never more so than in Brannenburg. The interior had a reception counter, behind which stood the surly proprietor. He was issuing keys to rooms opening off a long corridor on the first floor. The hotel consisted of nothing else, save a charmless breakfast room provided by a modern extension. Amazingly, there was almost a queue at the reception. Perhaps the proprietor reserved the worst room for me, the guest least likely to return. It was tiny and grim. The shower cubicle within the room was no better. The door to the balcony did not open and the only window was cracked. When I rejected the proprietor's recommendation of a pizza restaurant, he reluctantly gave me the name of a restaurant for locals, which I then identified on my map.

It lay on the outskirts of the town, quite a long walk in drizzling rain, but had a cheerful interior and a warm welcome. The menu was simple, either asparagus and beef or asparagus and fish. I chose the fish and it was excellent, as was the white wine. I returned to the hotel in a better mood and slept well. But any cheer was erased by the sight of steady rain and puddles in the sand of what seemed to be a yard for animals behind the hotel. Things got worse with a dire breakfast served by the proprietor's wife. Their commercial creed seemed to be to charge as much and to give as little as they could get away with. My only consolation was the knowledge that Booking.com would ask me for a review.

☞

Day 7 – 15 May 2019 – Brannenburg to Kufstein

I SET OFF into the dank dark day as soon as I could. Although the rain had eased, the low clouds not only obliterated the wonderful scenery but almost touched the face of the earth. I found the exit for the Jakobsweg beside the pizza restaurant and soon passed the little gothic church of St Agidius. This pretty path served only to dump me swiftly onto a main road linking Brannenburg with Nussdorf. Between the two lay the motorway and then the Inn. Those who design motorway junctions (and this was the Brannenburg exit) have little consideration for pedestrians. This hazard lies about a kilometre out of town and the crossing of the Inn which follows is comparatively easy. I had contemplated a Jakobsweg variant which follows the edge of the hills beyond Nussdorf. I might have been tempted on a fine day but as it was I turned immediately south having crossed the Inn to follow the Innradweg on the embankment. The river embankment provides the *Radweg* to Kufstein and beyond. Proximity to the river is a merit but not so the absence of nature and the unforgiving asphalt surface which is not easily mitigated.

The mighty Inn is comparable to the Drau; although both are tributaries of the Danube, both are great rivers in their own right. Hence the Jakobsweg generally follows the rivers and they both become familiar companions. Here the Inn runs very straight and from the elevation of the embankment seems to stretch almost to the horizon. Far ahead the river seemed to be girdled. Was it a bridge, a weir, or electricity generation? Only when I drew quite close did I see that it was a pontoon bridge. Spaced along its length were flat-nosed boats with engines running, pushing the pontoon against the river's flow. On each boat stood two soldiers controlling the thrust. I had come upon a military exercise rehearsing the crossing of the pontoon by an extensive convoy. On the far side stood a tank, its sombre flank emblazoned with a white German cross on a black ground. To me, with childhood memories of war with Germany in Europe, it had a sinister look. As I paused I saw the first vehicle in the convoy trundle down the far bank and onto the pontoon. It crossed ponderously and, reaching the end of the pontoon, breasted the bank and away. The convoy extended to vehicle after vehicle, tracked machine-gun carriers alternating with light lorries. Each machine gun was manned by an alert soldier, as if he were anticipating immediate engagement. I grew weary of watching after perhaps twenty minutes, and with no sign of an end I walked on.

To enable the pontoon to function, a broad scoop had been taken out of the embankment at each end and then tarmacked for transit. After walking on for perhaps a kilometre I saw ahead another pontoon position similarly scooped out of the embankment at either end. As I approached the scoop I saw in the undergrowth immediately to the left of my path a platoon of soldiers, motionless but alert, and facing the river as though guarding an imaginary pontoon. I felt them to be humans beneath their roles and greeted them with a smile and a wave. But for them I did not exist.

I came upon these dramas on the way between Nussdorf and Windshausen. Windshausen is no more than two or three farms on the east bank with the tiny *Wallfahrtskirche* Heilig Kreuz standing apart from and above the hamlet, its visibility enhanced by its white painted walls against the green of the adjoining forest. After Windshausen is a long stretch beside the river until the way turns inland to reach the village of Erl.

Erl is famous for holding the oldest passion play, in competition with Oberammergau. It has been performed there since the beginning of the 17th century, once every six years through the summer months. In the 1950s a substantial theatre was built to house the performance. It lies outside the village and dominates the landscape, again an effect enhanced by its brilliant white painted exterior. Given the weather and my early morning decision to reach Kufstein I forwent a closer inspection of Erl. I could see from my map that it was in reality a detour rejoining the Innweg at Mühlgraben. To continue on the river path was a shorter and simpler solution.

All morning the Autobahn had been thundering beside the Inn on its west bank and at Mühlgraben we were to cross the river, pass beneath the Autobahn and the railway line and then strike westwards into Germany again. It was a footbridge across the river, connecting Erl to the village of Reisach. Immediately after the motorway crossing, the Jakobsweg swings north to reach a schloss now serving as a health clinic. Here the road swings sharply westwards to reach the Carmelite monastery of St Teresa of Avila. This monastery was for me the highlight of the day's walk. Built between 1731 and 1738, it incorporates a church whose interior is the work of Johann Baptist Straub, completed between 1750 and 1760. The monastery, painted Austrian yellow, is all the more impressive for standing isolated on the valley floor with wooded foothills rising behind. Had I not been on the Jakobsweg I would have made more effort to penetrate its interior. As it was I saw only the monastery church, or as much as could be seen from behind the wrought-iron screen at the west end, which is all that the public is offered. J.B. Straub was the leading sculptor of the Munich court and his work is abundant in and around Munich. At Reisach he executed seven relief work altars, his fusion of two-dimensional ground and three-dimensional sculpted image of a kind I have not seen elsewhere. It is indeed striking. It was impossible to appreciate the altars from behind the grill but at least in the adjoining entrance hall postcards of most of the seven were available. The only sign of engagement with the populace was a notice that one of the community would direct something akin to a retreat on three named dates within the year. As I left the church I saw a door marked "Clausur", but there was no basis upon which I could knock. There was an open yard to the side but even here was a barrier marked "Privatgrund".

So I walked on across the fields under the railway to reach the substantial village of Niederaudorf. In the middle of the village was a curiously old-fashioned wholesale butcher and hotel. I suppose the two trades combine well. Entering through the main door I found a great hall, off which to the left was the dining room and, to the right, the kitchen. The dining room was full as it was the lunch hour. Waitresses scurried across the hall, between kitchen and dining room. I caught one in mid-flight with a request for a cup of coffee. She waved me to a table in the hall, soon served me and even offered their Wi-Fi code. It was about halfway to Kufstein so time and place were right for my only break of the day. After ten minutes I was on, heading south-west through attractive country to reach Agg. The landscape is unusual, a series of large mounds, like half an egg, all thickly wooded. On from Agg is a road walk, pleasant enough. A huge white hospital lies just off the road and it strikes a chill, suggesting a place of death rather than a place of healing. It is named Bad Trissl Klinik and it dominates the neighbourhood. It might provide the setting for a Thomas Mann novel. The lanes on the outskirts lead into suburban streets that suddenly emerge into the main street and square of Oberaudorf, awash with hotels, health cures and expensive shops. In the square I found the tourist information – or perhaps it found me. The helpful lady at the counter provided me with a town map and pointed to the left turn on the other side of the street marked Kufsteinerstrasse. Just by the turn was a top-class cake shop. I should have passed it by but resistance crumbled, although I made a minimum purchase. The cake was labelled *Karmelitener*. After Reisach that seemed the fit choice. It was a pastry envelope stuffed with a sweet walnut paste. I ate it slowly as I walked downhill and enjoyed every mouthful. It lasted me until I reached Mühlbach, where there is a handsome old house at the junction with Rosenheimerstrasse, the street that leads on to Kiefersfelden. Although this is a street walk of some 3 kilometres from Oberaudorf, it is pleasant enough; there is a *Fussweg* running alongside the tarmacked traffic street, with open farmland and fine scenery after you have passed through Mühlbach.

Kiefersfelden has little to recommend it, although the tourist office in the centre did me well. I was directed to take the next left at the traffic lights into Innstrasse, which would in turn lead into Romerweg. At a sharp bend at the bottom I was to look out for a footpath that would lead me across fields to reach the Innradweg. As the lady described it so I found and soon I had reached the cycle path and the left or German bank of the Inn. For here the Inn is the boundary and in the 16th century Kufstein provided one of the principal gateways to Habsburg lands. At the tourist office I had been advised to take the first available bridge, a pedestrian bridge which is also signed for the Jakobsweg. However, I preferred to stick to the cycle path and that bought me to a bridge of great significance, being the only road bridge and one that directly connects the railway station to the main square beneath the fortress of Kufstein. The fortress was built in the time of Maximilian on a bluff that even without the fortress would dominate the town and its surroundings. Topped by the fortress it inspires awe. Gross too is the railway station and its adjoining marshalling yards on the other side. The line carries all the southbound traffic and many trains stop here. So for most people their acquaintance with the fortress is the view that they get from their railway seat.

As I reached the marketplace it was already 5.30 and I knew that I had a choice between three hotels. I looked first at the Goldener Löwe; the exterior seemed dismal and did not meet the expectation created by the name. This impression was heightened by a glimpse of three roughs leaving the hotel. So I returned to the Auracher Löchl. I knew it to be the best hotel and was relieved to find that they still had one room available. I took it, although it was much above my normal budget. This good old hotel had been given a fashionable makeover by some unimaginative interior decorator. Each room had a country theme. My room was China, evidenced by a scatter of pseudo Chinese objects which might have been sourced from a Caritas shop. I rather liked the effect, however, which was after all only a 21st century return to what had been fashionable intermittently in the 17th century in Europe. Otherwise everything in the room was luxurious and the bed exceptionally comfortable. Furthermore, the windows commanded a panoramic view of the Inn, upstream and downstream. I had an excellent dinner in the restaurant attached to the hotel in the building across the street and slept like a log.

The weather had been so dank my camera had not left my pocket all day.

☞

Day 8 – 16 May 2019 – Kufstein to Breitenbach

I WAS FIRST into breakfast, anticipating a feast. I was not disappointed. In charge of the breakfast was a middle-aged man. He noticed my Moroccan babouche slippers. They pleased him greatly since he was, as he revealed, Moroccan. That gave me his undivided attention, to the slight prejudice of the other guests. I not only ate an excellent breakfast but prepared myself a fine picnic for the long walk to Breitenbach. The dreary weather of the day before had cleared away to give a day of sunshine and clouds blowing on the west wind. Crossing the bridge I tried without much success to photograph the fortress but the sun was all wrong. Kufstein is in a way unsuited to its ancient and important role, since there is only a narrow strip of level land between the river and the rock face that climbs through foothills to culminate in the Wilder Kaiser, whose peaks had thrilled me when I had seen their eastern flank. Strangely, although there is more suitable ground for development on the west bank, there is very little there save the railway station, all the town being confined to the long but narrow strip on the east bank.

My immediate challenge was to get beyond the railway station. I contemplated a direct assault but when I saw how huge the platforms were and the tracks beyond I thought better of it and, casting left, saw a covered stairway rising sharply. I took it to reach a bridge that carried me across all the railway ground and deposited me in a quiet street above and beyond. From the railway exit to open country was but a few hundred metres. As I walked on I met a charming scene: a quiet road with old houses to the left and nothing on the other side but an uninterrupted view across farmland to thickly wooded hills rising to fill the eye. Anyone lucky enough to own one of these houses has at the same time a sense of commanding an alpine scene in front and yet being within a five-minute walk of a rail link to all the cities of central and eastern Europe. At the end of this road the path dives steeply down to reach the banks of the Inn and there follows for about a kilometre an easy route between river on the right and motorway on the left. Then a sharp right turn carries the walker away from the river, which he will not see again until the day's end at Breitenbach. To lose the river is also to lose the motorway under which the Jakobsweg immediately passes; then comes quickly thereafter the railway, over which the Jakobsweg now passes. This endeavour to shake off the transport systems on the valley floor is not entirely successful, as ahead lies the L211 that connects Kufstein and Kirchbichl.

As I passed over the railway I was overtaken by a young woman on a bicycle with a seat for her child mounted over the front wheel. Just short of the main road was a farm on the right and on the left a wire netting enclosure almost 2 metres high within which there was a henhouse, assorted fowl and three goats or sheep, I was uncertain as to which. They were a family: one male, one female and one offspring. Here I met again the mother and child, both dismounted and feeding the animals through the wire. All three had long coats of straight hair, chestnut colour streaked with black. The male had well-developed horns. To the child this was clearly a favourite treat.

The animals were the attraction and the poor hens got nothing. I doubt that mother and child realised I was watching them.

All pleasure at this interlude faded as I reached the main road. There was a constant stream of traffic in both directions. Eight kilometres on from Kufstein I was hot and tired. The sun beat down and there was little shade. Almost at once I came to a bus stop. The timetable suggested that a bus was due in five minutes and that in less than another five it would cover the 2 kilometres to the edge of Schaftenau, where a wide junction marked the parting of the Jakobsweg from this charmless highway onto the village street, Obere Dorfstrasse. I was more than tempted. Only a masochist would have rejected this godsend. I settled down to wait and just as I was beginning to doubt my reading of the timetable the bus swung into sight. I requested the first stop in the Dorfstrasse and the driver to put me down. I hardly needed his help. The contrast between the highway and the Dorfstrasse was too obvious. He swung into the village and I duly alighted at the next stop. It would have been unprincipled to ride further. Indeed, the Dorfstrasse had much to recommend it: quiet and bordered by neat houses and gardens, all spaced out. This main artery of village life ran on into the adjoining village of Langkampfen. Here, at a junction, I swung right for Niederbreitenbach. By the turn was a bus stop and I decided to rest in its shelter and on its seat. Soon an old man shuffled up in a pair of the sort of plastic slippers worn by men and women working in the health service. Clearly he had come to catch a bus and he appeared suitably attentive, if somewhat confused. I had a view to my right of about 50 metres to a T-junction. As he stood facing the T-junction I glanced that way and saw a bus pass by without stopping. I guessed that he had chosen the wrong stop, a guess confirmed by his reaction as he shuffled off towards the junction. He looked helpless but there was little I could do to help him.

It is a pleasant country road that connects Langkampfen with Niederbreitenbach. The fields on either side are well farmed. Mowing for silage and hay had not yet begun so cuts to shorten a winding road were not possible. This comparatively late start surprised me as in Wiltshire a considerable acreage had been cut for silage in late April. The name of the village, Niederbreitenbach, seems surprising since it is a long way from Breitenbach and certainly not on the same *bach* or brook. In the village centre was a substantial *Gasthaus* which I penetrated in search of a drink. The restaurant off the entrance hall was very full of local working men eating the lunch of the day. I sat in the hall to drink a cup of coffee.

Reinvigorated, I set out on what was an unattractive stretch of about 2 kilometres to reach Mariastein, which I anticipated to be the highlight of the day's walk. I walked what seemed to have become more of a highway with frequent traffic in both directions and no escape from what had become a hot sun. It was a considerable relief to see a Jakobsweg waymark indicating a side road that led off to the left and rose steeply uphill through a belt of forest. After a modest climb the ascending byway emerged from the trees to reveal a spectacular fortress soaring up from a rocky spur above. Fifty metres ahead on the left stood a restaurant café which attracted me. But when I reached it there was a sign on the door informing all that it was their *Ruhetag*. On the deserted terrace there were some tables and chairs set for busier days. The terrace commands a magnificent view of the fortress and I settled down to eat the picnic that I had made that morning. Nothing marred the sense of perfection. I was undisturbed on a warm terrace with comfortable table and chairs, an unrivalled view of the tower, brilliant white against a full blue sky. The photograph I took is in the plate section. My picnic had been made with the best of ingredients. Even the knowledge that I had a long way to go did not spoil the indulgent moment. When I moved on it was to explore what appeared to be a castle built for war but which is marked as a *Wallfahrtskirche*.

The entry is signalled by a free-standing arch at the roadside. Through the arch the eye is caught by two painted warriors dressed to serve Maximilian I, one each side of a modest door. There was neither sight nor sound of another human and as I approached the door I fully expected to find it locked. When it opened, it admitted me to a courtyard formed by a flanking wall closing three quarters of a circle; the fourth quarter provided an entry from the car park below. The curtain wall sprang from the tower that was rooted in the rocks opposite the point at which I stood. I approached the modest door at the foot of the tower, again fully expecting it to be locked. Only the familiar notice on the door – *Bitte Türe schließen* – led me to think otherwise. Again the eerie opening admitted to a surprising space – this time a wooden staircase with walls on either side completely covered by portrait photographs of individuals who I took to be either pilgrims or departed loved ones of pilgrims.

The staircase led to the first floor, which consisted of a warren of interconnecting spaces, all devotional, and a small chapel.

The focus of devotion in the chapel was a medieval madonna. Within the circular space of the tower were two staircases offering ascent to the second floor. This was entirely given over to a chapel created or redecorated in the baroque period.

Again there were two staircases serving the third and top floor. Again the whole space was given to the Chapel of the Madonna of the Pilgrimage, in the power of which people had believed for more than six hundred years.

In part it must be because of the turbulent times of its construction in the 15th century that the place of pilgrimage should have been raised as a fortress. If the ultimate object of veneration was naturally nearest to heaven, the two lower levels were fittingly filled with emotional images to prepare the pilgrim for the ultimate goal. This venerated place had seen such surges of history: good times when the land was at peace and bad times when war, pillage and pestilence battered its foundations. It seemed to me a miracle in itself that the building and its original mission had survived. That is perhaps partly explained by the fact that it is in the joint charge of temporal authority (the Province of Tyrol) and spiritual power (the Archbishop of Salzburg).

Leaving Mariastein, I walked a few metres to the houses huddled at the crossroads above. Here I was forced to pause since the four alternatives offered seemed ambiguous and there was no sign of the heartening yellow shell on a blue background. Eventually I got a clue and soon found myself back on the way, walking through the woods. In due course a sign at a junction offered me a variant as a choice and I took it only because it was signed Baumgarten, which the guidebook told me was a village through which I must pass. I would not normally take a variant and I regretted having done so when I was evacuated from the woods onto a main road with no indication of the onward direction. I took the more probable right turn, which did lead me towards the large Gasthaus Baumgarten. But that reassurance evaporated a few metres further on when my suburban road met a highway at a T-junction. Again there was no waymark and little evidence to suggest right or left. I was loath to choose because error would be costly, particularly on an unattractive highway walk. I waited for an approaching pedestrian and asked for help. He understood my question, I understood sufficient of his answer to know that I should turn right and look for another right turn onto a side road in Angerberg. Fortunately Angerberg was not far on and I was relieved to leave the highway on a small road through undeveloped land to reach a modern wood-built chapel across the road from this junction. Here there was no alternative but to walk on what was again the L211, a relatively significant local road connecting all the villages east of the river from Kufstein on.

After a long slog the road passes within sight of Glatzham. This is significant as Glatzham is the junction between the main Jakobsweg river, which flows, metaphorically, from east to west across Austria, from Bratislava to Feldkirch, and the tributary that I was walking from Český Krumlov (or, in my case, Schlägl). Thus all before Glatzham was fresh and the walk from Glatzham I had walked before. I remembered the hard slog up from Wörgl and the desperation that had forced me to hitchhike soon after Glatzham. Fortunately, on this occasion I was out of neither stamina nor time, and I made on cheerfully to reach Kleinsöll. As a passenger in a car on my previous visit, the distance from Glatzham to Breitenbach had seemed but a brief hop. Now, as I crept antlike across the page of my guidebook, it seemed a true 8 kilometres and on the outskirts of Kleinsöll I was struck by the view of the Inn below (see the plate section). Next I was pleased to see a Jakobsweg blue and yellow marker pointing off the road, leftwards through farmland. The path ran downhill through several fields of pasture and then entered a wood where it dropped so steeply that at times I could hardly keep upright. On either side of the path the ground was thick with leaf which I instantly recognised as lily of the valley. But where were the lilies? I knew that they were in season because I had seen the flower in a garden earlier in the day. I did not resolve this attribution, and the leaves grew only at the top of the wood. As I scrambled down, all sorts of other floor cover emerged. This rapid descent terminated as I emerged from the wood onto a suburban street. Thinking that I was at journey's end, I stopped to reorganise my load and my appearance in the hope of presenting a picture of respectability as I entered the Gasthaus Rappold. As usual I was deceived, or rather had deceived myself, as I had nearly a kilometre of further road walking before I recognised the spire of the parish church, although it was now shrouded in scaffolding. I remembered Breitenbach church with affection and my heart filled with joy knowing that the Rappold lay only a hundred metres or so along the street from the church. Even so, my memory was again faulty and I did not find the Rappold easily nor recognise it at first sight. But I had been there only once and then only for a meal. On arrival I was given a simple room and later ate the good dinner that I had anticipated. Nothing is more conducive to a good sleep than ten hours of walking followed by a choice dinner.

☞

Day 9 – 17 May 2019 – Breitenbach to Strass im Zillertal
IF GLATZHAM WERE not my journey's end, undoubtedly Breitenbach was. However, Aura was forced to work a full day on Saturday at some trade show east of Vienna. How then should I spend Friday and Saturday? I was in no doubt that the greatest pleasure for me would be to walk another day from Breitenbach to Strass im Zillertal, where I remembered the excellent Hotel Post. In this choice I was rewarded.

As I left the Rappold it was a perfect spring day. The sun was up, there was not a cloud in the sky and a gentle breeze blew from the west. The departure from Breitenbach could not have been more perfect. Immediately opposite the Rappold is an entry by stile onto the fields that seem to surge into the heart of the village. After 800 metres of meadow, the path rises graciously through beech trees, which were bathed in sunlight on that perfect May morning. At the crest of the climb I looked back and tried to photograph the scene but it was hard to capture the essence of an early summer's day. After some 2 kilometres the path ran along the edge of the wood, with meadows falling away to the left. Here the harvest was just starting, with only a tractor mowing and, further on, a local gathering mown grass from under the shade of the trees at the field edge. I was sad to see that he was not using a rake but a powerful blower, petrol-driven and mounted on his back. It was fearfully noisy, even for me some 50 metres distant, and it must have weighed heavy. This was the Jakobsweg at its very best: easy walking through idyllic scenery without a waymark in sight, and only because none was needed. Towards the end of this interlude a milepost has been erected marking the precise distance to Compostela: 2,214 kilometres. Its photograph is in the plate section. The scenery just before and just after the shrine is uplifting and perhaps prompted the location of this sole pointer to an end beyond Austrian lands. I saw here an outstanding example of the beauty of an Austrian meadow awaiting the mower. That nothing in nature here has changed in the last century is proved by a painting by J. MacWirter, R.A., which was a great success when exhibited at the Royal Academy. Bought for the Tate Gallery and much reproduced, it is entitled "June in the Tyrol".

Shortly thereafter came a less welcome sign warning of the closure of the Jakobsweg because of a landslide, and a diversion was sternly marked: a stiff climb up to the right. This diversion had been in place when I had passed this way some years before and I cursed the idleness of those who had done nothing to restore the proper path. I panted and sweated as I zigzagged up to reach a depressing plantation of firs. Here there was not a path marked by the usage of ages and it appeared that the diversion had been largely ignored, for it was impossible to see which way to go or between which trees to pass. Eventually I emerged, cursing, by the back entrance to the Museum of Tyrolean Farm and Village Buildings. A sign on the five-bar gate forbade entry. I was familiar with the museum and therefore knew I had only to hop over the gate to find an easy walk up to the main entrance, but having no cause to make short cuts I continued on the diversion. I was soon regretting my obedience as the path meandered, following the circumference of the extensive museum grounds.

When I eventually reached the end of the diversion I was standing at the edge of the wood looking across a broad plain bordering the Inn, with Voldöpp in the distance. I descended a steep grass hill by a perilous path. At the foot was a sign for the museum, pointing the walker up the steep slope. I could not imagine who would voluntarily follow that invitation. Ahead of me lay perhaps 400 hectares of water meadow, all sown to grass. That description misleads, since meadows in Austria are seldom if ever grass, rather a random spread of wild flowers of every description. The only landmark between me and Voldöpp was an ancient ash tree, beside which a shrine and seat had been built. The tree had the *Denkmal* status, as it well deserved. Here I settled on the bench to eat the picnic which I had prepared at breakfast. As I ate I surveyed the frenzy of the harvest. Within 800 metres of me I counted eight tractors at work, some tedding, some mowing, some baling and some hauling. The rows for baling were created by a single sizeable circular rake that threw the rows against a rubber guard or shield. Down one way and back the reverse resulted in one thick row 10 metres from the last. The round bales were created and wrapped by one and the same machine. Bales were picked by a grab. Although the machinery in use here was not so advanced as would be seen in Wiltshire, still it was effective at achieving the same result, albeit more laboriously.

As I rested on that glorious May day, I only dimly remembered that I had rested at the same shrine almost five years before whilst on my way to Feldkirch. It had struck me even more forcibly then and I had photographed it as exemplifying a very Austrian tradition. (See First Walk, Day 25.)

Having finished my picnic, I had something over a kilometre to reach the outskirts of Voldöpp. At the edge of the village was a farmyard. Outside the yard two tractors had stopped to enable the drivers to converse. They stood between the two tractors, enormous middle-aged men but with childlike faces, burnt brick red by the weather. They must have been brothers, even more likely twin brothers. Although I had been to Voldöpp before, I took a little time to explore. Opposite the church stood a magnificent *Gasthof*, sadly converted into flats. The church stands prominently but, in my eyes, unprepossessingly. However, the interior is surprisingly rich. At the west end under the organ loft were some strange processional figures. They were life-sized and standing on processional carriages. There were four, all dressed like window models, in ancient clothing and with lifelike innocent faces. Particularly striking were the angel and child. Both were dressed with what I am sure was blonde human hair, but the passage of years had given it a sinister aspect. They were meant to represent the living but they had an aspect of the long dead.

From Voldöpp I remembered an easy footpath immediately into the north end of the famous town of Rattenberg. As usual my memory had gilded the lily. I had a long, hot walk through the outskirts of Voldöpp before reaching the footpath. That proved much longer than I had remembered and led to highways which had to be crossed before reaching Rattenberg's north end.

Rattenberg is perhaps unique among Austrian towns in having an Italianate appearance, achieved during its brief prosperity from the mining of silver. Since the collapse of the trade, the town has not had the wherewithal to develop or modernise and so it has emerged as a centre of tourism. Its long, wide main street accommodates countless cafés and even more shops retailing glass, in the making of which it now specialises.

After a cup of coffee at one of the many cafés, I decided to visit the parish church of St Virgil. Even more extreme than the squeeze in Kufstein, there is very little land between the Inn and the rock faces of the high ground closing the valley. The parish church was built on a rocky outcrop and so it stands more at first floor than at ground level. Gaining entry to the church is a puzzle. It presents only its west side to the town and it is easy to overlook the steps rising sharply from the street. I had seen something similar in Krems and also, I think, in Sighişoara, so I was confident at the foot of the stairs that they would ultimately lead to the church door. So it proved. Not to any main door at the west end, however, but to a modest door at the side. It was effective to admit to a strange church having a broad nave and one aisle only. Perhaps it was the limitation of the site which compelled such a lopsided design. The church is richly decorated with 17th-century stucco work and I particularly liked the rendering of Daniel in the Lion's Den above the high altar. At the back of the church is a strange shrine to a very local saint, St Notburga. She lived a seemingly unadventurous life in the 15th century as a servant in the household of the local feudal lord. In midlife she suffered injustice at the hands of his successor but in later life was restored to peace and plenty on his demise. At the end of a life of service and forbearance, she was carried across the river to be buried in the village of her birth. While hers had been an exemplary life, she did not seem to have the usual attributes that might lead to sainthood. In her shrine, however, there is an interesting 17th-century bust which presents her imaginatively as a stout woman in middle age.

From the church I set out on the long walk to reach my destination in Strass. Because I thought I knew the way I did not bother to look for signs, so subjected myself, doubtless unnecessarily, to a grubby walk through industrialised wastelands before and through Brixlegg. I continued only because I always had the Inn close on my right hand. Indeed, I think that it was the *Radweg* beside the Inn that I was following, and on the far side of Brixlegg I stopped for water in an open-sided kiosk for cyclists that mapped all the long distance rides into the Alpine uplands. As I walked on, the wastelands gave way to nature, the river to my right and long fields of pasture to the left.

Well over halfway to Strass, and approaching the castle on the hill which had so intrigued me on my first walk, I saw a sign to a variant which would pass the church of St Gertraudi. Since I was repeating a previous walk I was attracted to any variety and so turned left onto the variant. The modest church of St Gertraudi had invested in a Jakobsweg pilgrim stamp, with which I embellished the appropriate page in my guidebook. Leaving the church I found that I had an unattractive stretch along a village street. The only consolation was that it presented a view of the side of the castle, which emerged as a substantial ancient fortress, more or less in ruins, save for the tower visible from the path along the Inn. Worse was to come as the village street debouched onto the main highway, with fast-flowing traffic in both directions. Had I stuck to the main path this penance would have been avoided. It seemingly ended with a sign for the Jakobsweg right-handed off the highway, but as I took it I felt it was not right. As I anxiously looked at the map I saw a girl approach. I asked her if I were on the right path for Strass and she looked at me as if I were mad and walked on. I asked again with greater determination. At this she did answer but only with rude words. Her attitude was thankfully uncharacteristic. I ploughed on with ever-increasing doubt. I had a river to the left-hand side which I suspected was the Ziller and I walked in hope of a bridge. Fortunately I met a jogger, bathed in sweat, who kindly told me that I must return to the highway and continue the road walk until reaching on the left the minor road leading to the centre of Strass. I followed his directions and perhaps forty-five minutes later found myself approaching the parish church in Strass. It is dedicated to St Jakob and of course I entered as a dutiful pilgrim to offer thanks and to mark my passage with a stamp. Beside the stamp was a visitors' book and I was not surprised to see that since the previous September there had been only six entries in the book. I added a seventh. From the parish church I knew my way to the Hotel Post, opposite the station serving the villages of the Zillertal and connecting them to the main line in Jenbach. The Post was not busy and they gave me a much better room than I had booked. I had a good dinner in the restaurant and a sound sleep.

The following day, Saturday, provided an ideal opportunity to record my memories of my last three days on this tributary pilgrim path that had started in the Czech lands. It was best written up while the memory was fresh. I knew that I did not need to leave the hotel until late afternoon. But my unusually firm resolution was dogged by misfortune. After breakfast I worked all morning in the sun in the hotel garden. Only when I got home did I realise that there was no tape in the dictation machine. I did it a second time, producing a tape that was blank for the transcriber, who advised me that the tape was faulty. I did it a third time. Unbelievably, since I had tested the tape when halfway through, it was again blank. This time I was advised that it was the machine that was at fault. So, for my fourth attempt to recapture the walking days, I am equipped with a new machine and a new tape. Surely this time I will not be again in despair.

☞

The End of the Road

HAVING COMPLETED SIX years of intermittent wandering on Austria's pilgrim way I should perhaps feel some sense of satisfaction and achievement at reaching a goal which did not exist at the outset but rather, like a seed sown in good soil, emerged tentatively, then grew stronger and stronger as it developed. Certainly, little credit is due to my persistence; my great good fortune is having the capacity to persist. If I anticipated feelings of relief, satisfaction, or even triumph, I have been disappointed. I have felt even grief and mourning, as though at the death of a familiar friend. The pilgrim paths have given me such frustration, anxiety, delight and excitement that I have only a profound sense of their loss. Ageing involves forsaking parts of a faceted life, some small, some great. Gradually the distances close in; each loss, each retiring, each resignation diminishes the whole. All that I will be left with is memories, sharpest when the moment and the place were coloured by strong emotion. Memories of the Jakobsweg come upon me unbidden and unexpected. Seldom can I place them in their true time and place. Which year was it? Which of the three journeys? What was the sequence of days from which this memory, this image in the mind's eye, has sprung? Partly in an endeavour to remedy this frailty, I am preparing in more permanent form the words that I wrote at the time and the photographs that I took of things that struck my eye as I walked.

Last week – 10 July 2019, to fix the moment more precisely – I was given the brochure for the pilgrim ways in Upper Austria by the tourist office in Linz. It was not new to me as I had used it to supplement the Kompass guides when walking the main pilgrim way through Upper Austria. Then, I would only turn to the pages covering that day's journey. Last week I was on a mission that was not, with one exception, going smoothly. I had planned to reconnoitre the abbeys of St Florian and Wilhering for *Country Life* and was unable to make Kremsmünster my base as the abbey was hosting a major conference. So I based myself in Dörnbach. Attempts to arrange visits to the abbots were difficult even with the full support of the Kremsmünster office. So I had time on my hands and in Dörnbach Bauernhof I read the brochure from cover to cover and found a paragraph referring to the Innviertel Jakobsweg. I had not read the paragraph before but I had seen the thin red line of the route from Passau to Salzburg. The Kompass guide which I had thought covered this walk did so only to Schärding, then turned westwards into Bavaria, returning to Austria shortly before Kufstein and on to Innsbruck. The Innviertel Jakobsweg from Passau south to Salzburg is an Austrian pilgrim path and that was always the path I intended to walk until I confused the two paths. So, having completed the Austrian kilometres of the Austro-Bavarian path I discover in Dörnbach more than a hundred kilometres of unwalked Austrian path, from Schärding south to Salzburg.

The one exception to the general run of frustration or failure throughout that July week was that on the train from Vienna to reach Dörnbach on 6 July I had been rescued from an altercation with the guard by the stranger sitting opposite. I offered her coffee from the passing trolley, which she declined. I offered coffee in Vienna on my return on 13 July, which to my surprise and pleasure she tentatively accepted. And so we met again at the Albertina Café a week later on a perfect morning of high summer. From such an improbable beginning, Aleksandra entered my life.

And so, is it really the end of the road or come the autumn will I once again be in my boots and on my way?

THE FOURTH WALK

The Innviertel Jakobsweg

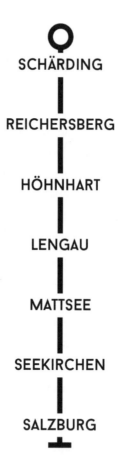

SCHÄRDING

REICHERSBERG

HÖHNHART

LENGAU

MATTSEE

SEEKIRCHEN

SALZBURG

SCHÄRDING TO SALZBURG

I HAD THOUGHT that I had walked every metre of the available Jakobsweg pilgrim routes in Austria when I reached Breitenbach in May 2019. It was only by chance that I had discovered the Innviertel Jakobsweg. I had long suspected its existence but that was only confirmed by a passing reference in a brochure promoting the Jakobsweg in Upper Austria. That chance discovery while staying in Dörnbach in July I have explained already. I then surmised that I might be drawn to a fourth Jakobsweg in the autumn, and indeed I was.

The Innviertel Jakobsweg runs from Passau in the north to Salzburg in the south. I did not need to start in Passau. Schärding was my start point, as I had covered the walk from Passau when walking south from the Czech border.

The route was problematic, however. There was no published guide. The central tourist office for the Innviertel region held nothing other than a single A3 sheet which delineated the towns and villages through which the route passed. For three of those towns I also received a tourist map. They were Reichersberg, Altheim and Maria Schmolln. All three had on the reverse the same map covering the Innviertel region.

I had never before walked with so little to go on, but in my imagination I envisaged a lovely walk along the Inn valley and in true country. It was not to be. As so often, my imagination had coloured what was in truth a monochrome.

☞

Day 1 – 16 September 2019 – Schärding to Reichersberg

I HAD SPENT a weekend of golden glow, more summer than autumn, at Schönbrunn, discovering that the park I had so often dismissed is in reality a place of great distinction and beauty. Aleksandra was my guide and to her I owe a great debt for showing me the wonders of these gardens.

I left the Park Hotel at just before eight o'clock to catch the 08.47 from Meidling station. In Linz I changed onto the local train for Passau. It stopped at innumerable stations along the way, passing through country that was unspectacular. I had hoped that the line would run close to the Inn, for my plan was to spend the first night at the monastery in Reichersberg some 25 kilometres south of Schärding, leaving the train at the stop before Schärding and thus abbreviating the walk. It was not to be. The line ran through Ried and only at Schärding did it join and then follow the Inn northwards. So, at just before eleven o'clock, I found myself on a deserted platform as the train continued on towards Passau. Not only was the platform deserted but so were the station surrounds. I knew Schärding well from past visits and sensed that the station was well out of the town. A solitary taxi on the forecourt at least enabled me to make enquiries and to conclude that the only public transport was the post bus, which stopped at Antiesenhofen, within walking distance of the monastery. Had I correctly understood? Would the bus leave in about an hour? I couldn't risk it. I got the driver to take me to the tourist office, which I well remembered to be beside the bridge in Schärding. There, a helpful girl dispelled all anxiety. She confirmed all that I had understood from the taxi driver. She printed the timetable for the bus. She telephoned the monastery and booked me a room, warning me that I must arrive no later than five o'clock.

With anxiety dispelled and confidence restored I walked the kilometre and a half back to the station and boarded the bus, which, ten minutes later, departed with me as its only passenger. Although we stopped at a number of settlements, these stops were token as I remained the only passenger to the end. Since I was riding kilometres that I should have been walking, I paid close attention and noted the fine medieval church in St Florian, the tower of which resembled a stack of building blocks, each slightly smaller than the one below. All the blocks were buttressed on their corners to remarkable effect. In the next village, St Marienkirchen, was again a medieval church, the church of a monastery built on a bluff high above the Inn. By contrast Antiesenhofen, when we reached it, was a long straggling street, just right for the shoot-out in a Clint Eastwood epic. I was dumped down at what passed for a railway station and, having no idea where to go, I headed south. As I walked on I could see a church in the distance and a lady pruning her garden shrubs that overhung the pavement. Of course I asked her for the Jakobsweg and she could not have taken more care. We soon switched from German to English and she with hesitation but ultimately precision explained that I must choose between three possible routes. Two passed by the church and then on cross-country to the centre of Reichersberg. Those routes were direct and pleasant enough, but her personal recommendation was to take a much longer route through Viehausen and on to the banks of the river. That route would take me through the hamlet of Minaberg and then into the north end of Reichersberg where lay the Stift. Since I had ample time and was not quite comfortable with my resort to the post bus, I accepted her recommendation.

It was a road walk to Viehausen but once through that hamlet I was soon on a path separated from the river by a narrow belt of woodland. So to my right stood the trees and to my left rich farmland, quite generally sown, either to maize or to grass. I knew that I needed to keep an eye out for a pilgrim chapel, which my guide told me venerated a spring of healing waters that were reputed to cure eye infections and even blindness. This sanctuary was regularly signposted as the Bründl in Viehausen. So I had no difficulty in recognising the steep flight of granite steps descending from the path to the chapel. The chapel is small, rustic and built of wood. The builders had considerately added a picnic table outside the door. Here I settled and ate half my provisions garnered from the ample breakfast at the Park Hotel. It seems that the chapel was built and is maintained by the six farmers in the parish of Viehausen. On the leaflet they are all named, as are their farms. The spring is a few steps below the chapel. Naturally it twinkles out of the rock face but it has also been piped so that it falls with the force of a kitchen tap into a sink below. I reflected on the journey for these healing waters. After a fall of some 9 metres they reach the Inn. That great river carries them all the way to Passau, where they flow into the mighty Danube. Then theirs is a long journey, until eventually they reach the Black Sea at the Danube Delta in Romania.

The farmland both before and after the shrine seemed exceptionally rich, with fine loam bearing maize crops towering well over 3 metres high. On the headland of maize fields was planted a 3-metre strip of mixed flowers: sunflowers, scabious, marigolds and cosmos daisies. And sometimes the headland was sown with pure white clover. But both had the same purpose, to provide nectar for the bees. This concern for every aspect of nature's bounty seems to me characteristically Austrian. I doubt an English farmer would be bothered. This being the season, fungi were also abundant at the edge of the wood. For the first time I turned over a white cap to reveal pink gills and, had I been at home, I would have been in no doubt that I had found a horse mushroom. But in Viehausen I could not be sure and I left it for a greater expert.

My recommended route doubled the distance and it was a good two hours before I saw the spire of the monastery church rising ahead and half right. In Austria a monastery often stands as if it were a large island in the surrounding sea of the town. On first arrival it is difficult to guess where the main gate of entry will be. Approaching from the north-east, I sensed that the gate would be at the south end but I was too tired to reject the first door that I came on. It gave on to what seemed to be an exhibition gallery, completely deserted. So I headed on and duly came upon the main gate at the head of a picturesque high street, a uniform survival of late 17th-century town houses. To the left of the main gate was the shaded terrace of the *Stiftschank*, which commanded a fine view of fields down to the river and all Bavaria stretching out beyond.

I soon discovered that the vigour of the monastery lies in its secular life, with well-developed facilities for tours, conventions, groups, retreats and casual visitors. There was an ample administrative staff in a large office. I was directed to my room just as though I had arrived at a hotel. They did not appear to expect me to show any interest in the spiritual life of the community and seemed almost unsure of when and where vespers would be said and mass celebrated on the following day. More confident was the manager in saying that I could not have breakfast before seven o'clock and he equally surely pointed out the door leading to the guest accommodation and a different door leading to breakfast.

Having settled in, I went in search of the six o'clock vespers. Approaching the church I was greeted by a hubbub of many voices coming from brick-built cellars at the foot of a flight of steep steps. Descending, I found myself in a room with perhaps a hundred people all seated facing a dais, which I assumed was for the community. Seeing a young monk enter I asked him if this was the place for vespers. "Heavens, no," he said, "that's in the church." I have no idea what I was leaving behind in the cellar as I hurried up the steep steps, turned left and entered the church to find that vespers was indeed already underway. I was alone in this large church save for four monks in the chancel who recited rather than chanted the texts. Even from the front pew it sounded like the droning of bees, sometimes placid, sometimes threatening. Suddenly the recitation ceased, the four elderly men departed and someone switched off the chancel lights. The possible presence of a congregation, even a congregation of one, seemed not to be anticipated. I left unfulfilled and explored the high street and what was once the monastery garden, now known as the Herrengarten. It has become effectively a public park. It is said to be a baroque garden in the English style. Its form is a square with four cross paths leading to a central fountain. Along the boundaries are pleasant allées of old and twisted trees. I had the impression that the spiritual life of the community had shrunk within the *Clausur* and that there was no interaction between that diminished spirituality and the burgeoning secular and commercial life of the abbey in the hands of able businessmen and, in the case of the *Schank*, a gifted and ambitious chef. Adaptability includes the surrender of a ten-acre private garden for which the community had neither use nor, perhaps, the means to maintain.

After my tour of the garden I took the last table on the terrace overlooking the river and had an excellent supper served by a huge and grumpy waitress. I was soon asleep but thereafter frequently roused by the high jinks of a large group of visiting teenagers exploring every aspect of puberty.

☞

Day 2 – 17 September 2019 – Reichersberg to Höhnhart
MASS IN THE morning was little different. Three monks and a server in the chancel, a congregation of four. The engagement between the two groups was restricted to the distribution of the

host. Within the church there seemed to be no perceptible spirit or warmth. I found the door to breakfast, which opened to a short passage leading to the kitchen. I glimpsed the dining room laid for many, but that was the group that had disturbed my sleep. A space had been cleared at a table at the kitchen door and there I was served my breakfast with kindness. I ate an egg and wrapped the rest for my rucksack. The office must have opened early because I paid my bill and set off just before eight o'clock.

Immediately after the *Gemeindeamt* I turned right, taking the lane that ran abruptly downhill and on to the outskirts of the town. There, at a Y-junction, I would have followed on to the left had a man not shouted to me from his garden. He pointed to a faint track down a grassy bank. If ever a waymark were needed, it was here. I followed his instruction with some hesitation until overtaken by a local couple out for a morning walk. We fell into conversation and walked together until we had crossed marshy ground and reached the *Radweg* on the banks of the Inn. Here we parted, with their assurance that I had 2 easy kilometres to reach Obernberg. And so it proved. Well short of the town the path turned sharp left and uphill, carrying me away from the Inn to reach the outskirts of the town, which stands on a bluff above the river. By the first houses I took a short detour to reach the advertised panorama point, where I dutifully photographed the mighty river. Not much further on was another distraction, a drive leading to what appeared to be a community centre. Two 17th-century buildings stood apart on what had been the site of a medieval castle. The castle wall commanded the same view of the river and I photographed the two manor houses that added distinction to the promontory. Not far on lay the magnificent marketplace, entirely surrounded by multicoloured baroque facades. In one corner of the irregular shape I found the post office and the stamps I would need once I had found postcards. The traditional Gasthof Goldenes Kreuz looked as if it might offer an agreeable weekend stay. Soon after leaving the marketplace the street lost its charm and as it descended revealed a fantastic development, still incomplete but with surrounding walls topped with golden balls and enclosing an array of golden domes arising from an extensive range. It looked like a circus, recently erected and soon to be dismantled. But it must have been designed to generate a substantial return on the investment. Less than a kilometre further on was a sign for a nightclub, pointing down a quiet suburban street. Out of curiosity I followed the sign until I lost patience after several hundred metres. As I returned to my path I wondered if the fantasy on the hill was to be the nightclub.

I was again on the banks of the river and I could see from the map that the river would lead me all the way to the next town, Kirchdorf. It proved to be typical of so many river routes: long, straight stretches of level asphalt walking; see the plate section for the picture of one stretch. Well short of Kirchdorf I took the path away from the river, which was clearly way-marked although the map suggested it was a variant. Just before leaving the river I photographed this witch's house; see the plate section. This alternative route led me inland to Katzenberg before swinging back into Kirchdorf.

With only a map and possessing no guidebook, I assumed that Kirchdorf would share the antiquity and charm of its neighbours on the riverside. But I found a mean and dispiriting place. I was in need of coffee but the only *Gasthof* looked as if it were closed, not for the day, but for eternity. Opposite stood a modest *Gemeindeamt* and I was made to feel an intruder when I asked where I might find a café. The woman at the counter, after all the representative of the community, should surely not have seemed so satisfied when she informed me that there was nowhere in Kirchdorf. This was dispiriting news since I could see from the map that I faced a long walk on a main road to reach the next byway, which led from Gimpling to the substantial town of Altheim. So, cursing Kirchdorf, I set off with resignation and without pleasure on a long walk only marked with the hamlet of Graben at the halfway point. Graben turned out to be a welcoming hamlet. At the first house on the left was a garden produce stall and the invitation to take with or without payment. I picked up a few chillies and a handful of walnuts to take to Aleksandra. This was about 100 metres short of the bus stop in the middle of the hamlet. Of course I checked the timetable just in case, but there was nothing for me save a wayside seat beside a tree. Feeling some attachment to the place I settled on the bench and ate my breakfast salvage. Before moving on I returned to the produce stall and doubled my helping of walnuts, paying what I thought was a fair price. I was accustomed to buying walnuts, which when fresh in the autumn, are often on sale at farm gates. Felicitas has a walnut tree in her garden and there I had discovered that they are exceptionally delicious. They are also large in size with shells that crack easily. Why they are so vastly superior to an English walnut I do not know.

This pleasant stay in Graben restored my sense of well-being and I made the next point to Gimpling in good spirits. Shortly after the crossroads in Gimpling, my footpath led off to the left and uphill. To reach Altheim I would walk over Gallenberg. The map suggested that the walk should be easy enough: I would cross a railway line and then, short of Altheim, the main road outside Danglfing. A substantial bridge carried the footpath over the railway and shortly thereafter brought me to a most unusual farmstead. What appeared to be pedigree sheep grazed in the surrounding field, the house itself appeared more decorative than functional, and the surrounding outbuildings were lavish. My curiosity aroused, I paid insufficient attention to the map, which clearly showed that I should not deviate so it was a folly that took me on a circular exploration of the property. The more I saw the more obvious it became that it was a hobby farm, the indulgence of some affluent professional or artist. There was no fence between the farm road and the farm garden, and on the edge of the garden I found an explosion of mushrooms, or so they appeared. I walked cheerfully on, thinking that this must be the road that connected the property to Altheim. Fortunately I had not gone far when I saw the railway line converge with my road. This sight sent me back to the map and my error was immediately apparent. I retraced my steps and by a wayside shrine at the farm gates saw the waymark which I had earlier neglected. This was an elementary and inexcusable error and I resumed the adjacent, true path. About a kilometre and a half on, I crossed a farm track which was being consolidated by a heavy roller. My path converged with that of the approaching roller as I reached the track and the driver got off for a chat. The conversation was one of my most successful. I explained who I was, my day's journey, my destination and my homeland. He was a strong man in middle age with a most genial face. He assumed that I was a fluent German speaker and I succeeded in concluding our exchange without revealing my limitations. I walked on with his good wishes and with some self-satisfaction. The route from there to Altheim, crossing the highway, was both literally and metaphorically downhill.

Despite having a detailed street map, I still managed to get lost in Altheim and was rescued eventually by turning right, against all indications from the map, to arrive in the marketplace. From the marketplace to the *Rathaus* I could not go wrong and I knew that within the *Rathaus* was a substantial tourist office. The office was run by a good-looking woman, more strong than beautiful, to whom I outlined my needs; immediately coffee but more substantially a bed within reasonable walking distance. According to the map Rossbach appeared to be as far as I could go, given that it was now approaching four o'clock. Of course, had I had a guidebook I would have known for myself that there was no accommodation in Rossbach. Without a guidebook, local tourist offices become vital for survival. Knowing the area, she recommended the village of Herbstheim or, failing that, Höhnhart. This was not good news as effectively she was doubling the distance I would have to walk. She set to ringing first Herbstheim and then several numbers in Höhnhart, all without success. The result, she said, was that there remained only a *Privatzimmer* which she seemed to think I would not accept. She clearly had not appreciated that I was in no position to refuse any offer. When I explained that I must have a bed, any bed, she telephoned and reported that she had successfully reserved the last room in the house in Höhnhart. She wrote out for me the family name (Gatterbauer), their address and their telephone number. For coffee she could only suggest a cup from the office machine, which I gladly accepted, and before I could intervene she had charged the machine with her own money. With someone waiting at her door, she hurried back to work and I endeavoured to extract a second cup using my own coin. The result was a predictable disaster with more coffee on the floor than in my cup. With some embarrassment, since I had no means of clearing up, I made off and was soon on my way out of town heading for St Laurenz. This was less than a mile on and, at the road junction beside the church, I could see that the main road to Höhnhart bore left and that to the right ran the road to Stern. The third alternative was cross-country to Diepolding, which provided more of a country walk and would also end in Stern. Although tempted at that late hour to walk the main road direct to Höhnhart, I could not justify such an unprincipled solution. By way of compromise I chose to reach Stern by the road, knowing that from Stern onwards lay forest paths. In Stern there was a lot of development underway and a confluence of many roads. The one I needed was the smallest, leading on to Lüfteneck at the edge of the huge Gaugshamer Wald. From Stern the tarmac was soon replaced by the softer surface of the promised *Forststrasse*. I was hot and dry and stopped to extract what juice I could from windfall black plums at the boundary of more than one garden.

The wood I then entered was huge, stretching all the way from Stern to Rossbach. I could see from the map that my way through the wood was by no means straight, with one long and seemingly pointless loop westwards at the halfway mark. The wood I had entered was a pure conifer plantation. As such, sunlight was excluded and there was neither sight nor sound of any living thing as I walked on. Obviously there were mammals but they would lie hidden. Surprising was the absence of any sight or sound of the birds that I would have expected to nest and feed there. It made me think of the wood approaching the racecourse at Goodwood which my father maintained was known as "the birdless grove". There seemed also to be no insect life. It was me and the trees. I could see from the map that it was a long walk, but underfoot the going was good and I made on. I photographed my shadow in a glade at a quarter to five; see the plate section.

After about ninety minutes I sensed that I was nearing the edge and I should emerge onto the main road on the outskirts of Rossbach. As I left the wood, I saw the road about a hundred metres ahead and my heart was glad. At the roadside stood a house and I could hear voices in the yard beyond. As a policy I always ask, if only to seek confirmation and reassurance. I was in no doubt that I was in the hamlet of Buch. Again, had I given more attention to the map I would have concluded that on the other side of the wood should be not open farmland but more forest. But I had not looked at the map with care and I was sure that my orientation would be confirmed. In the courtyard were three women, and the youngest was quick to understand my question and to read the map which I offered her. Without hesitation she showed me that I was miles from Buch. Somewhere in the midst of the forest I had swung eastwards and in consequence I had emerged not at the southern end but halfway down the eastern flank. She pointed to my precise location on the map and advised that if I wanted to be in Rossbach I had little alternative but to follow the local road from her house to Grünau and thence on the main road that I had rejected in St Laurenz. This was terrible news. It was already nearly 5.30. I was at least a kilometre and a half from Grünau and Grünau would be further from Rossbach than we were as we spoke. Probably a local would have found a better way, but for me Grünau was the only sure one. I set off with the determination that crisis induces. At the halfway point I passed a farm and asked again in the hope of some relief. A group discussion followed in which clearly the debate lay between what was possible for a local and what was possible for a stranger. They concluded that what was there for them would be too difficult for me and sent me on. On the outskirts of Grünau was a man picking vegetables in his garden. Yes, he said, ahead lay the main road and I could not go wrong. Rossbach was within reach. Well, it proved to be a long reach, and as I entered the village the church clock struck six o'clock. If I took the Jakobsweg it would be two hours on to Höhnhart. If I took the road it would still be an hour on to Höhnhart in the dusk. In the daylight all the way from Grünau I had thumbed each passing car and, although there were many at that rush hour, not one had even slowed. At least I had Frau Gatterbauer's telephone number and to my relief she answered my call. She swiftly grasped who I was and my predicament. There was only one solution and she did not hesitate to offer it. We agreed that I would walk on and she would come in her white car to collect me. Of course, as I walked every approaching car seemed to be white and as each passed I worried that I had not been seen. But there was no need to worry: the third white car slowed and in a moment Frau Gatterbauer was shaking my hand. She packed me in the car, retrieving some vital papers which had fallen from my rucksack that I had carelessly left open, and ten minutes later we drove through Höhnhart and on to her house about a kilometre and a half beyond the village. She showed me a windowless room in the basement but it was next door to the bathroom and beyond that was a kitchen, where she prepared me a supper of dumplings in clear soup and a ham sandwich. I feared that I would be alcohol-free but to my relief she added a bottle of beer. With all this inside me I slept well enough in my cell to find breakfast awaiting me at seven.

☞

Day 3 – 18 September 2019 – Höhnhart to Lengau
THE PRICE OF bed and breakfast was €28 and I had considerable difficulty in persuading Frau Gatterbauer to accept €40 to cover my rescue and my supper.

Leaving the house I could have seen that I had only to continue on the main road out of Höhnhart but in my mind I was sure that the Jakobsweg passed the church. Indeed it did, but only to reach the Gatterbauer hamlet. So walking down to the church was a luxury but for me a church was magnetic. As I approached the church the bells rang twice and only when I entered the church did I realise that they had rung for the consecration. Clearly I had arrived in the course of the eight o'clock mass and I quietly joined the congregation from the Our Father to the conclusion of the service. Although I had no regrets, I still had to walk all the way back uphill to reach the Gatterbauer hamlet and then along a road until I could find the Jakobsweg turning left into the country. I found what I believed to be the left turn, and walked uphill beside a wood to reach a small road. Here I turned right, believing myself to be on course. After about 1.5 kilometres I saw to my horror a sign announcing that I was entering Windschnur. At once I could see from the map that I had fallen into grievous error. To avoid worse I could only retrace my steps, returning to the path beside the wood, this time downhill. This was an hour wasted, partly my fault but more generally the fault of the absence of any consistent waymarking for the Jakobsweg. I certainly was not going to try again to find a left turn off the highway but continued until the sign pronounced that I was entering the village of Thannstrass. Here I photographed a curious structure which at first sight I took to be a summer room elevated at the top of a spiral staircase but in the end concluded was something to do with the electricity line. I photographed it and also the local *Wirtshaus* attached to one of the farms in the village; for the latter, see the plate section. After Thannstrass I needed a left turn and fortunately selected one that at least took me safely to Sollach. This was unorthodox but from the Sollach roundabout it is but a short walk to reach the ancient church in Maria Schmolln.

Maria Schmolln is about halfway between Höhnhart and Mattighofen. It is a small town but distinguished as a place of pilgrimage since the Middle Ages. Beside and connected to the parish church is a Franciscan monastery. The monastery garden is carefully tended and open to the public. I had a good look round and took this view of the handsome Franciscan house from the garden; see plate section. A medieval church is dark and cool on a hot day. While the glorious weekend weather had continued on Monday, Tuesday had been overcast and light drizzle had accompanied my morning walk. On Wednesday, however, the glorious weather was back and Maria Schmolln at midday had an almost Mediterranean air.

Perhaps because of its eminence as a place of pilgrimage, it has a proper tourist office in the *Gemeindeamt*. There, a young girl took the greatest care to map out the day ahead and my overnight rest. Her conclusion was that I must be sure in leaving Maria Schmolln not to miss the Jakobsweg through the huge forest which stretched south-eastwards for thousands of hectares. The road to the village of Schalchen was perilous for pedestrians because of the traffic. I must cross the forest westerly to reach Schalchen, which had become almost a suburb of the considerable town of Mattighofen. We concluded that it was pointless to walk through Mattighofen, which stretched for miles from Schalchen in the north almost to Munderfing in the south. This area would offer barely a kilometre of country walking, nor anywhere to attract an overnight stay. So the plan that we developed was for me to walk to Schalchen and then the comparatively short distance to the railway station in Mattighofen. The Salzburg train stopped there once an hour on the hour and fourteen minutes later would stop at Lengau. The plan may have been unprincipled but it was extremely practical, taking me from one desirable place, Schalchen, to another, Lengau.

This same kind girl took care of my immediate needs. Pointing out of the window she said that I would get a good cup of coffee across the street. Then, to ensure I left the town on the true path, I must take the side road that turned left from the high street at the kindergarten. I drank the coffee outside in the hot sun and heard the Angelus from the church. I found the kindergarten and duly turned left downhill. There were a number of pitfalls between the kindergarten and the forest on the far side of the valley. It was clear from the map that I had to cross the main road at the bottom of the valley but finding the crossing point was not easy and I would have gone wrong had I not had the good fortune to meet a farmer on his way home. After he had set me right I was soon across the main road, across the valley floor, across the brook and entering the forest for an uphill climb that led to a forest crossing of the main road from Maria Schmolln to Schalchen. This was the road the girl had advised me not to walk because it was fast and dangerous. It was easy to find the point of crossing but not straightforward to choose which of the number of tracks and footpaths that fanned out from the crossing point was the one I needed. It was important that I avoided 317 and made sure that I took 315 and 316, which ran together for some way. Shortly after the road crossing the forest thinned and opened into a clearing of perhaps 200 hectares of arable land. On the arable land there was no possibility of error since there was only one path which carried 315 and 316 across to re-enter the forest on the far side. From this point of re-entry the forest stretched unbroken to the outskirts of Schalchen. This was a lovely forest, with a mixture of beech and pine. The sunlight illuminated the clearings and also penetrated the lighter cover of the beech. It was such a lovely walk that I made many attempts to capture its essence with the camera.

Although the forest in its entirety is immense, I was only crossing the neck of the forest at its north-west end. Perhaps it was a walk of about 8 kilometres but in a forest there are many tracks and paths, some ancient and some essential to extract the timber. Nowhere is waymarking more vital and at first the marker seemed to have laid his marks regularly and consistently. At a point where I had begun to think that Schalchen could not be far I saw ahead a car parked at a considerable crossroads. To my dismay I found there was not a mark at any of the four ways of the crossing. This was ominous because through the forest there had consistently been marks not only for the Jakobsweg but also for new arrivals: the Via Nova and another pilgrim route, the Marienweg. What I had come to was a crossroads for vehicles that offered nothing for the pedestrian. I cast about in every direction, in vain. I could be certain that a driver would return to the car but that might not be before evening. My instinct was to take the right-hand path but then I realised I must use the compass offered by the sun. I needed to travel westwards and for that I must have the sun to my left. Of the four paths only the left hand offered that possibility. I was on the point of deciding to reject my instinct and instead to follow the sun when I saw, approaching towards me from the one direction that I had not contemplated, a man with a basket. I waited for him and, as I expected, saw that his basket was filled with fungi and a serrated knife. It followed that he must be both local and knowledgeable in the ways of the forest. I explained my mishap and my destination. He reassured me that I would have no difficulty provided I followed the path to the left. Without his reassurance I would have walked anxiously on the left-hand path, but with his guidance came confidence. Eventually, I came to a point in the forest that I recognised: the path that I had been following an hour before swung left-handed and sharply downhill. I had of course followed it, needing no waymark to guide me. There was a smaller path that diverged to the right but it would require a strong waymark to persuade the walker to diverge. There had been some attempt to waymark but not at the junction and only 20 metres beyond. This carelessness had caused me anxiety at the crossroads and cost me an hour that I could not afford. I made on as best I could and survived another challenge where the proper path at a crossing was not only unmarked but clearly unused and blocked by fallen saplings.

As I emerged from the forest Schalchen and Mattighofen were both laid out before me. I could see the spire of the church in Schalchen but how to get there? I stood beside a road that led only south and north. As I hesitated a man walked up from behind carrying a loaded bucket overflowing with fungi. He asked me a question which revealed only that he was not a native German. When, to excuse myself, I said that I was an English visitor, he then said that he was Polish. There was something decidedly shifty about his appearance and his approach. This impression was strongly confirmed when I asked him to repeat his question. He denied he had asked a question and appeared to prepare for flight. I decided not to let him go and persisted. Eventually he said that his question was whether I could direct him to Mattighofen. This was hardly convincing because he could see Mattighofen as well as I could. I suggested he take the left turn, and I took the right. It was with some difficulty that I eventually found the church in Schalchen dedicated to St James. As so often in a town or city, a church spire appears and disappears, leading and then misleading. True to its dedication, the church held a Jakobsweg stamp and also a good choice of postcards celebrating both its dedication and its 17th-century statues of the martyrdom of St Barbara. Now I could marry the stamps I had bought in Obernberg with these postcards.

From the church to the station in Mattighofen seemed to be an easy and straightforward walk. It was easy so long as I could follow the local road that ran alongside the stream, but when I reached the main road I mistakenly turned south and only after half a mile did I doubt my direction. Back to the map again, which led me only to regret that I had not used it earlier. I had to walk back to the junction, cross the main road and walk further west. I soon found myself in suburbia and without much idea of how to proceed. I reached a main road and there saw a group gathered round the boot of a car. At once I saw the shifty Pole and that he was one of a gang loading the car with fungi under the direction of a blonde woman who gave her orders from the steps of the house. I retreated before I was recognised and soon reached a road junction and the rail track. Clearly I had to take the road that ran beside the track.

My road soon brought me to a building on the far side of the track that I was assured was the station but the manoeuvre to reach it required either local knowledge or signs which were nowhere apparent. Almost unfathomable was the only route, which entailed crossing the track at the next level crossing then taking the next right turn and walking northwards on the west side of the track until reaching a platform. The station building on the other side of the track is apparently disused; although Mattighofen is a considerable town, it appeared that its station is almost unneeded and little used.

I had missed the 16.00 by a country mile and as I waited for the 17.00 two or three other passengers straggled in. But this was Austria, so to the minute and in accordance with the timetable the train arrived and I was able to see how little I had lost by executing the plan. To walk the length of Mattighofen would have been a depressing hour. To resume onwards to the south would have been a road walk through uninteresting arable land to the west of the railway track. Immediately east of the track stretched the great forest, here unused by the designers of the Jakobsweg. The journey took precisely the fourteen minutes timetabled and the station at Lengau was no more than a platform beside the track.

Lengau is no Mattighofen. It is just another Austrian village – a collection of big farmhouses randomly grouped round an ancient church. I took the view of the church from my room in the hotel and a view of one of the farms with the milking cows in the adjoining. In Austria, even in summer, the cattle are not turned out to graze between milkings but are kept in the parlour with fresh-cut grass put before them.

From the station to the church is a walk of about a kilometre. Beside the church I saw an elderly householder closing her front door. I called to her for guidance as to where I could find accommodation, fearing that she would tell me that there was nothing short of Lochen, which would have required another hour's walk. "Oh," she said, "you have only to go to the Jägerwirt." This I had already passed, a considerable modern hotel development which advertised itself as a conference centre. I had assumed that it was not there for passing trade. However, with her encouragement I walked in and with some difficulty persuaded the receptionist that I could afford the charge of €68 for bed and breakfast. I was then a happy man. The bedroom was excellent, the dinner delicious and breakfast the next morning no less good. At dinner I had had the incomparable local dish of chanterelles in a cream sauce supporting two bread dumplings. I wrote a dozen postcards over dinner and posted them in the box opposite the hotel.

The next morning, the guard on the Salzburg train put me off after two stations and assured me that after a very short wait I would be able, to pick up the Vienna express. Thus I saved mileage, time and expense, arriving at Meidling in good time to meet Aleksandra at the end of her day.

The walk from Schärding to Salzburg is 125 kilometres and it was obvious I could not do it in the three days then available. Only by twice using public transport had I reached Lengau. Unless I had returned I could never claim to have walked the Innviertel Jakobsweg. I would not be in Austria again until mid-November, and the days are too short then and the weather too uncertain. So I resolved to return the following

May. The walk from Lengau to Hallwang on the outskirts of Salzburg appeared to be beautiful and to deserve the month of May. It measures about 31 kilometres and therefore could be done in a day, but if I gave it two days I could add some of the eleven kilometres between Hallwang and Salzburg.

So I thought, always optimistic and never anticipating or allowing for the possibility of impediment or setback, let alone catastrophe. It is now May. I have not seen Aleksandra since February and I have no idea when I will see her or Austria again. What prevents me is beyond the bounds of the foreseeable. I returned to Vienna on Thursday 18 rather than Friday 19, as I had originally intended, in order to be with Aleksandra. I do not regret that decision but the consequence is indefinite delay in reaching my journey's end.

August 2020

WHEN I LEFT Lengau in autumn 2019 I had no doubt at all that I would return in the early spring to complete the few remaining miles that separated me from journey's end in Salzburg. That certainty endured all through the winter. Even in early March I was planning the week in late April when I would walk. I have always been an optimist and fond of speculation. I have a lifetime's experience of confident assumptions and predictions turned to dust but never have my plans and assumptions been shattered as Covid-19 has shattered them. Its force and effect were so unexpected and so sudden. In two weeks we all descended from well-ordered normality into chaos.

This return at the end of August was far from ordered normality. On 20 August, well after I was booked and committed, England imposed a fourteen-day quarantine on any traveller returning from Austria. At least entry into Austria, which had been opened on 28 July, remained unrestricted. The British Airways flight to Vienna on 28 August was all I needed and, having left the house at 4 a.m., I duly arrived at Schwechat at 10.20, ahead of schedule. But, for Aleksandra's peace of mind, I had agreed to a voluntary submission to the coronavirus test available at the airport.

I had left London in autumn chill and arrived in Vienna in the blaze of summer. I had expected an official testing station within the terminal but as I passed through without any sign a friendly policeman explained that the only testing facility was a private clinic beside the hotel outside the terminal. Clothed in Hebridean tweed and carrying all my luggage I struggled to locate the clinic, but once there joined a considerable queue for what proved to be an extremely efficient commercial service. My throat swab would be analysed and a result available on the clinic's website before midnight. At the airport I was free to catch the midday express bound for Salzburg which reached Wien Haubtbahnhof some ten minutes later. Aleksandra came to meet me to exchange my *Wanderstaub* for my suitcase and Hebridean tweed. We parted and, more suitably dressed, I boarded the Bregenz express with just my rucksack. I was lucky to get a seat and dozed until reaching Salzburg just after five. There I picked up the local service that stopped at Lengau just before six. The day was fading and I had no reservation. So it was an anxious walk from the station to Gasthof Jägerwirt, my only chance of a room. I was at once relieved by a warm reception, a comfortable room and a dish of *Eierschwammerl* and dumpling. To my amazement, the waitress remembered me and would hardly believe that it was a year since my previous visit. She warned me that after many hot days rain was forecast for the weekend.

Day 4 – 29 August 2020 – Lengau to Mattsee

DAYBREAK FULLY ENDORSED her prediction. Light drizzle fell from a leaden sky. I was totally unprepared. In order to lighten the load on my back I had gambled on fine weather. Without a change of clothing, I decided to delay my departure from the warmth of Jägerwirt, something I had never done before.

This first return to the Jakobsweg after a break of almost exactly twelve months proved to be more a new beginning than a continuation of the past. I had never before had any fear of getting wet. Then, perhaps because of the late start, I had no clear goal. The guide to the Jakobsweg in the Salzburg region suggested a 27 kilometre stretch from Lengau to Eugendorf. That goal was clearly lost before I even started. Setting out without a goal, I had a new-found freedom: to walk without haste and to stop at whatever took my fancy. So I looked at the fine old church in Lengau before following the field route across rolling country to reach Intenham. The helpful tourist office in Salzburg had supplied me with a quiverful of maps including the map for Lochen am See. It proved an invaluable guide. On the 4 kilometres from Lengau to Intenham I only checked once to ask for help, and without the guidance I was then given I would have lost heart in crossing a wood where the path had been swamped by thickets of Himalayan balsam.

Intenham is a hamlet very close to Lochen and it only earns my special mention for two farmhouses that, unlike almost all others, have avoided the Austrian urge to modernise. When I reached the church in Lochen I noted that I had taken two hours to cover a 4 kilometre field walk. The rain had cleared but it was hot and humid. After admiring the baroque altar in the church I stopped for half an hour in the *Gasthof* opposite for mineral water and coffee. I was careless in leaving the village, taking the road to Feldbach when I should have taken the road to Astätt. A kind man to whom I appealed in Feldbach gave me good advice: take a right turn in about 200 metres. Thereafter my map guided me without quandary or error across country to Wichenham where I met the Jakobsweg running south from Astätt. As I walked down to the junction I had my first view of Mattsee – the lake, not the town. From the junction I had a road walk of perhaps 2 kilometres to reach Gebertsham. This was on a small local road almost free of traffic and I was able to walk on the loose gravel in the verges. Gebertsham is famous for its *Filialkirche*, which has a remarkably fine flying altar from the 16th century. The door to the tiny church stood wide open, and clearly it and the grounds around the church were in the loving care of two ladies living beside the church. My photograph of the flying altar is in the plate section.

The road ran on from Gebertsham until the edge of a great wood where the road swung left and I followed a Jakobsweg sign for a track into the ancient wood with its many fine beech trees. The path that ran through the wood was as ancient as the wood itself, perhaps many centuries old. From being a *Forststrasse* it quickly became only a footpath. The great trees on either side had spread their roots, which were then exposed by human passage. These roots enhance the way by providing safe footfalls, particularly on descent to and ascent from gullies and water courses. I noticed again the silence; the only bird I heard all day was a single wood pigeon. Nor is there much insect life: no butterflies, no dragonflies. Perhaps we should be thankful for the absence of attacking flies and particularly mosquitoes. On such a warm, damp day the midges in Scotland would have been terrible. The exit from the wood marks the return to open land with wide views of the lake below. Soon the path joins a local road serving intermittent homes and farms. Properties here must be sought after for their wide views over the lake. One in particular caught my eye with its roadside boundary. This was a most expensive endeavour to exclude intrusion or even the curious gaze; first a high, evergreen hedge, then a cast-iron panel fence, outside which ran a second iron barrier with sharp spikes, all supplemented by frequent warnings of CCTV cameras in operation. If the purpose had been inclusion rather than exclusion it would have been a prison fence. When I reached the heavily boarded entrance gate I was able to peep in to catch a restricted view of a most expensive property. Nothing could have been less warm and homely. I thought of it as a prison from which the prisoners were nevertheless free to come and go at will.

From here the town of Mattsee appears almost as a dreamlike vision: harbour, schloss, *Stift*, all against the backdrop of a small wooded mount. I took this view and it is included in the plate section, but the bleak grey light does not do it justice. But to reach this paradise there was still a long road walk around an inlet of water at the end of the lake. A Jakobsweg mark had earlier appeared, as it were miraculously, directing the walker off the road and into the great wood. Now, out of the great wood, waymarks appeared only intermittently and, on the approach to the town, a final waymark took me off the road and into an extensive park which at its far end led directly into the attractive *Marktplatz*. Handsome houses surround it but all are dwarfed by the great *Stiftkirche*. It was half past four and I was parched. I almost fell into the excellent Café Konditorei Neuhofer. It was crowded and at one table was a wedding party with the bride in her white finery and the men all in black. I watched an old man unconvincingly courting a younger woman. After coffee and cake the waitress confirmed that there were two *Gasthöfe*, one at each end of the *Martkplatz*. By the church stood Gasthof Post. At the other Gasthof Kapitelwirt, where, she said, one ate well. Its facade proclaimed that it had been a *Gasthof* since 1375. I was soon installed in Room 9. For supper I ate the best *Eierschwammerl* and dumpling that I had ever tasted. I guessed that the secret of its excellence lay in the addition of fine white onion and thyme to the mushrooms before their blending into the cream sauce.

Day 5 – 30 August 2020 – Mattsee to Seekirchen

I HAD RESEARCHED, after my coffee and cake in Neuhofer, to find that there was no vigil mass but Sunday mass at eight o'clock. That I attended amidst many elderly locals. The celebrant was not robed but wore what is now described as "smart casual". This distorted and abbreviated the mass when the central core of consecration was omitted. He rushed to the

Agnus Dei and the distribution of the host which he had taken from the Tabernacle. In an age of few vocations this may be commonplace but it was a surprise to me. After mass I had an excellent breakfast at Kapitelwirt. I asked the kind proprietress for the *Eierschwammerl* recipe. She was at first diffident, explaining that it was her husband who was the chef. But then she warmed to the subject: cook the mushrooms and onions together before adding the herbs – oregano, not thyme – and the cream.

Again the day had started wet and drear. It was pointless to set off in the rain and it was not until 10.45 that the cloud lifted. I set out without much idea but found a way through the suburbs that brought me to the shore of the Obertrumer See. I saw little of the lake itself since the ribbon development of lakeside homes was served by a road behind that was the only route for all, including the Jakobsweg. It was a hard slog on tarmac all the way to reach the main road running south, the L101. Immediately beside the main road a tarmac track had been laid for bicycles. For the Jakobsweg walker this is a very poor solution. Its only merit is separation from the fast-flowing traffic on the busy main road. But what is lost is the quiet, which is one of the Jakobsweg's greatest attractions. The hamlet of Mitterhof has a notable *Gasthof*, where I stopped for my habitual intake of coffee and mineral water. Mitterhof also marks the end of the uneasy partnership between the Jakobsweg and the main road. From this point of separation, the Jakobsweg takes a direct line to the parish church of St James in Obertrum am See. Although a field walk and blessedly peaceful it is still tarmac all the way.

Obertrum is a handsome town and the parish church is ancient but was unsympathetically restored in the 19th century. In the porch there is a visitor's book for the pilgrim but curiously no *Stempel*. Across from the church is the massive Braugasthof Sigl. It has an extremely welcoming appearance, suggesting tradition and excellent service. I was sorry that I had no need of it after the recent stop in Mitterhof. I had noticed in the churchyard an enormous family vault, quite out of scale with all other family plots in size and design. It proclaimed that it held at rest only members of the Sigl family.

Obertrum is compact and uncomplicated so it was as easy to enter at its heart and to leave without any guidance other than that offered by the map. But again the exit is a long tarmac trail laid out as a running track. This peters out after 2 kilometres, but the tarmac continues relentlessly, following the main road to Katzelsberg and beyond. I needed to leave this road short of Katzelsberg to take a left turn across country to another junction with the L101 at Fürnbuch.

As I sought this essential left turn, things went badly wrong. First the map was misleading in promoting a turning for Grabenmühle instead of Petermühle. This would not have mattered but for a strange coincidence. At the critical junction the waymark for the Jakobsweg had sheered one of its fixings so that it sagged to point not left but straight ahead. Before discovering these traps I had stopped at a farmhouse and had a proper picnic, something I would never have done on the Jakobsweg before. The sun shone, I had a wonderful view down the valley. I lingered without a qualm. My energy restored, I followed the sign to Grabenmühle, only to find that it was a dead end. I had no choice but to walk back to the main road. I asked a passing family for help. Parents are invariably thrown by any appeal that involves map reading. It is always the children who seize the map, size up the situation and give advice. The children's insistence that I must walk through Petermühle was so inconsistent with the map that I decided to reject their advice and try my luck with a cast up towards Katzlsberg. Here I had the good fortune to walk into a farmyard just as the farmer's wife drove out. I signalled and she stopped. When I explained my dilemma she simply confirmed what the young children had said. Seeing that I was still dithering she offered to drive me to the crucial turning. I clambered in and within moments she had put me down. It was then that I discovered the wayward waymark that had confused me.

Although I was now set fair swinging down to Petermühle, it was hard going on the tarmac, especially on the long climb from Petermühle to Köllern. In bright sunlight the temperature rose and I was soon winded. So it continued until I reached Fürnbuch and the L101. Fürnbuch would have been a hamlet of three farms, had not a very modern factory been built for Mattig Präzision on the other side of the road and beside it an enormous DPD depot. These interminglings of agriculture and industry in Austria always surprise me.

Fortunately, the return to the L101 was only for some 400 metres before another left turn onto a minor road, but still relentless tarmac. Shortly after the turn, I stopped at a farmhouse to diminish the mineral water I had bought at a Billa on the outskirts of Obertrum. I was tired out and lay flat on my back with my left leg on the rucksack, a good foot higher than my head.

With the blood flowing in the right direction I dozed for fifteen minutes and then set out on quiet roads through rich farmland. The places I passed hardly matter but they were Unteraigen, Kreuz and Koppelton. Koppelton leads to Waldprechting, which has almost been absorbed into Seekirchen. However, it still has its striking church of St Nicholas declaring its independence. The waymark at that point declares 1.7 kilometres to the centre of Seekirchen. I hammered on with a light heart since it was downhill all the way, and because it would be folly to continue beyond Seekirchen. Partly that was because it was almost five o'clock and partly because clouds were gathering and the rain was beginning to fall. Seekirchen is a considerable town and has the benefit of being at the head of Wallersee. So it was a surprise to find the centre curiously dead. The main café was shut, as was the main *Gasthof*. I asked and was told the only alternative was the Gasthof Post. I found it but as it was Sunday it was shut for its *Ruhetag*. I had passed an unpleasing hotel, Il Mollino, as I approached the church, which claimed to be inspired by Italy. I was not in a position to make a choice. I willingly accepted a poor room at an elevated price to be paid in cash in advance and with no breakfast. I ordered a Mollino salad to avoid all the pizza and it turned out to be surprisingly good.

So ended my second day, much like the first. I had started late and had struggled to cover the ground. In six hours of walking I had covered little more than 12 kilometres.

Day 6 – 31 August 2020 – Seekirchen to Salzburg
I QUIT THE hotel like a shadow, seeing no one and leaving no mark. In the main street was a baker where I was well served

with coffee and fresh bread. Soon there was a sign left onto a narrow street. This carried me through the woodland Am Pfaffenbühel to a crossroads where the Jakobsweg bears right for Mühlberg. Mühlberg is only a farm and a fine church dedicated to St Leonhard. I photographed the scene. From the church there is a sharp descent to meet and cross the main road. The path follows the main road briefly before bearing right uphill towards Eugendorf and, shortly before reaching the parish church, there is an attractive looking *Gasthof*, Neuwirt. The centre of the village is dominated by the parish church. I walked downhill through the town to reach a right turn for the Jakobsweg, which then sets forth over open land towards Hallwang. This walk was across rich farmland; the road connected the farms with each other and with the village but essentially served no other purpose. Although of limited use it was nevertheless tarmac and the grass was either too long or too recently slurried to offer relief.

Having no map and without waymarks I went wrong in Einleiten. Whereas I should have turned right, I followed left to reach Döbring. Here I was in a complete quandary because at the junction with the road through the village there was no clue as to whether to turn right onto the village road or continue straight on. To continue would bring me almost at once to the motorway. I waited and fortunately a car came from behind and was obliged to stop at the junction. I asked for help and a kind lady sent me firmly on the road through the village. This was marked "Döbringerfeld" and it led me on seemingly nowhere. The town of Hallwang seemed to have disappeared without trace. I saw a minibus parked with a young driver at the wheel who was eager to help but offered me poor advice. As I attempted her option I caught sight of the Hallwang parish church. Clearly I needed the road she had rejected, which proved to be Dorfstrasse, and it took me swiftly to the centre of the village with the church in plain view. No harm had been done. I had simply walked 2 kilometres more than I should. As I walked up the High Street I saw the *Gemeindeamt* to my right. It was 11.50 so I guessed I had ten minutes of their time. In the front office was a kind lady who was only too willing to provide me with a map and useful advice in exchange for my view as to whether she should do a house swap with a family in Newcastle. She encouraged me to hasten on to Maria Plain and I in return encouraged her to make the exchange and explore the great county of Northumberland. Her plan for me was that I should walk up the hill to reach Maria Plain from Radeck and then descend the hill into Bergheim, where I could catch the Strassenbahn straight into Salzburg Hauptbahnhof. She said that in Berghein there were excellent places to eat. When I said that my immediate need was for coffee and mineral water she assured me I would find all that I needed at Gasthof Kirchbichl nearby. Such warmth is not unusual in a *Gemeindeamt* and I was almost overwhelmed by the scale and magnificence of Gasthof Kirchbichl. It spread far and wide on both sides of the crossroads. I tried every available entrance to find them all tightly shut. At last I found a door that opened and that led to the hotel reception counter. Yes, said the receptionist, we are shut. No explanation or apology. There was nowhere else in the town. However, I could use the automatic vending machine in the hall. My two-euro coin simply ran straight through the machine. I called for her help. She looked at my inadequacy with scorn and took my coin. To her surprise when she inserted it, it simply ran through the machine. To save face she fetched a key, unlocked the machine and extracted a bottle of water. The price of the bottle in Billa is fifty-nine cents. So in selling it to me for two euros she was amply rewarded for her trouble. I drank the water on the steps outside and left the empty bottle by her door.

The way out of Hallwang is easy. Take Kirchenstrasse downhill past the church and across the main road to enter Bergstrasse. Bergstrasse is again a tarmacked road to serve the farms that lie ahead and the settlement of Berg at the top of the hill. The climb up to Berg is steady rather than steep. Having gained the summit, I rested on a bench and then was rewarded with a long stretch downhill to meet and cross the local railway at Salzburg Maria Plain Station. On the two previous days I had taken no benefit from the descents but I was pleased on this third day to find that I could again stride out and double my speed on the descent. Across the railway line was an attractive avenue of trees marked Wickenburgallee that led into a street crossing the Kasern. As I walked on I was attracted by the pungent smell of cooking from what was clearly a popular local eating house, the Jägerwirt. I turned off, thinking I might get coffee there. This was a happy chance since beside the hedge I chanced to see a Jakobsweg sign pointing to a path to the side of the Jägerwirt. I followed it and it was indeed the entry into a wonderful walk, albeit all uphill, to the great pilgrim church of Maria Plain. It is the principal route to the church, ancient and meandering. On the climb I filched some ripe and juicy apples that had fallen from a garden tree onto the verge. Although ultimately the road climbs perhaps 500 metres this is achieved almost by stealth, with level stretches through pasture or woodland breaking up the ascent. It brings the pilgrim to the foot of the mount on the top of which the pilgrim church dominates the scene. The ascent of this final mount is the only trial of wind and limb. It is eased by a succession of late 17th-century pavilions each telling a moment in the crucifixion story. These are achieved in painted sculptured form. They are a fit introduction to the splendours displayed in the pilgrim church. Both its facade and its rich interior provide an important element in the wider history and culture of the city of Salzburg.

From the church I needed to find the footpath for Bergheim. There was no sign but little alternative. After I had dropped perhaps 200 metres from the summit, I saw a group of three – a husband and wife, clearly affluent, conversing with some condescension with a cyclist. I asked them for Bergheim and it was the cyclist who pointed me on. Dropping through the outskirts of Bergheim I reached the main road. Fortunately I saw an elderly lady working in a garden centre. The old in Austria are invariably kind and helpful. When I asked for the Strassenbahn she kindly corrected me to Straussenbahn and then pointed me up the street to reach the crossroads, where I would find a large hotel. There I should turn left and find my way under the main railway line to reach the station for the Lokalbahn. After warm thanks I set out and easily found the crossroads and the hotel, at which I turned left and walked on until reaching a bridge crossing the main railway line. I was not to go over the railway line but under it and how? As I stood there, perplexed, a bicyclist approached and slowed to stop beside me. To my amazement I saw that it was the very same man who had directed me at Maria Plain. Then ensued something of a struggle. I was determined to convey my need for directions and he was determined to believe that I was seeking the post office since I was still carrying in my hand the cards that I had bought in the pilgrim church. My voice was thin for want of water and he explained that he was deaf but in the end we succeeded and once he understood the problem he went wholeheartedly for its solution. He sped off on his bicycle to a couple who were about to go into a large house. Having discussed the question with them, he called me up and the three of them together explained what I had to do. It required explanation because the route that they recommended was far from orthodox and passed through what seemed to be somebody else's garden. Seeing my lack of confidence the bicycle brigadier set off to reconnoitre and to lead. When we reached a sharp descent, I kept pace with him by cutting off the hairpin bends and so we reached the tunnel under the main railway simultaneously. At the other side of the tunnel I was still quite unclear where I should go and was about to set off to join him when he gesticulated and, bicycling back, put me precisely on the path which almost at once had me on the platform. Such kindness sealed the final 400 metres of my long walk. There was a shelter for waiting travellers in which two men were in cheerful mood consuming large quantities of beer from Gösser cans. In their company I waited the twenty minutes until the train came and I was accelerating to Salzburg

Haubtbahnhof and thence to Wien Meidling on the express from Munich to Budapest.

☞

Journey's End

MONDAY 31 AUGUST 2020 measures seven years and seventy-one days since I first set out from Purkersdorf on 21 June 2013. In that span I have walked nearly 2,000 kilometres in completing the four principal stretches of the Jakobsweg in Austria (treating the Südtirol as reunited with its Austrian brothers). At the outset I was seventy-four years of age; now, at the conclusion, I am eighty-two. At the outset I was still sitting in the Court of Appeal and directing our participation in international family justice, although on the verge of retiring (perhaps at some level in walking the Jakobsweg I sought to mitigate the many losses that were about to come). More recent losses are now dwarfed by the coronavirus which has almost certainly terminated the consultancy I successfully developed once retired. So following the Jakobsweg has been the constant thread through inconstant years.

These reflections suggest I have reached a spatial end: there are simply no kilometres left to walk. But it may be that I have reached a physical end: I have exhausted my strength and stamina and, accordingly, were there yet more kilometres to walk, I would have to admit defeat. It is the last three days on from Lengau that have created this tension. I have never before walked so slowly. Yes, the weather was against me but not the terrain. The cause was either age or lack of fitness: the coronavirus had extended what should have been a winter break into a whole year without a walk. After reaching Seekirchen I had decided Anno Domini was the cause. But on the last day my stride lengthened and I was again fast downhill. So it had really only been want of condition, I thought. Now, a week on, I am sure it was an equal combination of both factors. This is a cheerful conclusion. It means that I have run out of strength just at the moment I have run out of road. Providence could not have designed a better end.

Significant achievements in life (and for me the completion of this pilgrimage is significant) call for celebration. The morning after a late return to Schönbrunn on 31 August, Aleksandra and I set off in her car for Gröbming in Steiermark. Three hours after leaving Vienna we were negotiating the hairpin bends that ascend Michaelerberg to reach a house glued onto the face of the mountain only 50 metres below the road's end. Here we settled for six glorious days of late summer. As over so much of upland Austria, pasture and forest alternate here. Any one of the *Bergwege* that radiate out from the road's end might have been a section of the Tyrolean Jakobsweg.

Here I learned from Aleksandra the skill of foraging the forest for fungi, a skill I had so often envied on the Jakobsweg when meeting locals returning home with laden trugs. Principally we prized *Eierschwammerl, Steinpilz* and *Herrenpilz*. But we also gathered a nameless yellow top with the robust profile of the *Steinpilz*. My contribution on any day was at most ten per cent of the bag. Aleksandra was so swift of foot and so sharp-eyed that nothing escaped her and nothing delayed her. I learned that what the insects have eaten is generally safe. I learned that a useful test is to cut the specimen in two and apply the tip of the tongue to the cut surface. If the taste is sour or bitter it must be discarded. A sweet or neutral taste is safe. Whatever is to be taken must be cut at ground level to leave the spores in the soil. The hunt is delightful and addictive. Nowhere in the forest is without prospects in season and after rain. Every night we feasted on our findings, sometimes three courses differently composed and differently cooked.

The views from high on the side of the Berg are sublime. Immediately below lie Moosheim and Gröbming. To the east the whole valley is in view to distant Liezen. To the west the view is much shorter but dominated by Dachstein, with its snow-covered summit. Half way to Dachstein, in the hills to the south, lies the picturesque mountain lake known as the Steirische Bodensee. It is well stocked with fish that are expertly cooked in the waterside restaurant. Aleksandra photographed our celebration; see the plate section. These six days were indeed a celebration and, for me, a respite and a reward.

THE HISTORY AND SIGHTS OF VIENNA

VIENNA

I ADD THIS eccentric guide since I have come to know Vienna better than any other city, apart from London, and to love it best.

There are three keys, I would suggest, to the history and the sights of Vienna and its territory, for Vienna is a province as well as a city. Those three keys are the monarchy, the Catholic church and the princes. I will start with the monarchy.

THE MONARCHY

AFTER THE REIGN of Maximilian I in the 15th and 16th centuries, and as a consequence of his achievements, the monarch would have required several heads to display simultaneously his majesty. These can be loosely and probably inaccurately listed as the Austrian Crown, the Crown of the Holy Roman Empire, St Stephen's Crown of Hungary, the Bocskay Crown of Hungary, the Crown of Bohemia and the Crown of Spain. Three of these are on display among the Secular Treasures in the Hofburg. Strictly, the Crown of Spain was lost in 1713 and the Crown of the Holy Roman Empire in 1806.

Maximilian had in fact split his empire between his sons, and for our purpose I need deal only with the eastern empire.

Brothers, and then cousins, ruling Spain and South America are only indirectly influential on a picture of Vienna.

So the visitor should think of the Habsburgs as more or less absolute rulers from the time of Maximilian at the end of the Middle Ages to Franz Joseph, who expired in 1916. His death ushered in disaster for Austria. He was succeeded by his great-nephew, Emperor Karl I, who threw away an early opportunity for Austria to exit the Great War without punishing reprisals. He later initiated secret negotiations duplicitously. His exile was the final ignominy. Spanish flu saved him from the risk of further folly. He was seen, however, as an exemplary husband and father and a devout Catholic, which must explain his beatification in 2004. The numbering of the Emperors is confusing because the sequence for the Habsburg Holy Roman Emperors vanished when Napoleon abolished the Holy Roman Empire. So the last Holy Roman Emperor, Francis II, became Francis I, Emperor of Austria. The last Emperor of Austria was Karl I, since previous Habsburg Karls had been Holy Roman Emperors.

The names and dates of those who came between the sovereigns whom I have chosen as Alpha and Omega can be left unexplored, save for Maria Theresa in the 18th century, the only woman, and one of the most illustrious of the Habsburgs.

So, even today after a century of the Republic, the possessions of the Habsburgs are the core of the Vienna experience.

First there are the royal palaces: the Hofburg in the city, Schönbrunn in what are now the western outskirts of the city, and, for the ardent, Schloss Hof, in the east, from the terrace of which there is a clear view of what was then Pressburg and what is now Bratislava. While Schloss Hof is a shell, the interiors of the other two palaces contain many of the Habsburgs' greatest treasures, the moveable possessions.

In the Hofburg is the Schatzkammer, or Treasury, which from earliest times has held the crown, the regalia and the inalienable possessions of the Habsburgs, both secular and sacred. The Schatzkammer is divided into two separate treasuries, the Secular Treasury and the Ecclesiastical Treasury. The division is an historic one; confusingly, many things in the Secular Treasury could just as well be included in the Ecclesiastical Treasury.

The Secular is of much greater importance but there are many outstanding works of art and craftsmanship in the Ecclesiastical. The Secular contains unimaginable treasures that come from the imperial trappings of the Holy Roman Emperor and the Burgundian Inheritance that came to the Habsburgs from the marriage of Maximilian I to the only child of Philip the Good of Burgundy. If I could choose one thing from the Schatzkammer it would be the fantastic Colombian emerald fashioned by Miseroni into an ointment pot. It derives from the Spanish territories in South America. The emerald mine in what is now Columbia was opened in 1558. This, the biggest known emerald, was the size of a male fist and had found its way to the Holy Roman Emperor, Matthias, before his death in 1619. It was Ferdinand III who had it cut into its present form by Dionysio Miseroni in Prague in 1640.

Elsewhere in the Hofburg are the many rooms given over to a memorial to the Empress Elisabeth, wife of Franz Joseph, to the display of imperial china and to the display of imperial silver. Here I have no favourites and covet nothing. I do not share the current enthusiasm for the Empress Elisabeth, nor am I sympathetic to the promotion of her cult. But in that respect I am out of step with the majority of visitors to Vienna.

Unfortunately, the portion of the Hofburg dating to the golden age of Maria Theresa is reserved for the use and occupation of the President of the Republic.

Other glorious sights within the Hofburg are the Spanish Riding School, the Chapel and the Imperial Library. Most visitors insist on a visit to the Riding School to see the Lipizzaners so skilfully put through their haute école paces. Equally, most will seek a ticket to hear the Vienna Boys' Choir sing in the Chapel. The Imperial Library is a less obvious attraction but it is easily accessible and certainly not to be missed. It is perhaps the grandest library in the whole world. The ascent to the upper floor library is by functional stairs that give no hint of the grandeur to which they lead. The central cupola has two adjacent wings. The commissioning emperor was Charles VI, the architect Fischer Von Erlach and the decorator Daniel Gran. His fresco within the cupola depicts the triumph of the House of Austria through Learning, with proper emphasis on the contribution of Emperor Karl VI. Everywhere, frescos and sculptures eulogise the House of Habsburg through the generations.

Beside the historic Hofburg lies the Neue Burg, that bombastic enlargement achieved by Emperor Franz Joseph. Within there are two collections. The first is Graeco-Roman, largely what the Austrian archaeologists sent back from their excavations at Ephesus. The second collection is the Habsburg

Arms and Armour. The first I would not recommend but the second is not to be missed. For in the 16th and 17th centuries arms and armour were still worn by kings and princes for display, if not for battle, and in the earlier age of Maximilian I for jousting, an art in which he excelled. So the finest metal workers in Europe lavished their art on arms and armour for royalty and some of their greatest achievements remain in the Habsburg collection.

The 19th century saw the dawn and midday enthusiasm for bringing works of art to public display in museums. Franz Joseph was a reactionary so he was not in the vanguard. But in middle age he reordered existing imperial public displays to create what is perhaps now the greatest museum in the world, the Kunsthistorisches Museum (generally abbreviated to "KHM"). I say "now" because its standing has been hugely advanced by the recent opening of rooms to display the Habsburg Kunstkammer. The division between Schatzkammer and Kunstkammer was relatively straightforward: the former was for Habsburg treasures and the latter for Habsburg works of applied arts. Although the Kunstkammer had been on display in the 19th century, its reappearance in modern times was much heralded prior to its eventual arrival.

Above the Kunstkammer stretch the great picture galleries. Within their palatial space Franz Joseph installed the family collection of western European art. The scale of the collection is huge and the quality unmatched. Particular treasures are the Bruegels and the Rubens. These riches result in no small part to the rule of the territories of the Dukes of Burgundy (Flanders and the Low Countries) and the zeal of one

Habsburg, Archduke Leopold Wilhelm. This archduke, the younger brother of the Emperor, was originally destined for the Church. But in the event he governed the Spanish Netherlands and collected on the grandest scale. When his collection was returned to Vienna there were 1,400 paintings and many other works of art. Within the picture galleries I would choose to live with the portrait of the composer Gluck. It would hang as comfortably in a home as in a museum.

As well as this world-famous gallery there is also the smaller but still choice collection in the Gemäldegalerie, which is the collection of the Academy of Fine Arts. The Academy was created as a teaching school by Karl the Sixth and its prestigious premises are only a short walk from the KHM. In London its history and ideals would be matched in the Royal Academy.

The Kunstkammer complements the picture galleries. It contains the Habsburg collection of works of art, not inalienable and mainly secular. Here is the Habsburg Wunderkammer. As the world beyond Europe opened, so kings and princes collected natural wonders such as shells and minerals. Ivory in abundance opened the way to ivory carvers of extraordinary skill who could be directed to the celebration in ivory of imperial majesty or to the creation of works of devotion.

Perhaps even more were the Habsburgs greedy for the hardstone carvings of the great Milanese masters. The riches of the Habsburg collection are in large part thanks to the eccentric life of Emperor Rudolf, who chose Prague rather than Vienna for his residence and court. Several members of the Miseroni family were tempted to move to Prague to work for him.

But the bounds of the Kuntskammer are almost limitless. Pre-Renaissance artworks open the display, which closes with Maria Theresa's gold table and toilet service and then some weak representations of the early 19th century. My choice amongst this extraordinary assembly would be, in common with many, the Cellini Salt Cellar, a marvellous masterpiece in gold and enamel. Fittingly, it was a gift to the Habsburgs from Francis I, King of France. My delight in the Kuntskammer never tires or diminishes.

Also within the KHM are collections of Egyptian and Roman antiquities as well as an extensive collection of coins. But these I mention only as a footnote.

Across the Maria Theresien Platz from the KHM is the matching Museum of Natural History. It too was designed to display the Habsburg collections in this field. They dominate the Platz and the Burgring like brothers. They are perhaps the foremost of the public buildings achieved by Franz Joseph. Beside these two museums rank the temples to music: the Musikverein and the Staatsoper. It is said that Franz Joseph, at the opening of the gigantic opera house, let fall some disparaging criticism. One of the two architects promptly committed suicide. On all future occasions thereafter Franz Joseph was wont to say that any novelty was "very nice".

The relationship between emperor and the Catholic Church is neatly expressed in the funerary etiquette. The body of the emperor was committed to the Crypt of the Capuchin Monastery, the heart to the Crypt of the Augustinian Monastery and the entrails to the Crypt of the Cathedral of St Stephen.

The entry of the royal and imperial corpse to the Kapuzinergruft is said to be accomplished according to a solemn ritual. The abbot stands within the locked and bolted door as the cortège approaches. The chamberlain then hammers on the door's exterior with his staff.

"Who seeks entry?" the abbot cries.

"His Royal and Imperial Highness, Emperor of Austria, King of Hungary" – and so on through the roll of titles in descending order of importance.

"We know him not," the abbot responds.

The exchange is repeated a second time.

When the question is asked a third time the chamberlain responds:

"Franz Joseph, a poor sinner."

Whereupon from the abbot:

"Enter, we know him well."

I hope this ritual was observed most recently for the burial in 2011 of the man regarded by monarchists as Emperor Otto. For he was the son of the last Emperor, Karl I. He was known, however, as Herr von Habsburg in his considerable public life as a politician and a member of the European Parliament.

THE CATHOLIC CHURCH

THIS RELATIONSHIP UNDERLINES the confusion and sometimes the struggle between temporal and spiritual powers. The spiritual potentate for this survey of the city and province must be the Cardinal Archbishop whose palace adjoins his cathedral, the great Stephansdom, so venerated that it has sailed through the centuries with little change to its medieval soul. So a cathedral visit is a necessity. The adjoining Diocesan Museum was for a long time closed but has recently been very successfully relaunched. It has some wonderful things, selectively presented in order to magnify their impact.

Any understanding of the houses of God in this province of Vienna must concentrate on the Counter-Reformation: the fight back from the losses to Martin Luther. Art and architecture were prominent in the Catholic war chest. In Rome, Bernini and Borromini developed a new architectural and sculptural language which expressed the divine not in austerity but in sensuality. These languages were then learned by the architects and painters practising north of the Alps, especially in Bavaria, Austria and Czechoslovakia. The Austrian new-build used the language but most of the churches predated its invention. So they received a heavy makeover that obliterated or disguised earlier decorative styles. Little has since changed, so Austria is a Mecca for the lovers of baroque theatricality.

This is well illustrated in the first district, Vienna within the Ring. Fischer von Erlach, the most accomplished Austrian architect of the baroque period, is represented by his Karlskirche, a highly original and accomplished work. It was commissioned by the Emperor Karl VI as a thanks offering for the relief of the plague of 1713. The Emperor commissioned the two extraordinary columns that front the church, inspired by the columns of Marcus Aurelius and Trajan in Rome. They symbolise Emperor Karl's motto: *Constantia et Fortitudine.*

St Peter's off the Graben is small, but perfectly achieves its aim. It is architect Lukas von Hildebrandt's triumph.

The Jesuitenkirche is my favourite and here the element of theatre is nowhere better illustrated than in the apparent but non-existent dome above the nave, the work of the Jesuit monk and architect Andrea Pozzo. Emperor Leopold I commanded these works. Choral high mass is celebrated here on many Sundays in the year at 10.30. The music chosen is predominantly and appropriately the work of Haydn, Mozart or Schubert (Schubert was at school in the adjoining building). These are both liturgical and musical celebrations. Behind the altar are massed the conductor, the soloists, the orchestra and finally the choir. As these supremely professional forces burst forth in the Gloria, who in the church is not moved? Because of the renown of this tradition it is advisable to arrive about half an hour before the mass to secure a seat in one of the gloriously decorative pews. Stephansdom and the Augustiner church also offer choral high mass at a slightly later hour, but their medieval antiquity does not so completely harmonise with the musical tradition that Vienna fostered in and after the reign of Maria Theresa.

Near the Jesuit church is the Dominikanerkirche, but this church is as close as the baroque approaches to an austere expression.

One of the miracles of Austrian Catholicism is the survival of prominent monasteries. The closures of Joseph II and the madness of Hitler were as strong winds that made the monastic candles gutter, but they did not extinguish them. So, for the traveller with the time, the city and province offer wonderful opportunities. In what are now the Vienna suburbs there is Klosterneuburg. Karl VI planned a great future for this ancient monastery, a future which was cut off by his death.

Not far from the city bounds is the monastery of Heiligenkreuz, made famous beyond Austria by the recordings of the monks' Gregorian chant.

To the west of Vienna, near St Pölten (it too has a baroque heart), lies the Augustinian monastery of Herzogenburg, dominating the surrounding town.

Not far beyond lies the world-famous valley of the Wachau, where Austria's finest white wines are raised and where in June its incomparable apricots ripen. At the east end of the Wachau towers the Benedictine monastery of Göttweig and at the west end the mighty Melk. Between these two flows the wide Danube.

Today all five monasteries are commercialised in varying degrees. All sell visits, some meals, and some accommodation. None is dependent on income from tourism. All retain assets which have survived the depredations of secular power. Income may come from forestry, fishing rights, farming, vineyards or brewhouses, but no doubt tourism provides a useful supplement. Some monasteries possess and display a treasury of sacred artworks. For instance, at Melk the patrimony is displayed with the most modern professionalism in what were the imperial quarters. The emperor and his court, in motion for whatever need, would lodge at monasteries en route. Hence in somet of the greatest monastic houses you find the Kaisersaal or the Marmorsaal, sufficiently palatial to make an emperor feel at home.

The Church, like the Crown, was a great patron of all the applied arts. Painters, sculptors, goldsmiths, stucco workers, cabinetmakers, woodcarvers, gilders, jewellers, tapestry factories, and no doubt other specialists, looked to prelates, churches and monasteries for their commissions. The Church was rich. Many cardinals, abbots and priests were of the aristocratic class. They knew how to commission, perhaps in rivalry with their elder brothers – which thought leads me to my final key, the princes.

THE PRINCES

I TAKE FIRST Prince Eugene of Savoy. Exiled as a young man from the court of King Louis XIV of France he turned what must have seemed disaster to triumph. Rising in war to command the imperial forces, he was credited with the final defeat of the Turkish invaders at the Battle of Zenta in 1697. Early in his military career, in the service of Leopold I, he became lay abbot of two abbeys in Savoy, which provided him with both a useful income and the obligation of celibacy. He was, besides, a great collector and his tastes reflected his grandeur. So we now must be thankful for the creation and preservation of his palaces, the Upper Belvedere, the Lower Belvedere and the Winter Palace. All three now provide galleries for the permanent collection and for temporary exhibitions in glorious rooms. Of his personal collection nothing remains. Being childless, he left his estate to his niece who swiftly disposed of her responsibility.

The interiors of all three palaces, however, even empty of contents, give a sense of the grandeur of Prince Eugen and his household, especially those rooms that are gilded from floor to ceiling and perhaps further embellished with oriental porcelain. The gardens that sweep down from the Upper to the Lower

Belvedere are a magnificent architectural deployment of space and have recently been restored. The timeless quality of the view from the Upper Belvedere, scanning the gardens and the city beyond, is evident from Belloto's painting from this point. Striking in his painting, and in the contemporary view, is the dome of the church of the Salesian Convent, which closes the view to the right. The Winter Palace was essentially his inner city palace, as opposed to his garden palace, the Belvedere. It is on Himmelpfortgasse and is one of the grandest secular baroque buildings in Austria. Especially distinguished is the grand staircase by Fischer von Erlach. The palace served as the Ministry of Finance and its relatively recent release and restoration have been a very significant addition to Vienna's cultural treasury. Prince Eugene's country palace was Scloss Hoff, which passed to the Emperor after his death.

My second prince, or grand duke, is of Liechtenstein. Again, there is the Garden Palace and the City Palace. Items in the collection seem to be offered holiday accommodation there when tired of life in Vaduz. However, public access to the Garden Palace has become more restricted than it was a decade ago and, although access to the City Palace has become possible, it is on a very restricted rota. Nevertheless, Vienna is much enriched by the continuing presence of the Liechtenstein principality. Of the two palaces my strong preference is for the Garden Palace, which stands nobly in its own grounds and is enhanced by the charm of the surrounding ninth district. The palace has its own café, offering rest and good food. The noble rooms of its interior perfectly set off the paintings, furniture and works of art displayed. The City Palace intimidates with its monumental exterior, and the interior decorative scheme is of a later date and over-lavish to my eyes.

My third prince is in reality a long dead archduke. He is Albert of Sachsen-Teschen, who married Maria Theresa's favourite daughter, Maria Christina (sister of the ill-fated Marie Antoinette). As Maria Teresa's son-in-law he had a favoured life, enhanced by a considerable inheritance from an elderly relative. With these advantages he was able to indulge his discerning eye. He amassed an outstanding collection of watercolours and drawings. He patronised the finest bookbinders, silversmiths, cabinetmakers, makers of scientific instruments and painters. He was able to create his own palace and repository by extending the Hofburg onto a bastion of the old fortifications of the city. When he died he left his possessions in perpetuity to a museum in his memory, the Albertina, where the staterooms he created are on view. There is a permanent collection. Special exhibitions of outstanding quality follow one after the other.

Of course, there were many great aristocratic families with palaces in Vienna besides those that I have chosen. The Schönborn-Batthyány, the Trautson, the Kinsky, the Czernin, the Harrach and the Lobkowitz palaces all survive but generally to accommodate ministries of state or for other institutional use. The Lobkowitz palace, however, is available as the home of the Theatre Museum and it remains possible to ascend the grand stairs of the Kinsky, which is now occupied by business tenants.

The grandest palace beside my three is the Schwarzenberg Palace, whose gardens almost equal those of the Belvedere, which it borders. But it has been a hotel in modern times and is currently undergoing major redevelopment, or perhaps restoration. The most famous of the many seats of the Schwarzenberg family is Český Krumlov in Bohemia, but the remarkable achievements of the family in the wider sphere of the empire merit their mark on modern Vienna. In front of the Palais comes the Schwarzenbergplatz, dominated by the equestrian statue of Field Marshal Schwarzenberg. Even greater than his military achievement was the political achievement of his descendant Prince Felix Schwarzenberg, who as prime minister in 1848 orchestrated the abdication of Emperor Ferdinand and the accession of the 18-year-old Franz Joseph. In the ensuing nine years he ran a programme of absolutism to reverse the influence of European revolution.

The Austrian aristocracy was legislated out of existence in the early years of the Republic, so that even the son and heir of the last Emperor Karl, regarded by monarchists as emperor, was officially "Herr Otto von Habsburg". So it is the modern Austrian equivalent, Herr Rudolf Leopold, that we must acknowledge as the creator of the MuseumsQuartier, which in a very Viennese way is situated in the former stables of the Hofburg, across the road from Maria Theresien Platz. Here you will find the Leopold Museum and the centre of modern art in Vienna.

☞

OF COURSE, I do not attempt an exhaustive list of Vienna's attractions. I have sought to identify only those which have my appreciation, my heart. There are innumerable others which may appeal to other hearts and which are there to be discovered.

MY THANKS

My thanks to my former wife Carola who introduced me, over the course of twenty years of marriage, to the German-speaking countries, their culture, and all the wonderful things they offer English visitors.

My thanks also to those in Vienna who accepted or reciprocated my love from 2013 to 2021. From them I set out on each venture; to them I returned at each venture's end. They were always the source of my hope and inspiration. Without them I would not have persevered.

I am very grateful to Lyn Nash who, though a specialist legal typist, readily and most reliably typed up the first draft of the text, as the many stages of the journey unfolded. I thank Edward Cazalet, who guided me to Robina Pelham Burn and James Nunn, warmly. Robina was necessarily strict with my loose English, but always ready to hear my defence. James's designs capture the book's spirit perfectly, and I cannot sufficiently express my admiration for his front cover. In one image he conveys so many pages of text. At Bradt Guides, Adrian Phillips has saved me from the anxieties of self-publishing, and it has been a pleasure to work with Anna Moores, the Head of Editorial.

Finally, I thank the many Austrians who over the years were tolerant, friendly and kind. In these virtues all at Kremsmünster Abbey excelled. Indeed, I cannot sufficiently express my gratitude to the Abbott, Pater Franz, Schwester Lydia, and to the whole community. It is a debt beyond repayment.

THE EUROPEAN ARTERIES TO COMPOSTELA